Measu the Success of Sales Training

A Step-by-Step Guide for Measuring Impact and Calculating ROI

ASTD PRESS

ROI INSTITUTE™

Patricia Pulliam Phillips, PhD
Jack J. Phillips, PhD
with Rachel Robinson

ASTD Press is an internationally renowned source of insightful and practical information on workplace learning, performance, and professional development.

ASTD Press
1640 King Street Box 1443
Alexandria, VA 22313-1443 USA

Ordering information: Books published by ASTD Press can be purchased by visiting ASTD's website at store.astd.org or by calling 800.628.2783 or 703.683.8100.

Library of Congress Control Number: 2012940627

ISBN-10: 1-56286-859-4
ISNB-13: 978-1-56286-859-8
e-ISBN: 978-60728-523-6

ASTD Press Editorial Staff:
Director: Glenn Saltzman
Manager and Editor, ASTD Press: Ashley McDonald
Community of Practice Manager, Sales Enablement: Mike Galvin
Editorial Assistant: Sarah Cough
Text and Cover Design: Ana Ilieva Foreman

Printed by Versa Press, Inc., East Peoria, IL, www.versapress.com

Table of Contents

Preface

With ASTD's investment in selling skills, it has never been more important to show examples of sales skills at work. The process to evaluate these skills is sometimes perceived as straightforward and routine, simply a matter of tracking the sales gains after the program has been conducted. Credibly evaluating sales training programs is a bit more involved than that. Four important issues often surface when developing a credible study. First, since many other factors influence sales, there must always be a step to isolate the effects of the sales training program on the sales—an omission in most studies. Second, when converting sales data to monetary values, only the profit margins of increased sales must be used, not the sales themselves—a mistake made by many. Third, the stream of monetary benefits for the increased profits must be conservative, usually representing only one year. Finally, the assumptions surrounding which costs to use in the ROI analysis are usually incomplete, inconsistent, and not conservative.

Sponsors need a credible, conservative approach to measuring ROI—one that meets these four challenges. Using the ROI Methodology, all of the case studies in this book will address these issues, providing examples and benchmarks for others to use to evaluate these important types of programs.

In our visits around the world each year, we have been impressed with the work with ROI outside the United States. We have also noticed that the issues involved in creating, developing, and sustaining a comprehensive evaluation system are very similar from one country to another. In other words, evaluation is a universal language.

This publication includes eight case studies from around the world that were developed to show the value of sales training initiatives in various functions. The authors of these case studies are diligently pursuing accountability in sales training programs. Through their writing, they share their experiences with a process that continues to be at the forefront of measurement and evaluation.

TARGET AUDIENCE

These case studies will be ideal for anyone involved in the design, development, implementation, facilitation, or support of sales training and development programs. These studies show how these programs can be evaluated, pinpointing specific success factors along the way. A secondary audience is the executives who need to know how this important investment is evaluated. This includes sales managers and vice presidents of sales and marketing who are always concerned about the success of training, development, meetings, and events. Finally, a third audience is professors and students in sales programs where there is a need to show the value of training and developing the sales team.

THE CASES

Most selected case studies have adhered to the standards supporting the ROI Methodology. Some have neglected to adhere to the standards, noting lessons learned by not doing so. We are pleased with the studies presented in this volume and believe that those who have followed the progress of ROI use would agree that these are the best to be published in the sales training arena.

Although there was some attempt to structure cases similarly, they are not identical in style and content. It is important for the reader to experience the case studies as they were developed to identify the issues pertinent to each particular setting and situation. The result is a variety of presentations with a variety of styles. Some cases are brief and to the point, outlining precisely what happened and what was achieved. Others provide more detailed background information, including how the need for the program was determined, the personalities involved, and how their backgrounds and biases created a unique situation. In addition, while all case studies have been translated into English, we have tried to leave the nuances of the various languages and cultures intact.

In some cases, the name of the organization is identified, as are the individuals who were involved. In others, the organization's name is disguised at the request of either the organization or the case author. In today's competitive world and in situations where there is an attempt to explore new territory, it is understandable why an organization would choose not to be identified. Identification should not be a critical issue, however.

CASE AUTHORS

It would be difficult to find a more varied and impressive group of contributors than those providing case studies for this volume. The authors presented in this book are experienced and knowledgeable, and represent the highest standard of professionalism. Collectively, they represent practitioners, consultants, researchers, and even students. Many have already made a local or global mark in sales and marketing, measurement and evaluation, or both. All of them are or will be highly successful in their field.

SUGGESTIONS

We welcome your input. If you have ideas or recommendations regarding presentation, case selection, or case quality, please send them to us at ROI Institute, Inc., P.O. Box 380637, Birmingham, AL 35238-0637, or send them via email to patti@roiinstitute.net.

ACKNOWLEDGMENTS

Although this casebook is a collective work of many individuals, the first acknowledgment must go to all the case authors. They are appreciated not only for their commitment to developing their case studies, but also for their interest in furthering the development and implementation of ROI evaluation in their organizations. We also want to acknowledge the organizations that have allowed us to use their names and programs for publication. We realize this action is not without risk. We trust the final product has portrayed them as progressive organizations interested in results and willing to try new processes and techniques.

We would also like to thank Mike Galvin and the rest of the publishing team at ASTD Press. We have enjoyed publishing more than 40 books with ASTD and look forward to many more in the future.

Finally, we want to provide a special thanks to Rachel Robinson, our senior editor. Once again, she has produced an excellent book, while juggling many projects at the ROI Institute. Thanks Rachel, for a job well done.

Patricia Pulliam Phillips
patti@roiinstitute.net

Jack J. Phillips
jack@roiinstitute.net

Part I

The ROI Methodology

A Credible Approach to Evaluating
Your Sales Training Programs

1

The Opportunity

MEASURING ROI IN SALES TRAINING: THE BASICS

What Are Sales Training and Sales Enablement?

The term sales has a far-reaching scope that goes well beyond car salesmen, department store clerks, or bank tellers. Sales professions have become prominent in a vast number of industries, spanning both the private and public sectors. Almost everyone has a product or service to sell.

More and more, companies are recognizing that sales is a profession, and thus an increased emphasis on sales training is imperative. All true professions have competencies and competency models to identify key knowledge, skills, and abilities (KSA). When KSAs are identified, hiring profiles are created, sales training curriculums are created that teach and reinforce these behaviors, and gap assessments are performed. Determining the ROI for these efforts is key to gaining buy-in from sales leaders and corporate executives and securing long-term commitment to continuous sales training activities.

With all of that in mind, ASTD conducted a two-year research project that resulted in the World-Class Sales Competency Model. The model views sales as a system with sales representatives, sales managers, sales coaches, and sales trainers. From that, ASTD has developed educational courses and content to reinforce a competency-based approach to sales organization improvement.

The concept of sales training has been expanded to include enablement processes to assist in the sales scenario. The enablement processes include tools, guides, videos, events, meetings, brief modules, and other just-in-time processes to identify prospects, apply appropriate selling skills, close the sale, and support the customer while keeping the customer engaged and satisfied.

What Is ROI?

Return on investment (ROI) is the ultimate measure of accountability. Within the context of sales training, it answers the question: For every dollar invested in sales training or enablement, how many dollars were returned, above and beyond the investment? ROI is an economic indicator that compares earnings (or net benefits) to investment, and is represented as a percentage. The concept of ROI to measure the success of investment opportunities has been used in business for centuries to measure the return on capital expenditures such as buildings, equipment, or tools. As the needs for greater accountability for training, demonstrated effectiveness, and value increase, ROI is becoming an accepted way to measure the impact and return on investment of all types of training programs, including sales training.

The counterpart to ROI, *benefit-cost ratio* (BCR), has also been used for centuries. Benefit-cost analysis became prominent in the United States in the early 1900s when it was used to justify projects initiated under the River and Harbor Act of 1902 and the Flood Control Act of 1936. ROI and the benefit-cost ratio provide similar indicators of investment success, though one (ROI) presents the earnings (net benefits) as compared to the cost, while the other (BCR) compares benefits to costs. Here are the basic equations used to calculate the benefit-cost ratio and the ROI:

$$BCR = \frac{Program\ Benefits}{Program\ Costs}$$

$$ROI\ (\%) = \frac{Program\ Benefits - Program\ Costs}{Program\ Costs} \times 100$$

What is the difference between these two equations? A benefit-cost ratio of 2:1 means that for every $1 invested, $2 in benefits are generated. This translates into an ROI of 100 percent, which says that for every $1 invested, $1 is returned after the costs are covered (the investment is recovered plus $1 extra).

Benefit-cost ratios were used in the past, primarily in public sector settings, while ROI was used mainly by accountants managing capital expenditures in business and industry. While ROI and BCR calculations can be, and are, used in both settings, it is important to understand the difference. In many cases the benefit-cost ratio and the ROI are reported together.

While ROI is the ultimate measure of accountability, basic accounting practice suggests that reporting the ROI metric alone is insufficient. To be meaningful, ROI must be reported with other performance measures. This approach is taken with the ROI Methodology, the basis for the studies in this book.

THE ROI METHODOLOGY

The ROI Methodology is comprised of five key elements, which work together to complete the evaluation puzzle. Figure 1-1 illustrates how these elements are interconnected to create a comprehensive evaluation system.

Figure 1-1. The Evaluation Puzzle

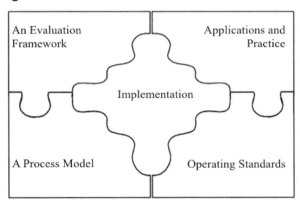

Evaluation Framework

The system begins with the five-level ROI framework, developed in the 1970s and becoming prominent in the 1980s (Phillips, 1983). Today, this framework is used to categorize results for all types of programs and projects.

- Level 1 *Reaction and Planned Action* data represent the reactions to the program and the planned actions from participants. Reactions may include views of the format, duration, facilitator effectiveness, and fit. This category must include data that reflect the value of the program, including measures of relevance, importance, amount of new information, and participants' willingness to recommend the program to others.

- Level 2 *Learning* data represent the extent to which participants have acquired new knowledge about their strengths, development areas, and the skills needed to be successful. The learning may include product knowledge, sales strategy, or marketing philosophy. This category of data also includes the level of confidence of sales professionals as they plan to apply their newly acquired knowledge and skills on the job.

- Level 3 *Application and Implementation* data determine the extent to which sales professionals apply their newly acquired knowledge and skills after the training program. This category of data also includes data that describe the barriers that prevent application as well as any supporting elements (enablers) in the knowledge transfer process.

- Level 4 *Business Impact* data are collected and analyzed to determine the extent to which applications of acquired knowledge and skills positively influenced key measures that were intended to improve as a result of the sales training experience. The measures include sales, new accounts, customer complaints, customer returns, customer satisfaction, market share, customer churn, and customer loyalty. When reporting data at this level, a step to isolate the program's effects on these measures from other influences is always taken.

- Level 5 *Return on Investment* compares the monetary benefits of the impact measures (as they are converted to monetary value) to the fully loaded program costs. Improvement can occur in sales, for example, but to calculate the ROI, the measure of improvement must be converted to monetary value (profit of the sale) and compared to the cost of the program. If the monetary value of sales improvement exceeds the cost, the calculation is a positive ROI.

Each level of evaluation answers basic questions regarding the success of the sales training or enablement program. Table 1-1 presents these questions.

TABLE 1-1. Evaluation Framework and Key Questions

Level of Evaluation	Key Questions
Level 1: Reaction and Planned Action	• Was the training relevant to the job and purpose of the participants' roles? • Was the sales training important to the jobs and success of the participants? • Did the sales training provide the participants with new information? • Do participants intend to use what they learned? • Would participants recommend the program or process to others? • Is there room for improvement with facilitator selection and match, training session duration and frequency, and the setting for the sales training work?
Level 2: Learning	• Did the participants gain the knowledge and insights identified at the start of the sales training? • Do participants know how to apply what they learned? • Are participants confident they can apply what they learned?
Level 3: Application and Implementation	• How effectively are participants applying what they learned? • How frequently are participants applying what they learned? • If participants are applying what they learned, what is supporting them? • If participants are not applying what they learned, why not?

Level 4: Business Impact	• So what if the application is successful—what impact does it have on the business? • To what extent does application of knowledge and insights improve the business measures the sales training program was intended to improve? • How does the sales training program affect output, quality, cost, time, customer satisfaction, employee satisfaction, and other measures? • How do you know it was the sales training that improved these measures?
Level 5: ROI	• Do the monetary benefits of the improvement in business impact measures outweigh the cost of the sales training initiative?

Categorizing evaluation data as levels provides a clear and understandable framework to manage the sales training programs' design and objectives and manage the data collection process. More importantly, these five levels present data in a way that makes it easy for the audience to understand the results reported for the program. While each level of evaluation provides important, stand-alone data, when reported together, the five-level ROI framework represents data that tell the complete story of program success or failure. Figure 1-2 presents the chain of impact that occurs as sales professionals react positively to a training initiative; acquire new knowledge, skills, and awareness; apply the new knowledge and skills; and, as a consequence, positively affect key business measures. When these measures are converted to monetary value and compared to the fully loaded costs, an ROI is calculated. Along with the ROI and the four other categories of data, intangible benefits are reported. These represent Level 4 measures that are not converted to monetary value.

Figure 1-2. Chain of Impact

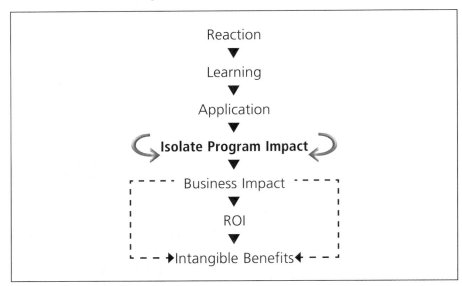

Source: Phillips, P.P., and J.J. Phillips. (2005). *Return on Investment Basics*. Alexandria, VA: ASTD Press.

ROI Process Model

The second part of the evaluation puzzle is the process model. As presented in Figure 1-3, the process model is a step-by-step guide to ensure a systematic approach to evaluating a sales training or enablement project. Each phase of the four-phase process contains critical steps that must be taken to ensure the output of a credible sales training evaluation. The ROI process is described in more detail in the next section.

FIGURE 1-3. ROI Methodology Process Model

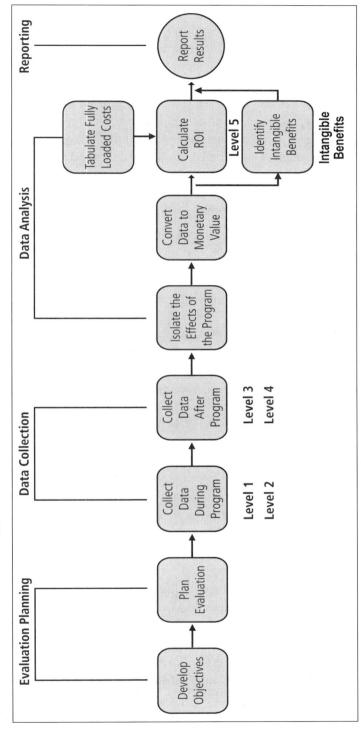

Operating Standards and Philosophy

This third part of the evaluation puzzle ensures consistent decision making around the application of the ROI Methodology. These standards provide clear guidance about the specific ways to implement the ROI Methodology to ensure consistent, reliable practice in evaluating sales training. When the 12 guiding principles shown in Table 1-2 are followed, consistent results can be achieved. Additionally, these guiding principles help maintain a conservative and credible approach to data collection and analysis. The 12 guiding principles serve as a decision-making tool and influence decisions on the best approach by which to collect data, the best source and timing for data collection, the most appropriate approach for isolation and data conversion, the costs to be included, and the stakeholders to whom results are reported. Adhering to the 12 guiding principles provides credibility when reporting results to executives.

TABLE 1-2. 12 Guiding Principles of the ROI Methodology

1.	When a higher level of evaluation is conducted, data must be collected at lower levels.
2.	When an evaluation is planned for a higher level, the previous level of evaluation does not have to be comprehensive.
3.	When collecting and analyzing data, use only the most credible sources.
4.	When analyzing data, choose the most conservative alternatives for calculations.
5.	At least one method must be used to isolate the effects of the solution/program.
6.	If no improvement data are available for a population or from a specific source, it is assumed that no improvement has occurred.
7.	Estimates of improvements should be adjusted for the potential error of the estimate.
8.	Extreme data items and unsupported claims should not be used in ROI calculations.
9.	Only the first year of benefits (annual) should be used in the ROI analysis for short-term solutions/programs.
10.	Costs of the solution/program should be fully loaded for ROI analysis.
11.	Intangible measures are defined as measures that are purposely not converted to monetary values.
12.	The results from the ROI Methodology must be communicated to all key stakeholders.

Case Applications and Practice

The fourth part of the ROI Methodology evaluation puzzle includes case applications and practice, which allow for a deeper understanding of the ROI Methodology's comprehensive evaluation process. Case application is a way to provide evidence of a sales training program's success. Thousands of case studies across many industries including business and industry, healthcare, government, and even community and faith-based initiatives, have been developed, describing the application of the ROI Methodology.

The case studies in this book provide excellent examples of application of the ROI Methodology. While practitioners who are beginning their pursuit of the ROI Methodology can learn from these case studies, as well as those found in other publications, the best learning comes from actual application. Conducting your own sales training ROI study will allow you to see how the framework, process model, and operating standards come together. Your first ROI study serves as a starting line for your track record of sales training program success.

Implementation

Finally, the last part of the ROI Methodology evaluation puzzle is implementation. While it is important to conduct a sales training ROI study, one study alone adds very little value to your efforts to continuously improve and account for your investments. The key to a successful sales training function is to sustain the use of ROI. Building the philosophy of the ROI Methodology into everyday decisions about your practice is imperative for attaining credibility and consistency in training effectiveness. Implementing the ROI Methodology requires assessing the organization's culture for accountability and its readiness for evaluating sales training programs at the ROI level. It also requires defining the purpose for pursuing this level of evaluation, building expertise and capability, and creating tools, templates, and standard processes.

ROI PROCESS MODEL

To evaluate a sales training program using the ROI Methodology, it is important to follow the step-by-step process to ensure consistent, reliable results. These 10 steps taken during the four phases of a sales training evaluation project make up the evaluation process model. Figure 1-3 presents the ROI Methodology process model.

Evaluation Planning

The first phase of the ROI process is planning. Having a plan allows you to know where you are going, and helps you define how you will know when you have arrived at your destination. The plan begins with developing and reviewing the program objectives to ensure that the application and impact objectives have been defined. Next, the data collection plan is developed, which includes defining the measures for each level of evaluation, selecting the data collection instrument, identifying the sources of the data, and timing of data collection. The baseline data for the measures you are taking should be collected during this time. The next step is to develop the ROI analysis plan. Working from the impact data, the most appropriate technique to isolate the effects of the sales training initiative on impact data is selected. The most credible method for converting data to money is identified along with the cost categories for the program.

Intangible benefits are listed and the communication targets for the final report are identified.

Data Collection

When the planning phase is completed, the data collection phase begins. Levels 1 and 2 data are collected as sales training takes place, using common instruments including end-of-course questionnaires, completion of exercises, demonstrations, and a variety of other techniques. Follow-up data at Levels 3 and 4 are collected after the training, when application of the newly acquired knowledge, skills, attitudes, and awareness becomes routine. After the application, the consequences are captured and the impact on key measures is observed.

Data Analysis

When the data are collected, the data analysis begins. As described earlier, the various methods for data analysis are defined in the planning stage; so data analysis is just a matter of execution. The first step in data analysis is to isolate the effects of the sales training on impact data. Isolation is often overlooked in evaluating the success of training programs, yet this step answers the critical question, "How much of the improvement in business measures is due to this particular sales training initiative or sales enablement program?"

Moving from Level 4 to Level 5 begins with converting Level 4 impact measures to monetary value. This step is easy because most of the data in sales and marketing are already converted to money. If not, there are some easy techniques to use. The fully loaded costs are developed during the data analysis phase. These costs include needs assessment (when conducted), design, participants' time, overhead, and evaluation costs.

Intangible benefits are also identified during the data analysis phase. Intangible benefits are the Level 4 measures that are not converted to monetary value. These measures can also represent any unplanned program benefits that were not identified during the planning phase.

The final step of the data analysis phase is the ROI calculation. Using simple addition, subtraction, multiplication, and division, the ROI and BCR are calculated.

Reporting

The most important phase in the evaluation process is the final report and the communication of results. Evaluation without communication is a meaningless endeavor. If you tell no one how the sales training is progressing, how can you improve the process, secure additional funding, and market programs to other participants?

While there are a variety of ways to report data, a micro-level report of the complete ROI impact study is important. This is a record of the success of the sales training program. A macro-level reporting process includes results for all programs, projects, and initiatives and serves as a scorecard of results for all initiatives. An important point to remember, however, is regardless of how detailed or brief the report may be, the information in it must be actionable. Otherwise, there is no ROI on conducting the ROI analysis.

BENEFITS OF ROI

The ultimate use of results generated through the ROI Methodology is to show value of programs, specifically the economic value. However, there are a variety of other uses for ROI data, including justification of spending, improvement of the sales training process, and gain of support for these types of programs.

Justify Spending

Being able to justify spending on sales training programs is becoming more commonplace than it was in the past. Managers of sales training programs are often required to justify investments in existing and new programs, as well as investment in changes or enhancements to existing training processes.

For those who are serious about justifying investments in new sales training programs, the ROI Methodology described in this book is a valuable tool. For new programs where a pre-program justification is required, there are two approaches that can be used: pre-program forecasts and ROI calculated on pilot implementation.

Calculating ROI in existing programs is more common in practice than forecasting success for new programs. Typically, ROI is used to justify continued investments in existing sales training programs. These are sales training programs that have been routinely conducted, but there is concern that the value does not justify continuation of the program.

Improve the Sales Training Process

The most important use of the ROI Methodology is to improve sales training programs and enablement processes. Often participants, as well as facilitators, believe that their performance is being evaluated in the program. Though they are sometimes asked to be accountable for applying their learning to improve business measures, the evaluation is improving the sales training and enablement process rather than evaluating the individual performance of the people involved in the program.

Set Priorities

In almost all organizations, the need for sales training exceeds the available resources. A comprehensive evaluation process, such as the ROI Methodology, can help determine which programs rank as the highest priority. Sales training initiatives with the greatest impact (or the potential for greatest impact) are often top priority. Of course, this approach has to be moderated by taking a long view, ensuring that developmental efforts are in place for a long-term payoff.

Eliminate Unsuccessful Programs

You hate to think of eliminating a sales training initiative—to some people this translates into the elimination of responsibility and ultimately the elimination of jobs. This is not necessarily true. Sometimes, one program is no longer necessary, but a need for a different process emerges. The ROI Methodology can be a tool to help decide which approach is eliminated and which alternative is selected as a replacement.

Gain Support

Another use for the ROI Methodology is to gain support for sales training and enablement. A successful sales training program needs support from key executives and administrators. Showing the ROI for programs can alter manager and executive perceptions and enhance the respect and credibility of all performance improvement processes.

Key executives and administrators are likely the most important group to influence with respect to the sales training program. They commit resources and show support for functions achieving results that positively affect the strategy of the organization. Executives and administrators are known for their support of development programs. To ensure that effective sales training programs are continued, it is necessary for the managers of sales training and enablement to think like the business—focusing programs on results and organizational strategy. ROI is one way this focus can occur. ROI evaluation provides the economic justification and value of investing in the sales training program selected to solve the problem.

Sales managers and supervisors can sometimes be antagonists of sales training programs because they often question the value of them. When this occurs, generally it is because the managers or supervisors have not seen success with a change in behavior in past sales training participants. Managers and supervisors aren't interested in what their participants learn; they are interested in what they do with what they learn. Sales training programs must take learning gained through the programs a step further by showing the effect on the job with outcomes in sales, new accounts, customer complaints, market share, and customer satisfaction. If the programs can show results linked to the business, managers and supervisors will provide increased support to sales training and enablement processes.

Participants and prospective participants should also support the program. Showing the value of sales training programs, including ROI, can enhance the credibility of the program. When the sales training process is achieving serious results, participants will view programs in a value-add way and may be willing to spend time away from their pressing duties. Also, by making adjustments in the sales training process based on the evaluation findings, participants will see that the evaluation process is not just a superficial attempt to show value.

FINAL THOUGHTS

This chapter introduced the concept of the ROI Methodology, which is a systematic and logical process with conservative standards that is being used by over 4,000 organizations. The process collects and generates six types of data: reaction, learning, application, impact, ROI, and intangibles. It also includes techniques to isolate the effects of the sales training or enablement program on the impact data, such as sales, new accounts, and market share. The next two chapters explain this process in more detail and they form the basis for the case studies presented in later chapters. Chapter 2 introduces the important steps of evaluation planning and the first major challenge, collecting data.

Evaluation Planning and Data Collection

ACHIEVING BUSINESS ALIGNMENT

As the sales profession has matured, accountability for sales training effectiveness has increased. In the past, we could provide nearly any talent development solution, including sales training, to clients and measure the success of that solution based on self-reports. But in a world of tighter budgets, less time, and fewer resources, this is no longer enough. Instead, the very real demands for sales training accountability require that we shift from an activity-based approach to a results-based approach to sales training, as outlined in Table 2-1. As a result of sales training, managers are now requiring a visible improvement in selling skills and a positive effect on the business with increased sales, new accounts, market share, customer satisfaction, and customer loyalty. In some cases, they want to see the financial ROI.

TABLE 2-1. Activity-Based vs. Results-Based Approach to Sales Training

Activity-Based Approach	Results-Based Approach
Business need is not linked to the sales training in terms of monetary impact.	Program is linked to specific business impact measures such as revenue, productivity improvement, new customers, etc.
Assessment of performance issues that will be addressed in sales training are not captured in a quantifiable, measurable manner.	There is an assessment of performance effectiveness that needs to improve.
Specific measurable, quantifiable objectives are not clarified.	Specific, measurable objectives for behavior change and the related business impact are identified.
Participants are not fully prepared to participate in the program.	Results expectations are communicated with and in partnership with participants.
The environment is not prepared to support the transfer of learning to behavior change and business impact.	Work environment is prepared to support transfer of learning to behavior change and business impact.
Partnerships with key managers to support the participant have not been identified and developed.	Partnerships are established with key managers and clients prior to training to ensure participation and support.

Continued on next page.

Table 2-1 continued.

Results or benefit-cost analysis in real, tangible, and objective measures—including monetary impact—are not captured.	Results and benefit-cost analysis are measured.
Planning and reporting is input focused.	Planning and reporting is outcome focused.

To ensure sales training programs lead to results, they must first be positioned for success. Positioning occurs through the establishment of objectives. Objectives are the starting point for implementation. They are also the first step in the ROI process, as shown in Figure 1-3 in chapter 1. Objectives drive the design of the sales training and enablement programs by describing what program participants will learn, what they will do with what they learn (including behavior changes based on newly acquired knowledge, skills, and insights), and the impact their efforts will have on key business measures. They tell facilitators and designers of the processes what elements go into the sales training program so participants and sales professionals can meet expectations. Objectives also tell evaluators which measures to collect during the evaluation process.

Objectives are core to business alignment, as shown in Figure 2-1. They evolve from the needs assessment process and drive the evaluation process. Objectives serve as the catalyst between what stakeholders want and need and what they receive and accomplish from a program or initiative. The first step toward developing objectives is clarifying stakeholder needs.

Clarifying Stakeholder Needs

Sales training programs originate from an observed need. The ultimate need for sales training is in the potential payoff of the investment. Several questions should be asked when deciding if and how much to invest in a sales training or enablement initiative:

- Is this program worth implementing?
- Is this a problem worth solving?
- Is this an opportunity worth pursuing?
- Is there likelihood for a positive ROI?

The problem or opportunity can be obvious, such as:

- Sales have decreased 30 percent from last year.
- Very low market share in a market with only a few competitors.
- Sales are flat—no growth.
- Product returns have increased 20 percent in six months.
- Customer satisfaction has declined two years in a row.

FIGURE 2-1. Business Alignment Process

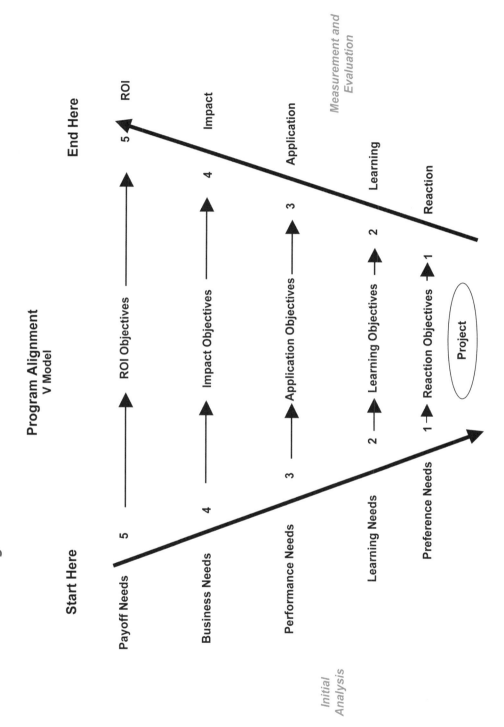

Or they may be less obvious, such as:
- We want our customers to be more engaged.
- The sales force should be more consultative.
- Every sales professional must have negotiation skills.
- We need more just-in-time training.
- Let's organize a business development conference.
- Create a great place to work for the sales team.

In either case, payoff needs are those problems or opportunities that if addressed, will ultimately help the organization make money, save money, or avoid costs, and deliver a positive ROI. When the payoff need is addressed, the specific business measures that need to improve to address the payoff need are identified. These "business needs" represent hard data, categorized in broad categories of output, quality, cost, and time; they may also represent soft data such as measures of satisfaction, image, and reputation. Examples of business measures in need of improvement may be sales, new accounts, market share, sales expense, customer satisfaction, customer loyalty, product returns, and customer complaints.

After the business needs are defined, the next step is to clarify the performance needs. These are behaviors, actions, or activities that need to change on the job to improve the business measures. The needs at this level can vary considerably and might include ineffective behavior, inadequate systems, and disconnected process flows. There are a variety of ways to identify gaps in performance including questionnaires, interviews, observations, brainstorming, nominal group technique, statistical process control, and other approaches, some more technical than others.

When performance needs are identified, the needs assessment addresses learning needs. When identifying learning needs, the basic question being answered is: What does the sales team need to know in order to change its behavior or actions on the job (performance need) to improve business measures (business need)? A variety of techniques are available including task analysis, job analysis, questionnaires, surveys, and interviews.

Next, the preference needs represent the preferred way in which the knowledge, skill, and information are delivered. This addresses the issue of preference for the training (or enablement) program from the sales team, the sales manager, and other stakeholders. This focuses on issues such as relevance, importance, and intent to use.

Finally, the project team determines the input needs, which simply represent the target audience, the required resource investment, and all other aspects of program implementation. With needs analysis complete, the next step is to develop objectives.

Determining Program Objectives

Program objectives reflect the needs of stakeholders. When implementing a sales training process, it is important to develop objectives at multiple levels of evaluation. These objectives tie the sales training initiative to meaningful outcomes. Program objectives represent the chain of impact, ensuring that designers, developers, facilitators, participants, supervisors and managers, senior leaders, and evaluators are aware of the potential for success.

Level 1 reaction objectives describe expected immediate satisfaction with the sales training program. They describe issues that are important to the success of sales training, including the relevance of the program and importance of the information or content shared through the process. In addition, these objectives describe expected satisfaction with the logistics of the sales training process from delivery to expected use.

Level 2 learning objectives describe the expected immediate and intermediate outcomes in terms of knowledge acquisition, skill attainment, and awareness and insights obtained through the sales training experience. These objectives set the stage for preparing participants for job transformation. It is important to note that even sales enablement tools (a non-learning solution) will still have a learning component and thus learning objectives.

Level 3 application objectives describe the expected intermediate outcomes in terms of what the participant is to do differently as a result of the sales training process. Objectives at this level also describe expectations as to the time at which participants should apply knowledge, skills, and insights routinely.

Level 4 impact objectives define the specific business measures that should improve as a result of the new behavior and actions occurring through the sales training process. Improvement in these intermediate (and sometimes, long-term) outcomes represent changes in sales, new accounts, sales costs, and response time measures as well as customer satisfaction and employee satisfaction measures. Objectives at this level answer the question, "So what?" as it relates to the investment in sales training. They describe to stakeholders the importance of the sales training process.

Lastly, the Level 5 ROI objective defines for stakeholders the intended financial outcome; it should be reserved for those programs evaluated at this level. This single indicator sets the expectation for how the benefits of sales training will relate to the cost (for example, will the increase in sales revenue generated from the program recoup the costs of its implementation?).

Evaluating the Program

This final phase of the alignment process is the basis for this book. Evaluation occurs based on the objectives of the sales training initiative. The more specific the objective, the easier it is to plan the evaluation. With clear objectives, the evaluator can determine what measures to take during the evaluation process, the sources of the data, the timing of data collection, and the criterion for success.

A critical step in the evaluation phase that validates the alignment of the sales training program to the business need is isolating the effects of the program. As you will read in the next chapter, this step is imperative if you want to report credible, reliable, and valid results. There are a variety of techniques available to isolate the effects of sales training. Clear, measurable objectives can help you decide which technique is best for your sales training intervention.

DEVELOPING EVALUATION PLANS

When planning a sales training program evaluation, two documents are completed in as much detail as possible. The data collection plan lays the initial groundwork and answers the five key questions outlined in Table 2-2.

TABLE 2-2. Data Collection Plan Key Questions and Descriptions

Key Question	Description
What do you ask?	The answers to this question lie in the program objectives and their respective measures.
How do you ask?	How you ask is dependent on a variety of issues, including resources available to collect data. For example, Level 2 data may require tests, role-plays, self-assessments, and facilitator assessments.
Whom do you ask?	Go only to the most credible source; sometimes this includes multiple sources.
When do you ask?	Timing of data collection is critical, particularly for application and impact measures. Select a point in time at which you believe application and impact will occur.
Who does the asking?	Typically, the sales training manager collects data at Levels 1 and 2. For the higher levels of evaluation, representatives of the evaluation team may be assigned specific roles.

By answering these questions as specifically as possible up-front, the scope of the data collection process is set. As you answer these questions, you will complete the data collection plan. An example of a completed data collection plan is shown in Figure 2-2.

The second planning document is the ROI analysis plan, which includes seven key areas outlined in Table 2-3.

FIGURE 2-2. Data Collection Plan

Program: _____ Responsibility: _____ Date: _____

Level	Broad Program Objective(s)	Measures	Data Collection Method/ Instruments	Data Sources	Timing	Responsibilities
1	REACTION and PLANNED ACTIONS • Positive reaction – 4 out of 5 • Action items	• Rating on a composite of five measures • Yes/No	• Questionnaire	• Participant	• End of program (3rd day)	• Facilitator
2	LEARNING • Learn to use five simple skills	• Pass/Fail on skill practice	• Observation of skill practice by facilitator	• Facilitator	• 2nd day of program	• Facilitator
3	APPLICATION/ IMPEMENTATION • Initial use of five simple skills • At least 50% of participants use all skills with every customer	• Verbal feedback • 5th item checked on a 1-to-5 scale	• Follow-up session • Follow-up questionnaire	• Participant • Participant	• 3 weeks after 2nd day • 3 months after program	• Facilitator • Store Training Coordinator
4	BUSINESS IMPACT • Increase in sales	• Weekly average sales per sales associate	• Business performance monitoring	• Company records	• 3 months after program	• Store Training Coordinator
5	ROI • 50%	Comments:				

23

TABLE 2-3. ROI Analysis Plan Key Areas and Descriptions

Key Area	Description
Methods for isolating the effects of the program	Decide the technique you plan to use to isolate the effects of the program on your Level 4 measures.
Methods for converting data to monetary value	Column identifying the methods to convert your Level 4 measures to monetary value.
Cost categories	Costs include the needs assessment, program design and development, program delivery, evaluation costs, along with some amount representative of overhead and administrative costs for those people and processes that support your programs.
Intangible benefits	Those measures you choose not to convert to monetary value are considered intangible benefits.
Communication targets for the final report	Identify those audiences to whom results will be communicated.
Other issues that may influence program impact or the evaluation itself	Anticipate any issues that may occur during the training process that might have a negative effect or no effect on your identified impact measures.
Comments or reminders to the staff managing the program	Put reminder notes of key issues, comments regarding potential success or failure of the program, reminders for specific tasks to be conducted by the evaluation team, etc.

These seven key areas are addressed in detail in the ROI analysis plan. Figure 2-3 shows a completed ROI analysis plan.

Planning in detail what you are going to ask, how you are going to ask, who you are going to ask, when you are going to ask, and who will do the asking, along with the key steps in the ROI analysis will help ensure successful execution. Additionally, having clients sign off on the plans will ensure support for the evaluation approach when the evaluation results are presented.

FIGURE 2-3. ROI Analysis Plan

Program: _____   Responsibility: _____   Date: _____

Data Items	Methods of Isolating the Effects of the Program	Methods of Converting Data	Cost Categories	Intangible Benefits	Communication Targets	Other Influences/ Issues
• Weekly sales per associate	• Control group analysis	• Direct conversion using profit contribution	• Facilitation fees • Program materials • Meals/ refreshments • Facilities • Participant salaries/benefits • Cost of coordination/ evaluation	• Customer satisfaction • Employee satisfaction	• Program participants • Department managers–target stores • Store managers– target stores • Senior store executives district, region, headquarters • Training staff: instructors, coordinators, designers, and managers	• Must have job coverage during training • No communication with control group • Seasonal fluctuations should be avoided

COLLECTING DATA: CONSIDERATIONS

There are a variety of data collection techniques that can be used to collect the desired data from the appropriate source at the right time. How data are collected will depend on a variety of factors, including validity and reliability, time and cost, and utility.

Validity and Reliability

Consider the technique that will provide the most valid and reliable results when selecting a data collection method. Keep in mind that you will have to balance accuracy with the cost of data collection. Never spend more on data collection than the cost of the sales training initiative. A good guideline to keep in mind is that the full cost of your ROI study should not exceed 5 to 10 percent of the fully loaded cost of the sales training process. All evaluation costs are included in the denominator of the ROI equation. So, what you spend on data collection reduces the ROI percentage; however, do consider the techniques and steps that will provide the best data. Always balance accuracy and cost.

A basic way to examine validity is to ask, "Are you measuring what you intend to measure?" Content validity can be determined using sophisticated modeling approaches; however, the most basic approach to determining the validity of the questions asked is to refer to your objectives. Well-written objectives represent the measures you will take. You might also consider the use of subject matter experts, along with additional resources, such as literature reviews and previous case studies.

While validity is concerned with ensuring you are measuring the right measures, reliability is concerned with whether people are consistent in their answers. The most basic test of reliability is repeatability. This is the ability to obtain the same data from several measurements made in the same way. A basic example of repeatability is to administer the questionnaire to the same person repeatedly over a period of time. If the person responds the same way to the questions every time, there is minimum error, meaning there is high reliability. If, however, the person randomly selected the answers, there would be high error, meaning there is low reliability.

Time and Cost

When selecting data collection methods, several issues should be considered with regard to time and cost. Consider the time required to complete the instrument. Also, consider the time required for managers to complete the instrument or time involved in assisting the participants through the data collection process. Everything spent on data collection, including time to develop and test the questionnaire, time for the completion of data collection instruments, and printing costs, is a cost to the program. Also, consider the amount of disruption that the data collection will cause employees; typically, interviews and focus groups require the greatest disruption, yet provide some of the best data. Balance the accuracy of the data you need to make a decision about the sales training program, with what it will cost to obtain that data.

Utility

Another consideration when selecting a data collection method is utility. How useful will the data be, given the type of data collected through the data collection process? Data collected through a questionnaire can be easily coded and put into a database and analyzed. With the help of automation, data generated through a questionnaire can be quickly summarized. Data collected through focus groups and interviews, however, call for a more challenging approach to analysis. While information can be collected through dialogue and summarized in the report, a more comprehensive analysis should be conducted. However, this requires developing themes for the data collected and coding those themes. This type of analysis can be quite time consuming and in some cases, it can be frustrating if the data are not collected, compiled, and recorded in a structured way.

Another issue with regard to utility has to do with the use of the data. Avoid asking too many questions simply because you can, and instead consider whether you really need to ask a question in order to obtain the data to make a decision about the program. Remember, data collected and reported lead to business decisions, regardless of whether the training programs are offered through a corporate, government, or nonprofit organization. How can you best allocate the resources for sales training programs to develop people or improve processes? With these issues in mind, if you can't use the data, don't ask the question.

COLLECTING DATA: THE METHODS

Given the considerations covered in the previous section, there are variety of methods and instruments available to collect data at the different levels of evaluation. Some techniques are more suited toward certain levels of evaluation than others, but in many cases the approaches to data collection can cut across all levels of evaluation. Table 2-4 lists the different data collection methods used to collect data at the different levels. The most-often used methods of data collection for ROI evaluation are questionnaires, interviews, focus groups, action plans, and performance records.

TABLE 2-4. Data Collection Methods

Method	Type of Data			
	Level 1	2	3	4
Surveys	✓	✓	✓	
Questionnaires	✓	✓	✓	✓
Observation		✓	✓	
Interviews	✓	✓	✓	
Focus groups	✓	✓	✓	
Tests/Quizzes		✓		
Demonstrations		✓		
Simulations		✓		
Action planning/ Improvement plans			✓	✓
Performance contracting			✓	✓
Performance monitoring				✓

Questionnaires

Questionnaires are the data collection technique used most often when conducting an ROI evaluation. Questionnaires are inexpensive, easy to administer, and depending on the length, take very little of respondents' time. Questionnaires can be sent via mail, memo, email, or distributed online through an intranet or one of any number of electronic survey tools available on the Internet.

Questionnaires also provide versatility in the types of data that can be collected. They are used to collect data at all levels of evaluation. You can collect data about the demographics of sales professionals, attitudes toward the training program, knowledge gained during the program, and how the salespeople apply that knowledge. You can also ask respondents to indicate how much a particular measure is worth, how much that measure has improved, other variables that may have influenced improvements in that measure, and the extent of the influence of those variables.

Questions in a questionnaire can be open-ended, closed, or forced-choice. Likert-scale questions are common in questionnaires, as are frequency scales, ordinal scales, and other types of scales such as paired comparison and comparative scales. Periodically, you'll see an adjective checklist on a questionnaire to give participants the opportunity to reinforce their attitude toward the program.

While questionnaires can be quite lengthy and can include any number of questions, the best questionnaires are those that are concise and reflect those questions that will allow you to gather needed data. Results from brief questionnaires are powerful when describing the impact of a sales training initiative as well as its monetary benefits.

Interviews

Interviews are an ideal method of data collection when details must be probed from a select number of respondents. Interviews allow for gaining more in-depth data than questionnaires, action plans, and focus groups. However, it is important to consider costs and utility, particularly when considering evaluation at Levels 1 and 2. Guiding Principle 2 says, when evaluating at a higher level, the previous level does not have to be comprehensive. For example, if you plan to evaluate the program to Level 3, it would not be feasible to use interviews to collect Level 1 reaction data.

Interviews can be structured or unstructured. Unstructured interviews allow for greater depth of dialog between the evaluator and the respondent. Structured interviews work much like a questionnaire, except that there is a rapport between the evaluator and the respondent. The respondent has the opportunity to elaborate on responses and the evaluator can ask follow-up questions for clarification.

Interviews can be conducted in person or over the telephone. Interviews conducted in person have the greatest advantage because the person conducting the interview can show the participant items that can help clarify questions and response options. In-person interviews also allow for observation of body language that may indicate that the participant is uncomfortable with the question, anxious because of time commitments, or not interested in the interview process. Unlike the situation with a paper-based or email questionnaire where the disinterested respondent can simply throw away the questionnaire or press the delete key, in an interview setting, the evaluator can change strategies in hopes of motivating respondents to participate. Interviews are used when the evaluator needs to ask complex questions or the list of response choices is so long that it becomes confusing if administered through a questionnaire. In-person interviews are conducted when the information collected through the interview process is viewed as confidential or when the respondent would feel uncomfortable providing this information on paper or over the telephone.

While interviews provide the most in-depth data, they are the costliest. Scheduling interviews can be a challenge; and getting through the executive's gatekeeper can prove even a greater challenge than putting the interview on the executive's schedule, once you do make it to that point. If possible, consider hiring a professional interviewer, skilled at both interviewing as well as the ROI Methodology. The interviewing process can be daunting, especially when asking questions related to Level 4 business impact measures, isolation, and data conversion. A third-party interviewer skilled in these techniques can ensure that the data obtained are accurate and credible when presented to stakeholders during the reporting phase.

Focus Groups

Focus groups are a good approach to gather information from a group of people when dialogue among the group is important. Focus groups work best when the topic on which participants are to focus is also important to them. High-quality focus groups and the questions that you ask produce discussions that address exactly the topics you want to hear about. The key to successful focus groups is to keep focused. A fair amount of planning goes into designing the protocol for the focus group. The conversations that transpire during the focus group are constructed conversations focusing on a key issue of interest.

Action Plans

In many cases, action plans are incorporated into the sales training program. They are used to collect both Level 3 and Level 4 data. Prior to the sales training, participants identify specific business measures they need to improve as a result of the process. Through the process they, along with their facilitators, identify specific actions they will take or behaviors that they will change to target improvement in those measures.

Performance Records

Performance records are organizational records. Data found in performance records represent standard data used throughout the organization in reporting success for a variety of functions. Using performance records as a method of data collection can save time and money. Sales records and quality data are generally easy to obtain. However, not all measures in which there is interest are readily available in the record. It would be a wise investment of your time to learn what data are currently housed within the organization and can be utilized or referenced for the sales training program.

GENERATING HIGH RESPONSE RATES

An often-asked question when considering the data collection process is, "How many responses do you need to receive to make the data valid and useable?" The answer is, as many as possible! Guiding Principle 6 says, if no improvement data are available for a population or from a specific source, it is assumed that no improvement has occurred. While it is unlikely that 100 percent of potential respondents will provide data, it is important that a plan is in place to gather as many responses as possible. Inference is not made to non-respondents, so if 20 participants are involved and data are only provided by 10, results are only reported for the 10. This conservative standard ensures that reliable and credible results are reported.

If we report for non-respondents, then we inflate the results on an assumption for which we have no basis. However, because we also adhere to Guiding Principle 10, costs of the solution or program should be fully loaded for ROI analysis, we will account for the cost of training all 20 sales professionals. So, the key is to develop a strategy to obtain responses from as many potential respondents as possible.

Table 2-5 lists a variety of action items to take to ensure an appropriate response rate. Start by providing advanced communication about the evaluation. Clearly communicating the reason for the evaluation ensures that training participants understand that the evaluation is not about them, it is about improving the sales training program. Identify those people who will see the results of the evaluation and assure them that they will receive a summary of the evaluation. When using a questionnaire as your data collection instrument, keep it as brief as possible by only asking questions that are important to the evaluation. If possible, have a third party collect and analyze the data so that participants feel comfortable that their responses will be held in confidence and anonymity will remain.

TABLE 2-5. Increasing Response Rates

- ☐ Provide advance communication.
- ☐ Communicate the purpose.
- ☐ Identify who will see the results.
- ☐ Describe the data integration process.
- ☐ Let the target audience know that they are part of a sample.
- ☐ Add emotional appeal.
- ☐ Design for simplicity.
- ☐ Make it look professional and attractive.
- ☐ Use the local manager support.
- ☐ Build on earlier data.
- ☐ Pilot test the questionnaire.
- ☐ Recognize the expertise of participants.
- ☐ Consider the use of incentives.
- ☐ Have an executive sign the introductory letter.
- ☐ Send a copy of the results to the participants.
- ☐ Report the use of results.
- ☐ Provide an update to create pressure to respond.
- ☐ Present previous responses.
- ☐ Introduce the questionnaire during the program.
- ☐ Use follow-up reminders.
- ☐ Consider a captive audience.
- ☐ Consider the appropriate medium for easy response.
- ☐ Estimate the necessary time to complete the questionnaire.
- ☐ Show the timing of the planned steps.
- ☐ Personalize the process.
- ☐ Collect data anonymously or confidentially.

IDENTIFYING THE SOURCE

Selecting the source of the data is critical in ensuring accurate data are collected. Sometimes it is necessary to obtain data from multiple sources. A fundamental question should be answered when deciding on the source of the data: Who (or what system) knows best about the measures being taken?

The primary source of data for Levels 1, 2, and 3 is the participants. Who knows best about their perception of the course, what they learned, and how they are applying what they learned? Although at Level 3, it may also be important to collect data from other sources, such as the manager to validate or complement the findings.

Performance Records

Given the variety of sources for the data, the most credible data source is the organization or internal performance records. These records reflect performance in a work unit, department, division, region, or organization. Performance records can include all types of measures that are usually readily available throughout the organization. This is the preferred method of data collection for Level 4 evaluation, since it usually reflects business impact data.

Participants

Participants are the most widely used source of data for ROI analysis. They are always asked about their reaction to the program and the extent to which learning has occurred. Participants are often the primary source of data for Levels 3 and 4 evaluation. They are the ones who know what they do with what they learned and what happened that may have prevented them from applying what they learned. In addition, they are the ones who have insight to what impact their actions have on the business.

While many people perceive participants as a biased option, if they understand the purpose of the evaluation and that the evaluation is not about them, it is about the program, they can remove their personal feelings from their answers and provide objective data.

Participants' Managers

Managers of the participants are another important source. In many cases, they have observed the participants as they attempt to use the knowledge and skills. Those managers, who are actively engaged in a learning process, will often serve as support to the participant to ensure that application does occur. Data from managers often balance the participants' perspectives. In gathering data from the managers, keep in mind any potential bias that may occur from this source of information.

Participants' Peers and Direct Reports

In evaluating at Level 3, participants' peers and direct reports are a good source of data. The 360-feedback evaluation provides one of the most balanced views of performance because it considers the perspective of the participants, their managers, their peers, and their direct reports. While gathering input from peers and direct reports can increase the cost of the evaluation, their perspective may add a level of objectivity to the process.

Senior Managers and Executives

Senior managers and executives may also provide valuable data, especially when collecting Level 4 data. Their input, however, may be somewhat limited if they are removed from the actual application of the knowledge and skills applied. However, senior managers and executives may play a key role in the data collection process when implementing a high-profile, leadership development program in which they have invested.

Other Sources

Internal and external experts and databases provide a good source of data when trying to convert business impact measures to monetary value. The ideal situation is to gather monetary value for the business impact measures from the standard values currently available. However, sometimes it is necessary to resort to the experts or the databases outside of the organization's records.

DETERMINING THE TIMING OF DATA COLLECTION

The last consideration in the data collection process is the timing of data collection. Typically, Level 1 data are collected at the end of the sales training program, and Level 2 data are collected during or at the end of the program.

Levels 3 and 4 data collection occur sometime after the new performance has had a chance to occur—the time in which new behaviors are becoming routine. Do not wait until the new behavior becomes inherent and sales professionals forget they were even involved in the training process. However, do not collect data while the facilitator is still involved, as this influence could affect results. Typically, Level 3 data collection occurs three to six months after the sales training program is complete. Some sales training programs, in which skills should be applied immediately upon conclusion of the program, should be measured earlier—anywhere from 30 days to two months after the program. Level 4 data can be a little trickier, however. With Level 4 data, timing may be different than timing for Level 3 evaluation, depending on data availability, the stakeholder requirements, and opportunity for the measure to improve.

While the ROI calculation is an annual benefit, it is unlikely that you will wait a full year to capture Level 4 data. Senior executives usually want to see results sooner than later. If the sales training program was introduced to solve a problem (such as, unsatisfactory sales revenue), the concern will either go away, executives and senior managers will forget, or a decision will be made without the data about the sales training program. Collect the Level 4 measures either at the time of Level 3 data collection or soon after, when impact has occurred. Then, convert those measures to monetary benefits and include them in the ROI calculation.

Sound data collection strategy is imperative for achieving credible results. Ensuring that the most appropriate methods, sources, and timing are employed in the data collection process will yield results that are reliable and useful to stakeholders. However, it is through the analysis that the real story of sales training success is told. Analysis begins with isolating the effects of sales training on improvement in business measures.

FINAL THOUGHTS

This chapter introduced the concept of achieving business alignment, which is important for any program, particularly those with significant business impact such as sales training. It also discussed the importance of evaluation planning (to maintain alignment throughout the evaluation) and data collection. The various methods of data collection were outlined. By using these methods of data collection, you will be able to gather the most credible and timely data and can begin the data analysis, which is discussed in chapter 3.

3

ROI Analysis

ISOLATING THE EFFECTS OF SALES TRAINING

In order for the data collected during the data collection phase to be credible and usable, it must be analyzed. When using the ROI Methodology, data analysis should include the isolation of program effects on the data, calculation of fully-loaded program costs, conversion of data to monetary values when appropriate, and the ROI calculation.

Isolating the effects of a sales training or enablement program on business impact data is one of the most challenging, yet necessary, steps in the ROI Methodology. When addressed credibly, this step links learning from sales training directly to business impact.

Other Factors Are Always Present

In almost every situation, multiple factors affect business results. During the time that sales training programs are implemented, many other functions within the organization may be attempting to improve the same metrics addressed by the sales training program. For example, marketing programs are designed to improve sales; and, while sales training should help a sales professional positively affect sales, the marketing program should also be positively affecting sales. In addition to internal factors, external factors may be affecting business results during the time that the sales training is occurring.

Without Isolation, There Is Only Evidence, Not Proof

Without taking steps to show the contribution of sales training, there is no clear business linkage; instead, there is only evidence that sales training may have made a difference. When business results improve during training, it is possible that other factors may have contributed to that improvement. The proof that the sales training program has made a difference on the business comes from isolating the effects of the program or initiative.

Other Factors Have Protective Owners

The owners of the other functions that influence business results are convinced that their processes or programs make the difference. Other processes or programs, such as promotions, advertisements, events, sales commissions, and job redesign all have protective owners, and their arguments are plausible. Therefore, owners of sales training programs are under pressure to build a credible argument for their case to claim value-add to the organization.

To Do It Right Is Not Easy

The challenge of isolating the effects of the sales training program on the business is critical and can be done; but it is not easy for complex programs, especially when strong-willed owners of other processes are involved. It takes a determination to address this situation every time an ROI study is conducted. Fortunately, a variety of approaches is available.

TECHNIQUES TO ISOLATE THE EFFECTS OF SALES TRAINING

Before reviewing the specific methods, it is helpful to highlight two important issues.

First, although it is possible to isolate for the effect of the sales training program at Level 3, application, isolation is usually applied to Level 4, impact. The business impact connected to the program is the key issue because when calculating ROI, the improvement in business measures is reported in monetary terms and more than any other level, it must be credible. After the business impact data have been collected, the next step is to isolate the effects of the program. This step demonstrates the proof that the sales training program made a difference, whereas reporting results along the chain of impact only presents evidence of the connection between sales training and results.

Another important issue is to attempt to identify the other factors that have contributed to the improvement in the business results measures. This step recognizes that other factors are almost always present and that the credit for improvement is shared with other functions in the organization. Just taking this step is likely to gain respect from the management team.

Several potential sources can help identify these influencing factors. The sponsors of the project may be able to identify the factors. Subject matter experts, process owners, and those who are most familiar with the situation may be able to indicate what has changed to influence the results. In many situations, sales professionals know what other factors have actually influenced their performance. After all, it is their direct performance that is being measured and monitored.

By taking stock in this issue, all factors that contributed to improvement are revealed, indicating the seriousness of the issue and underscoring how difficult it is going to be to isolate the effects of programs, projects, and initiatives. A variety of techniques can help address the isolation issue, discussed next.

Comparison Group Analysis

The most accurate and credible approach to isolate the effects of a sales training program is a comparison group analysis, known as the control group arrangement. This approach involves the use of an experimental group that participates in the sales training program and a control group that does not. The composition of both groups should be as similar as possible, and, if feasible, the selection of participants for each group should be on a random basis. When this is possible and both groups are subjected to the same environmental influences (such as market growth, economy), the differences in the performance of the two groups can be attributed to the sales training program. As illustrated in Figure 3-1, the control group and experimental group do not necessarily have pre-program measurements. Measurements are often only taken after the program is implemented, rather than prior to the program and then again after the program. The difference in the performance of the two groups shows the amount of improvement that is directly related to the sales training program.

FIGURE 3-1. Control Group Design (Post-Test Only)

For the comparison group analysis to be used, five conditions must exist.
1. One or two outcome measures represent the consequence of the sales training program. This is the business measure in question.
2. In addition to the sales training program, the factors that influence the outcome measures can be identified.
3. There are enough participants available from which to select the two groups.
4. The program can be withheld from the control group without any operational problems.
5. The same environmental influences affect both groups during the experiment (except that one group receives the sales training program).

If these assumptions can be met, then there is a possibility for a control group arrangement.

Problems and Opportunities With Comparison Groups

Inherent problems with the control group arrangements exist, which may make it difficult to apply in practice. When addressed properly, the problems become opportunities. The first major problem is that the process is inappropriate for many situations.

For some types of sales training programs, it may not be proper to withhold the program from one particular group while it is conducted in another. This particular barrier may prevent many control groups from being implemented. However, in practice, there are many opportunities for a naturally occurring control group arrangement to evolve in situations where sales training is implemented.

The second problem is that the control groups must be addressed early enough so that similar groups can be used in the comparison. Dozens of factors can affect employee performance, some of them individual and others contextual. To tackle the issue on a practical basis, it is best to select three to five variables that will have the greatest influence on performance.

A third problem with the control group arrangement is contamination, which can occur when participants in the sales training program influence others in the control group. Sometimes the reverse situation occurs when members of the control group model the behavior from the experimental group. In either case, the experiment becomes contaminated because the influence of sales training filters to the control group.

Closely related to the previous problem is the issue of time. The longer a control group and experimental group comparison operates, the greater the likelihood that other influences will affect the results. More variables will enter into the situation, contaminating the results. On the other end of the scale, there must be enough time so that a clear pattern can emerge between the two groups. Thus, the timing for control group comparisons must strike a delicate balance of waiting long enough for their performance differences to show, but not so long that the results become seriously contaminated.

A fifth problem occurs when the different groups function under different environmental influences. Because they may be in different locations, the groups may have different environmental influences. Sometimes the selection of the groups can help prevent this problem from occurring.

A sixth problem with using control groups is that it may appear to be too research-oriented for many business organizations. For example, management may not want to take the time to experiment before proceeding with a program, or they may not want to withhold a sales training program from a group just to measure the impact of an experimental program. Because of this concern, some practitioners do not entertain the idea of using comparison groups.

When implementing a control group to study the effect of a sales training program, it is important for the program impact to be isolated to a high level of accuracy; the primary advantage of the control group process is accuracy.

Trend-Line Analysis

Another technique used to isolate the impact of sales training programs is trend-line analysis. This approach has credibility when it is feasible. It is a simpler alternative to the control group arrangement.

A trend line is drawn using pre-program performance as a base and extending the trend into the future. After the sales training program is implemented, actual performance is compared to the projected value, the trend line. Any improvement of performance over what the trend line predicted can then be reasonably attributed to the sales training program. For this to work, the following assumptions must be verified:

- Pre-program data are available. Data represent the impact data—the proposed outcome of the program.
- Pre-program data should be stable, not erratic.
- The trend that has developed prior to the program is expected to continue if the sales training program is not implemented to alter it.
- No other new variables entered the process after the program was conducted. The key word is "new," realizing that the trend has been established because of the variables already in place, and no additional variables enter the process beyond the sales training program.
- When the variance of the data is high, the stability of the trend line becomes an issue. If this is an extremely critical issue and the stability cannot be assessed from a direct plot of the data, more detailed statistical analyses can be used to determine if the data are stable enough to make the projection. The trend line can be projected with a simple formula available in many software packages.

The key element in this approach is to track the trend using historical data; project where the trend would be without help from a program; then after the sales training occurs, track the actual data over the same period of time as the pre-program data. Then the comparison can be made between what the forecast data show and what the actual data show.

Figure 3-2 shows an example of a trend-line analysis taken from a sales department of a book distribution company. The percentage reflects the level of actual sales compared to sales goals. Data are presented before and after program implementation in July. As shown in the figure, an upward trend on the data began prior to program implementation. Although the program apparently had an effect on sales, the trend line shows that some improvement would have occurred anyway, based on the trend that had previously been established. Program leaders may have been tempted to measure the improvement by comparing the average six months' sales prior to the program (87.3 percent) to the average six months after the program (94.4 percent), yielding a 7.1 percent difference. However, a more accurate comparison is the six-month average after the program compared to the trend line (92.3 percent). In this analysis, the difference is 2.1 percent. Using this more conservative measure increases the accuracy and credibility of the process to isolate the impact of the program.

FIGURE 3-2. Sample Trend-Line Analysis

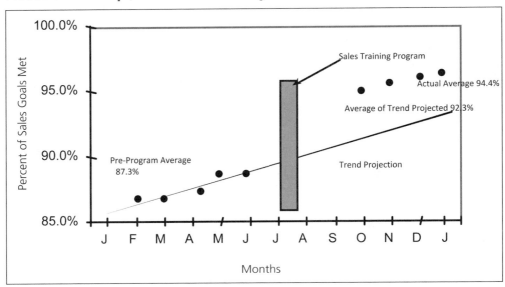

The primary advantage of this approach is that it is simple and inexpensive. If historical data are available, a trend line can quickly be drawn and differences estimated. While the approach is not exact, it does provide a quick assessment of a sales training program's potential results.

A disadvantage of the trend-line approach is that it is not always accurate. The use of this approach assumes that the events that influenced the performance variable prior to the sales training program are still in place after the program, except for the implementation of the program. Also, it assumes that no new influences entered the situation at the time the sales training was implemented. This is seldom the case.

Forecasting Methods

A more analytical approach to trend-line analysis is the use of forecasting methods that predict a change in performance variables based on the correlation of other variables. This approach represents a mathematical interpretation of the trend-line analysis when other variables enter the situation at the time of sales training.

The primary advantage of forecasting is that it can predict performance in business measures with some level of accuracy, if appropriate data and models are available. While there are no absolutes with any technique, using an appropriate level of statistical analysis can provide credible, reliable results.

A major disadvantage with forecasting occurs when several variables enter the process. The complexity multiplies, and the use of sophisticated statistical packages for multiple-variable analyses is necessary. Even then, a good fit of the data to the model may not be possible. Many organizations have not developed mathematical relationships for output variables as a function of one or more inputs. Without them, the forecasting method is difficult to use.

Expert Estimation

An easily implemented method to isolate the effect of sales training is to obtain information directly from experts who understand the business performance measures. The experts could be any number of individuals. For many sales training programs, the participants are the experts. After all, their performance is in question and the measure is reflecting their individual performance. They may know more about the relationships between the different factors, including the impact of training, than any other individual.

Because of the importance of estimations from participants, much of the discussion in this section relates to how to collect this information directly from them. The same methods would be used to collect data from others. The effectiveness of the approach rests on the assumption that participants are capable of determining how much of a performance improvement is related to the sales training initiative. Because their actions have produced the improvement, participants may have an accurate perception of the issue. Although an estimate, this value will typically have credibility with management because participants are at the center of the change or improvement.

When using this technique, several assumptions are made:

- A sales training program has been conducted with a variety of different activities, exercises, and learning opportunities, all focused on improving performance.
- Business measures have been identified prior to the program and have been monitored following the program. Data monitoring has revealed an improvement in the business measure.
- There is a need to link the sales training program to the specific amount of performance improvement and develop the monetary effect of the improvement. This information forms the basis for calculating the actual ROI.
- The participants are capable of providing knowledgeable input on the cause-and-effect relationship between the different factors, including learning and the output measure.

With these assumptions, the participants can pinpoint the actual results linked to the program and provide data necessary to develop the ROI. This can be accomplished by using a focus group or a questionnaire.

Focus Group Approach

The focus group works extremely well for this challenge if the group size is relatively small—in the eight to 12 person range. If much larger, the group should be divided into multiple groups. Focus groups provide the opportunity for members to share information equally, avoiding domination by any one individual. The process taps the input, creativity, and reactions of the entire group.

When conducting a focus group, the following steps are recommended to arrive at the most credible value for sales training impact:

1. Explain the task.
2. Discuss the rules.
3. Explain the importance of the process.
4. Select the first measure and show the improvement.
5. Identify the different factors that have contributed to the performance.
6. Identify other factors that have contributed to the performance.
7. Discuss the linkage.
8. Repeat the process for each factor.
9. Allocate the improvement.
10. Provide a confidence estimate.
11. Ask the participants to multiply the two percentages.
12. Report results.

Participants who do not provide information are excluded from the analysis. Table 3-1 illustrates this approach with an example of one participant's estimations. The participant allocates 50 percent of the improvement to the sales training program. The confidence percentage is a reflection of the error in the estimate. A 70 percent confidence level reduces the estimate to an adjusted percentage of 35 percent (50% x 70% = 35%). In essence, this error adjustment assumes the lowest percentage in improvement given a range. If a person is 70 percent confident in their estimate, that means they are 30 percent uncertain. Given this level of uncertainty, the margin of error is 50% x 30% = 15%. With a margin of error of +/– 15 percent, the range of improvement is 35 to 65 percent. To be conservative, the lowest end of the range, 35 percent, is reported as improvement.

TABLE 3-1. Example of a Participant's Estimation

Factors That Influenced Improvement	Percentage of Improvement	Percentage of Confidence Expressed	Adjusted Percentage of Improvement
1. Sales Training Program	50%	70%	35%
2. Change in Promotions	10%	80%	8%
3. Market Growth	10%	50%	5%
4. Revision to Incentive Plan	20%	90%	18%
5. Increased Management Attention	10%	50%	5%
Total	**100%**		

The use of expert estimations provides a credible way to isolate the effects of sales training when other methods will not work. It is often regarded as the low-cost solution to the problem because it takes only a few focus groups and a small amount of time to arrive at this conclusion.

Questionnaire Approach

Sometimes focus groups are not available or are considered unacceptable for purposes of isolating the effects of sales training. The participants may not be available for a group meeting, or the focus groups may become too expensive. In these situations, it may be helpful to collect similar information via a questionnaire. With this approach, participants address the same issues as those addressed in the focus group, but now on a series of impact questions imbedded into a follow-up questionnaire.

The questionnaire may focus solely on isolating the effects of the sales training program, as detailed in the previous example, or it may focus on the monetary value derived from the program, with the isolation issue being only a part of the data collected. Using questionnaires is a more versatile approach when it is not certain exactly how participants will provide business impact data. In some programs, the precise measures that will be influenced by the sales training program may not be known. This is sometimes the case in programs involving selling skills, customer service, communications, negotiations, up-selling, closing, and other types of sales training initiatives. In these situations, it is helpful to obtain information from participants on a series of impact questions, showing how they have used what they have learned and how the work unit has been affected. It is important for participants to know about these questions before they receive the questionnaire. The surprise element can be disastrous in this type of data collection. The recommended series of questions is shown in Table 3-2.

TABLE 3-2. Recommended Series of Questions for Isolating Program Results

1.	How have you and your job changed as a result of attending this program (skills and knowledge application)?
2.	What effects do these changes bring to your work or work unit?
3.	How is this effect measured (specific measure)?
4.	How much did this measure change after you participated in the sales training program (monthly, weekly, or daily amount)?
5.	What is the unit value of the measure?
6.	What is the basis for this unit value? Please indicate the assumption made and the specific calculations you performed to arrive at the value.
7.	What is the annual value of this change or improvement in the work unit (for the first year)?
8.	Recognizing that many other factors influence output results in addition to the learning gained in training, please identify the other factors that could have contributed to this performance.
9.	What percentage of this improvement can be attributed directly to the application of skills and knowledge gained in the program? (0%–100%)
10.	What confidence do you have in the above estimate and data, expressed as a percent? (0% = no confidence; 100% = certainty)
11.	What other individuals or groups could estimate this percentage or determine the amount?

Although this is an estimate, the approach has considerable accuracy and credibility. Four adjustments are effectively used with this method to reflect a conservative approach:

- According to Guiding Principle 6, the individuals who do not respond to the questionnaire or provide usable data on the questionnaire are assumed to have no improvements.
- Extreme data and incomplete, unrealistic, and unsupported claims are omitted from the analysis, although they may be included in the intangible benefits.
- Since only annualized values are used, it is assumed that there are no benefits from the program after the first year of implementation.
- The confidence level, expressed as a percentage, is multiplied by the improvement value to reduce the amount of the improvement by the potential error. This is Guiding Principle 7.

Collecting an adequate amount of quality data from the series of impact questions is the critical challenge with this process. Participants must be primed to provide data, and this can be accomplished in several ways.

- Participants should know in advance that they are expected to provide this type of data along with an explanation of why the information is needed and how it will be used.
- Ideally, participants should see a copy of this questionnaire and discuss it while they are involved in the program.
- Participants should be reminded of the requirement prior to the time to collect data.
- Participants should be provided with examples of how the questionnaire can be completed, using likely scenarios and types of data.
- The immediate manager should guide participants through the process and review and approve the data, if necessary.

These steps help keep the data collection process with its chain of impact questions from being a surprise. It will also accomplish three critical tasks.

- **The response rate will increase.** Because participants commit to provide data during the session, a greater percentage will respond.
- **The quantity of data will improve.** Participants will understand the chain of impact and understand how data will be used. They will complete more questions.
- **The quality of the data is enhanced.** With up-front expectations, there is greater understanding of the type of data needed and improved confidence in the data provided.

The estimation process is an important technique to isolate the effect of sales training programs; however, the process has some disadvantages. It is an estimate and, consequently, does not have the accuracy desired by some managers. Also, the input data may be unreliable since some participants are incapable of providing these types of estimates. They might not be aware of exactly which factors contributed to the results or they may be reluctant to provide data. If the questions come as a surprise, the data will be scarce.

Several advantages make this strategy attractive. It is a simple process, easily understood by most participants and by others who review evaluation data. It is inexpensive, takes very little time and analysis, and thus, results in an efficient addition to the evaluation process. Estimates originate from a credible source—the individuals who actually produced the improvement.

The advantages seem to offset the disadvantages. Isolating the effects of sales training programs will never be exact, but this estimation process may result in data accurate enough for most stakeholders.

SELECTING ISOLATION TECHNIQUES

With several techniques available to isolate the impact of sales training programs, selecting the most appropriate techniques for the specific program can be difficult. Estimates are simple and inexpensive, while others are more time consuming and costly. When attempting to make the selection decision, several factors should be considered:

- feasibility of the technique
- accuracy provided with the technique, when compared to the accuracy needed
- credibility of the technique with the target audience
- specific cost to implement the technique
- the amount of disruption in normal work activities as the technique is implemented
- participant, staff, and management time needed with the particular technique.

Multiple techniques should be considered if reliability of one technique is in question. When multiple sources are used, a conservative method is recommended to combine the inputs. A conservative approach builds acceptance and credibility. The target audience should always be provided with explanations of the process and the various subjective factors involved. Multiple sources allow an organization to experiment with different techniques and build confidence with a particular technique.

Because it is not unusual for the ROI in sales training programs to be extremely high, the audience should understand that, although every effort was made to isolate the impact, it is still a figure that is not exact and may contain error. It represents the best estimate of the impact given the constraints, conditions, and resources available.

By isolating the effects of sales training, the outcomes are clearly connected to the intervention, accounting for other factors. By ignoring this step, the reported results lack credibility. To calculate the ROI of your sales training program, you must next convert business impact data to money.

TYPES OF DATA

ROI is developed through the comparison of the monetary benefits of a program and the cost (or investment) in that program. It is an economic indicator, meaning that the metric indicates the financial return on the investment. To develop this measure, impact data (Level 4 results) are converted to monetary value then compared to the cost of the program. Before we describe the development of the ROI calculation, it is important to review the ways in which impacts are often described.

Hard Data vs. Soft Data

Data fall into one of two categories. They are either referred to as hard data or soft data. Hard data are easy to measure, quantifiable, objectively based, and immediately credible with management. They represent rational, undisputed facts and are usually easy to capture. Hard data can be broadly categorized as output, quality, cost, and time. For the sales area, these are sales, new accounts, market share, time to revenue, sales cycle time, number of deals, customer complaints, product returns, sales transaction errors, and customer churn.

Soft data represent measures that are difficult to measure and quantify; they are subjectively based and behaviorally oriented. Compared to hard data, these measures, while important, are often perceived as less reliable or less credible when converted to monetary value, due to the inherent level of subjectivity. Soft data are categorized as customer satisfaction, customer loyalty, brand awareness, and reputation.

Tangible vs. Intangible Data

Two other categories by which data are often referred are tangible and intangible data. On the surface, measures such as customer satisfaction, teamwork, and creativity may seem like difficult soft data items to measure, but consider the following:

- Though customer satisfaction seems like a soft measure, quantitative values are assigned to customer satisfaction to create an index. These numbers quantify customer satisfaction.
- When sales executives apply their newly acquired leadership skills, it may result in improved teamwork. Take that a step further to realize that improved teamwork likely yields greater productivity, leading to increased sales and reduced costs—both measures considered as hard data.
- When sales representatives are more creative, this new creative thinking may lead to more efficient business development meetings, which results in time savings that can be quantified.
- Employee engagement may seem like a soft measure, but when engagement results in more sales or customer loyalty, it can be quantified.

Ultimately, soft data lead to hard measures. Many people suggest that hard data represent tangible measures; others suggest that soft data represent intangibles. But this is not the case. Both tangible and intangible measures may evolve from either hard data or soft data. This is why to categorize a measure as hard or soft is ambiguous. An alternative categorization scheme is tangible versus intangible.

Tangible benefits of a program are those benefits that have been converted to money. Intangible benefits of a program are those benefits that have not been converted to money. Hard and soft data can be converted to monetary value. Hard data have a direct link to their monetary value, while soft data are converted by tying soft measures to hard measures. Then the measures are converted to money either by associating the measure with cost savings, cost avoidance, or revenue, which is then converted to profit, as shown in Figure 3-3.

FIGURE 3-3. Data Conversion

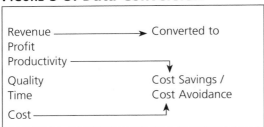

While all measures can be converted to money, several factors should be considered as listed below:

- **Cost to convert the measure:** The cost to convert data should not cost more than the evaluation itself.
- **Importance of the measure:** Some measures, such as customer satisfaction and employee satisfaction, stand alone quite well. When that is the case, you might think twice before attempting to convert the measure to money.
- **Credibility:** While most business decisions are made on somewhat subjective data, the source of the data, the perceived bias behind the data, and the motive in presenting the results are all concerns when data is somewhat questionable. Don't risk credibility just to calculate ROI. For those times when it is difficult to decide whether or not to convert a measure to monetary value, complete the four-part test shown in Figure 3-4.

FIGURE 3-4. When to Convert a Measure to Monetary Value

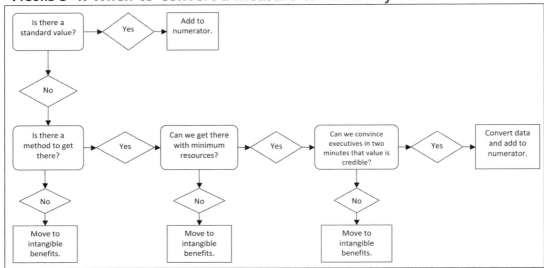

DATA CONVERSION METHODS

There are a variety of techniques available to convert a measure to monetary value. These are listed in Table 3-3 in order of credibility. The success in converting data to monetary value is knowing what values are currently available. If values are not available, it is possible to develop them. The use of standard values is by far the most credible approach, because standard values have been accepted by the organization. Following those, however, are the operational techniques to convert a measure to money. In the case of sales training, the improved measure is generally increased sales, and often is already in monetary form. When this is not the case, the following methods can be used.

TABLE 3-3. Techniques for Data Conversion

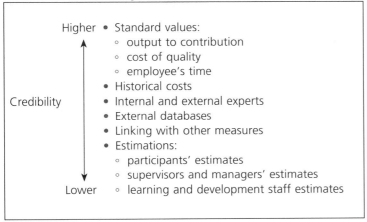

Standard Values

Many organizations have standard values for measures of turnover, productivity, and quality. Those organizations that are involved in Six Sigma or other quality initiatives have many measures and the monetary values of those measures. Look around the organization and talk with people to discover what is being measured in various functional areas of the organization. It may be possible to find a monetary value developed and accepted by the organization for a measure you are working with.

Standard values are defined as output to contribution, quality, and time. When considering output to contribution, look at the value of an additional output. For example, organizations that work on a for-profit basis consider the profit contribution, the profit from the sale in monetizing an additional sale. Most organizations have a profit margin readily available.

The cost of quality is another standard value in organizations. Quality is a critical issue and its cost is an important measure in most manufacturing and service firms.

Placing the monetary value on some measures of quality is quite easy. For example, waste, product returns, and complaints are often monitored in organizations and already have a monetary value placed on them. Other measures, such as errors, can be converted to monetary value by looking at the cost of the work. For example, when employees make mistakes and errors in the reporting, the cost of those mistakes—the value of those mistakes—is the cost incurred in re-working the report.

The third category of standard value is employees' time, probably the simplest and most basic approach to data conversion. If time is saved due to a program, the first question to consider is, "Whose time is it?" Then, to convert time to monetary value, take time saved multiplied by labor cost and add the percentage of additional value for employee benefits. This benefits factor can easily be obtained from the human resources department. A word of caution: When considering employee time as a benefit, the time savings is only realized when the amount of time saved is actually used for productive work. So, if a manager saves time by reducing the number of ineffective meetings he or she attends, the time saved should be applied to more work that is productive.

Historical Costs

When no standard values exist, historical costs can be utilized by considering what the incident has cost in the past. Using this technique often requires more time and effort than desired. In the end, however, it is possible to develop a credible value for a given measure. This monetary value can eventually become a standard value.

Internal and External Experts

When standard values are unavailable and developing the monetary values through historical costs is not feasible, the next option is to utilize internal or external experts. Using this approach, ask the expert to provide the cost for the value of one unit of improvement for the measure under investigation. Internal experts have knowledge of the situation and the respect of management. External experts are well published and have the respect of the larger community. In either case, these experts have their own methodologies to develop the values. Therefore, it is important for the experts to understand the intent and the measure for which to develop the monetary value.

External Databases

Sometimes there are no standard values or resources available to develop a monetary value using historical costs. Additionally, there are times when there is no internal expert and it is not possible to locate an external expert who can provide the necessary information. When this is the case, go to external databases. The Internet can provide a wealth of information through online databases and research. External databases provide a variety of information, including the monetary value of many different business impact measures.

Linking With Other Measures

Another technique to convert a measure to monetary value is linking the value of that measure with other measures that have already been converted to monetary values. This approach involves identifying existing relationships showing a correlation between the measure under investigation and another measure to which a standard value has been applied. In some situations, the relationship between more than two measures is connected. Ultimately, this chain of measures is traced to a monetary value often based on profits. Credibility of data becomes an issue when the assumptions increase as the chain of measures develops further from the actual monetary value. Using this methodology based on the monetary value of other measures is often sufficient for converting measures when calculating the ROI of sales training programs.

Estimations

When the previous methods are unavailable or inappropriate, use an estimation process that has been proven conservative and credible with executives in a variety of organizations. The estimates of monetary value can come from participants, supervisors, managers, and even the training program staff. The process of using estimation to convert a measure to monetary value is quite simple. The data can be gathered through focus groups, interviews, or questionnaires. The key is clearly defining the measure so that those who are asked to provide the estimate have a clear understanding of that measure.

FIVE STEPS TO DATA CONVERSION

When it has been decided to convert a measure to monetary value and you've chosen the technique that you are going to use to calculate the monetary value, follow the five steps to complete the data conversion process.

1. **Focus on the unit of measure.** The first step is to review one unit of the measure under investigation. For example, if evaluating a measure of productivity and the output is one more credit card account, then one credit card account is the unit of measure.
2. **Determine the value of each unit.** In determining the value of each unit, use standard values or one of the other operational techniques. For example, if one new account is worth $1,000 and that figure is based on standard values using profit contribution, the value is $1,000 in profit.
3. **Calculate the change in the performance of the measure.** Step three is actually taken during the evaluation process. For example, change

in performance or the improvement in the number of credit card accounts is determined during the Level 4 evaluation. How many new credit card accounts were due to the program? For this example, assume that an average five new credit card accounts were established per month (after isolating all other factors).

4. **Determine the annual improvement in the measure.** Annualize the improvement in the measure. Remember that Guiding Principle 9 says that for short-term programs, report only first-year benefits. You do not necessarily need to wait one year to see exactly how many new credit card accounts are achieved due to the program. Rather, pick a point in time to obtain the average improvement to that date and then annualize that figure. In the credit card account example, the unit of measure is one account and the value of the unit is $1,000. After establishing that the change in performance of the measure due to the program (after isolating the effects) is averaging five new accounts per month, determine the annual improvement in the measure by simply multiplying the change in performance by 12 months. So, five new accounts per month multiplied by 12 months equal 60 new accounts due to the program.

5. **Calculate the total monetary value of the improvement.** Take the number from step four, annual improvement in the measure (60 in the example), and multiply it by the value of each unit using the standard profit margin ($1,000 per credit card account in the example). This provides a total monetary value of improvement of $60,000. This annual monetary benefit of the sales training intervention is the value that goes in the numerator of the equation.

FULLY LOADED COSTS

The next step in the move from Level 4 to Level 5 is tabulating the fully loaded cost of the program, which will go in the denominator of the ROI equation. When taking an evaluation to Level 4 only, this step is not necessary; although regardless of how the sales training programs are evaluated, it should be common practice to know the full costs of them. Fully loaded costs mean *everything*. Table 3-4 shows the recommended cost categories for a fully loaded conservative approach to tabulating and estimating costs.

TABLE 3-4. Project Cost Categories

Cost Item	Prorated	Expensed
1. Initial analysis and assessment	✓	
2. Development of solutions	✓	
3. Acquisition of solutions	✓	
4. Implementation and application		
Salaries/benefits for L&D team time		✓
Salaries/benefits for coordination time		✓
Salaries/benefits for participant time		✓
Program materials		✓
Hardware/software	✓	
Travel/lodging/meals		✓
Use of facilities		✓
Capital expenditures	✓	
5. Maintenance and monitoring		✓
6. Administrative support and overhead	✓	
7. Evaluation and reporting		✓

Initial Analysis and Assessment

One of the most underestimated items is the cost of conducting the initial analysis and assessment. In a comprehensive program, this involves data collection, problem solving, assessment, and analysis. In some programs, this cost is near zero because the program is conducted without an appropriate assessment. However, as more program sponsors place increased attention on needs assessment and analysis, this item will become a significant cost in the future. All costs associated with the analysis and assessment should be captured to the fullest extent possible. These costs include time, direct expenses, and internal services and supplies used in the analysis. The total costs are usually allocated over the life of the program.

Development of Solutions

One of the more significant items is the costs of designing and developing the sales training program. These costs include time in both the design and development and the purchase of supplies, technology, and other materials directly related to the solution. As with needs assessment costs, design and development costs are usually fully charged to the program. However, in some situations, the major expenditures may be prorated over several programs, if the solution can be used in other programs.

Acquisition Costs

In lieu of development costs, some executives purchase solutions from other sources to use directly or in a modified format. The acquisition costs for these solutions include the purchase price, support materials, and licensing agreements. Some programs have both acquisition costs and solution-development costs. Acquisition costs can be pro-rated if the acquired solutions can be used in other programs.

Application and Implementation Costs

Usually, the largest cost segment in a program is associated with implementation and delivery. Eight major categories are reviewed below:
- salaries and benefits for learning team time
- salaries and benefits for coordinators and organizers
- participants' salaries and benefits
- program materials
- hardware/software
- travel, lodging, and meals
- facilities (even in-house meetings)
- capital expenditures.

Maintenance and Monitoring

Maintenance and monitoring involves routine expenses to maintain and operate the program. These represent ongoing expenses that allow the new program solution to continue. These may involve staff members, additional expenses, and may be significant for some programs.

Support and Overhead

Another charge is the cost of support and overhead, the additional costs of the program not directly related to a particular program. The overhead category represents any program cost not considered in the above calculations. Typical items include the cost of administrative/clerical support, telecommunication expenses, office expenses, salaries of client managers, and other fixed costs. This is usually an estimate allocated in some convenient way based on the number of training days, then estimating the overhead and support needed each day. This becomes a standard value to use in calculations.

Evaluation and Reporting

The total evaluation cost should be included in the program costs to complete the fully loaded cost. Evaluation costs include the cost of developing the evaluation strategy, designing instruments, collecting data, analyzing data, preparing a report, and communicating the results. Cost categories include time, materials, purchased instruments, surveys, and any consulting fees.

ROI CALCULATION

As explained in chapter 1, ROI is reported in one of two ways—the benefit-cost ratio (BCR) and the ROI percentage. In simple terms, the BCR compares the economic benefits of the program with the cost of the program. A BCR of 2 to 1 says that for every $1 invested, $2 is returned.

The ROI formula, however, is reported as a percentage. The ROI is developed by calculating the net program benefits divided by program costs times 100. For example, a BCR of 2 to 1 translates into the ROI of 100 percent. This says that for every $1 spent on the sales training program $1 is returned, after costs are captured. The formula used here is essentially the same as ROI in other types of investments where the standard equation is annual earnings divided by investment.

For example, if after you convert Level 4 measures to money and you follow the five steps described above, you find that the monetary benefits of a sales training intervention result in a sales increase of $350,000 and the training intervention cost $200,000, your BCR and ROI are:

$$BCR = \frac{\$350,000}{\$200,000} = 1.75 \text{ or } 1.75{:}1$$

$$ROI = \frac{\$350,000 - \$200,000}{\$200,000} \times 100 = 75\%$$

The BCR explains that for every $1 invested in sales training, the total financial benefit returned is $1.75. The ROI explains that for every $1 invested in sales training, that $1 is recovered plus a net return of $0.75. ROI is the "return" on the investment, where the BCR is the total benefit including the investment itself.

So when do you use which? Many times both metrics are reported to give both perspectives. Because the BCR comes from the public sector, it is more often used in public sector reporting. However, the ROI is gaining traction in those settings. For private sector organizations, the ROI is the primary metric.

Occasionally, a stakeholder will ask to see the time at which an investment will "pay off." This payoff period is the estimated time at which a program will break even. It is then assumed that any time after that period will result in added benefit. The payback period equation is simply the BCR equation turned upside down. Take the total investment of the sales training program, and divide it by the benefits. Using the previous numbers as the basis for the example, the payback period for the initiative would be:

$$\text{Payback Period} = \frac{\$200,000}{\$350,000} = .57 \times 12 \text{ months} = 6.85 \text{ months to payback}$$

This indicates that in approximately seven months, you can expect to break even on the investment.

INTANGIBLE BENEFITS

As described earlier, intangible benefits are those benefits that are not converted to monetary value; but they are important and sometimes just as important as the actual ROI calculation. Typical intangible benefits that are not converted to monetary value are job satisfaction, organizational commitment, teamwork, and customer satisfaction. These could be converted to monetary value; however, when job satisfaction, organizational commitment, teamwork, and customer satisfaction are improved, the organization is satisfied enough with the improvement in these measures that the dollar value with that improvement is not relevant.

When you report ROI, always balance it with the intangible benefits. This balance places the ultimate benefits of the sales training initiative into perspective.

FINAL THOUGHTS

This chapter discussed the various important aspects of ROI analysis. After following the steps in chapter 2 to collect data, it is important to analyze the data in a credible way. Perhaps the most important aspect of analysis is the isolation of the effects of the sales training program on the data. It is crucial to know how this particular program affected the data, outside of other influences. Another important part of data analysis is the conversion of data to monetary value. Various methods are discussed. Finally, the chapter discussed intangible benefits, or those not converted to monetary values. All of these items are critical in the ROI analysis. The next chapter deals with the communication of results of the analysis.

4

Reporting and Using ROI Data

THE IMPORTANCE OF REPORTING RESULTS

After the analysis has taken place, perhaps the most important step in the ROI process model is communicating the results of the evaluation to stakeholders. The results from the study will not provide insight into the effectiveness of the training program, help secure funding for future programs, or build credibility for the ROI Methodology unless they are properly communicated to the appropriate stakeholders.

This final step in the ROI Methodology is critical. Evaluations of sales training programs are essentially useless if the results are never communicated. Communicating the evaluation results of the sales training program allows for improvement and provides the necessary feedback to those interested in the outcomes of the training programs. In this way, others in the organization can understand the value the programs bring to the organization. Communication can be a sensitive issue—there are those who will support the sales training program regardless of the results. There are others, however, who are skeptical regardless of what the data show. Some will form their opinions about the program based on how the results are communicated. Different audiences need different information, and the information needs to be presented in a variety of ways to ensure that the message comes across appropriately. There are five steps to take into account when planning your communication strategy:

1. Define the need for the communication.
2. Identify the audience.
3. Select the media.
4. Develop the report.
5. Evaluate the results.

IDENTIFY THE NEED

There are a variety of needs that can be addressed through the communication process. Those needs range from getting approval for sales training programs, to satisfying curiosity about what the program is all about. Sometimes it is necessary to gain additional support and affirmation for programs, or to gain agreement that a change or improvement in a sales training program needs to occur. Often, the purpose of communicating the results of the sales training program is to build credibility for the program. Many times, the report reinforces the need to make changes to the system to further support the transfer of learning to implementation and business impact. Communicating the results can also serve to prepare the learning and development department for changes in the organization or, better yet, to apprise the staff of opportunities to help them develop their skills.

Communication is often conducted to enhance the entire process as well as to emphasize a specific program's importance to the organization. The communication process is used to explain what is going on, why something might or might not have occurred, and the goals to improve a sales training program when it results in a negative ROI.

When a pilot sales training program shows impressive results, use this opportunity to stimulate interest in continuing the program as well as stimulate interest for potential future program participants. The communication process can also be used to demonstrate how tools, skills, or new knowledge can be applied to the organization. Table 4-1 provides a list of possible needs that can be addressed through the communication process. Once you are clear on why you are reporting results of your evaluation, identify the audience who can best help you address that need.

TABLE 4-1. Reasons for Communicating Results

1. Reasons related to the sales training program:
   - Demonstrate accountability for client expenditures.
   - Secure approval for a program.
   - Gain support for all sales training programs.
   - Enhance reinforcement of the sales training program.
   - Enhance the results of future sales training programs.
   - Show complete results of the sales training program.
   - Explain a sales training program's negative ROI.
   - Seek agreement for changes to a sales training program.
   - Stimulate interest in upcoming sales training programs.
   - Encourage participation in sales training programs.
   - Market future sales training programs.

2. Reasons related to management:
   - Build credibility for the staff.
   - Prepare the staff for changes.
   - Provide opportunities for the staff to develop skills.

3. Reasons related to the organization:
   - Reinforce the need for system changes to support learning transfer.
   - Demonstrate how tools, skills, and knowledge add value to the organization.
   - Explain current processes.

IDENTIFY THE AUDIENCE

Once the purpose for communicating results is clear, the next step is to determine who needs to hear the results in order to satisfy the communication need. If the need for communicating results is to secure approval for a new sales training program, consider the client or the top executive as the target audience. If the purpose of communication is to gain support for a sales training program, consider the immediate managers or team leaders of the targeted participant group. If the purpose of communication is to improve the sales training program, including facilitators provided as well as the environment and process, target the staff that oversees the sales training program(s). If it is important to demonstrate accountability for the sales training program(s), then the target audience would be all employees in the organization. It is important to consider the purpose of the communication to determine the appropriate audience. Listed below are the key questions to ask to make this determination:

- Is the potential audience interested in the sales training program?
- Does the potential audience really want to or need to receive this information?
- Has someone already made a commitment to this audience regarding communication?
- Is the timing right for this message to be presented to this audience?
- Is the potential audience familiar with the sales training program?
- How does this audience prefer to have results communicated to them?
- Is the audience likely to find the results threatening?
- Which medium will be most convenient to the audience?

There are four primary audiences who will always need the results of the ROI studies communicated to them:

- **The learning and development team** should receive constant communication of the results of all levels of evaluation. Levels 1 and 2 data should be reported to the learning and development team immediately after the sales training program. This provides them the opportunity to make adjustments to the program prior to the next offering.
- **Participants are a critical source of data.** Without participants, there are no data. Levels 1 and 2 data should always be reported back to participants immediately after the data have been analyzed. A summary copy of the final ROI study should also be provided to participants. In doing so, they see that the data they are providing for the evaluation are actually being used to make improvements to the sales training program. This enhances the potential for additional and even better data in future evaluations.
- **Participants' managers** are critical to the success of sales training programs. Without managers' support for a sales training program, it will be difficult to get participants engaged in the program, and it will jeopardize the successful

transfer of learning in sales training to changes in behavior when sales professionals return to work. Reporting the ROI study results to the managers demonstrates to them that employees' participation in the programs yields business improvement. Managers will see the importance of their own roles in supporting the training process from program participation to application.

- **The client** (the person or persons who fund the program), should always receive results of the ROI study. It is important to report the full scope of success, and clients want to see the sales training program's impact on the business as well as the actual ROI. While Levels 1 and 2 data are important to the client to some extent, it is unnecessary to report this data to the client immediately after the sales training program. The client's greatest interest is in Levels 4 and 5 data. Providing the client a summary report for the comprehensive evaluations will ensure that the information clearly shows that the program is successful and, in the event of an unsuccessful program, a plan is in place to take corrective action.

SELECT THE MEDIA

Consider the best means for asking what is needed. As in other steps in the ROI Methodology, there are many options—meetings, internal publications, electronic media, program brochures, case studies, and formal reports. The choice of media is important, especially in the early stages of implementing the ROI Methodology. It is important to select the appropriate medium for the particular communication need and target audience.

Meetings

When considering meetings as the medium for communication, look at staff meetings and management meetings. If possible, plan for communication during normal meeting hours so as to avoid disrupting audiences' regular schedules. However, this approach does present the risk of having to wait to present the report until some future meeting when it can be added to the agenda. But, key players will be so interested in the ROI study that getting a slot on the earliest possible meeting agenda should not be a problem. Another meeting might consist of a discussion that includes a participant and maybe a participant's manager to sit on a panel to discuss the sales training program. Panel discussions can also occur at regularly scheduled meetings or at a special meeting focused on the sales training program. Best practice meetings are another opportunity to present the results of the sales training program. The meetings highlight the best practices in each function within the organization. This might mean presenting the ROI study at a large conference in a panel discussion, which includes managers who oversee sales training programs and managers from a variety of organizations. Business update meetings also present opportunities to provide information about the program.

Internal Publications

Internal publications are another way in which to communicate to employees. Use these internal publications—newsletters, memos, postings on break room bulletin boards—to report sales training program progress and results as well as to generate interest in current and future programs. Internal hard copy communications are the perfect opportunity to recognize sales training program participants who have provided data or responded promptly to questionnaires. If incentives were offered for participation in a sales training program or for prompt responses to questionnaires, mention this in these publications. Be sure to accentuate the positive and announce compliments and congratulations generously.

Electronic Media

Electronic media, such as websites, intranets, and group emailing, are important communication tools. These are often used to promote programs, such as sales training programs and processes being implemented in the organization. Take advantage of these opportunities to spread the word about the activities and successes related to these programs. When using group email, whether organization-wide or to certain target audiences, make sure that message content is solid and engagingly crafted.

Brochures

Sales training program brochures are another way to promote training activities and offerings. Reporting results in a brochure that describes a sales training program's process and highlights successes can generate interest in a current program, stimulate interest in coming programs, and enhance respect and regard for the team who oversees the sales training programs.

Case Studies

Case studies are an ideal way to communicate the results of your sales training evaluation. You can use case studies to demonstrate the value sales training brings to the organization or to provide others an opportunity to learn from your experience. There are multiple outlets for case studies, including books (such as this one) and training courses offered within an organization. The ROI Institute uses case studies as a key component in training others in evaluation. Through case studies, others can learn what worked and what didn't.

Formal Reports

A final medium through which to report results is the formal report. There are two types of reports—micro-level reports and macro-level scorecards—that are used to tell the success of programs. Micro-level reports present the results of a specific program and include detailed reports, executive summaries, general audience reports, and single-page reports. Macro-level scorecards are an important tool in reporting the overall success of sales training programs.

DEVELOP THE REPORT

There are five types of reports to develop to communicate the results of the ROI studies. These include the detailed report (which is developed for every evaluation project), executive summary, general audience reports, single-page reports, and macro-level scorecards.

Detailed Reports

The detailed report is the comprehensive report that details the specifics of the sales training program and the ROI study. This report is developed for every comprehensive evaluation conducted. It becomes the record and provides the opportunity to replicate the study without having to repeat the entire planning process. It is possible to save time, money, effort, and a great deal of frustration by building on an existing study. The detailed report contains six major headings:
- need for the program
- need for the evaluation
- evaluation methodology
- results
- conclusions and next steps
- appendices.

Need for the Sales Training Program

Define and clarify the objectives for the sales training program, making sure that the objectives reflect the five levels of evaluation. Objectives should relate to the participants' perspective, describe what participants are intended to learn, reflect how they are intended to apply what they have learned, and reflect the outcomes that the knowledge and skills gained in this sales training program will have on the organization. Objectives also present the target ROI and how that particular target was determined.

Need for the Evaluation

Typically, if the sales training program is intended to influence Level 4 measures, this presents a need. But, in some cases, it may be that the Level 4 measures were never developed so the intent of the evaluation is to understand the influence the sales training program has had or is having on the organization. The intent of the evaluation may be to understand the extent to which the sales training program successfully achieved the objectives. The need for the evaluation may be dependent upon the request of an executive. Clearly state the reasons in the report. Although this report will be distributed to key audiences, it is also the report that serves as the tool to refer to in future evaluations and to describe what happened during this particular evaluation.

Evaluation Methodology

This clear and complete description of the evaluation process builds credibility for the results. Provide an overview of the methodology. Then, describe each element of the process, including all options available at each step, which option(s) were chosen, the reasons for those choices, all actions and activities related to each element of the process, and each step taken. For the data collection section of the report, detail how the data were collected, why those data were collected, from whom the data were collected, why the data were collected from that particular source(s), when the data were collected, and why those data collection procedures were selected. Also display a completed copy in detail of your data collection plan. After the data collection plan has been described, explain the ROI analysis procedures. Explain why the isolation method was selected. Clearly state the various ways the effects of the sales training program could be isolated and explain why the method chosen was selected. In essence, answer the question, "Why did you do what you did?" When explaining data conversion, describe how the monetary values for the Level 4 Impact measures linked to the program were developed, again explaining the range of possibilities for data conversion. After describing the possible data conversion methods, clearly explain why the techniques selected were chosen. Address the cost issue and provide the cost categories included in the ROI analysis. At this point, do not include the actual cost of the program. If the cost of the program is introduced too early, the audience will focus solely on the cost and their attention will be lost. As with data collection, provide a detailed copy of the ROI analysis plan so that the audience can see a summary of exactly what happened.

Results

In this section, the sales training program that has undergone a rigorous evaluation will shine! Provide the results for all levels of evaluation beginning with Level 1, reaction, satisfaction, and planned action. Explain the intent for gathering reaction data, providing the specific questions the reaction data answers, and report the results. Then move on to Level 2, learning. Explain why it's important to evaluate learning and the key questions that learning data answers and report the results. Next, move on to Level 3, application and implementation. This is one of the greatest parts of the story. Provide evidence that what was taught was used. Discuss how effectively knowledge and skills gained in the sales training program have been applied by the training participants and how frequently they have applied their new knowledge and skills. Discuss how the support system enabled participants to apply what they learned. Discuss the barriers to the transfer of learning, to behavior change, or implementation and application. It is important to explain what happened. For example, if the work environment did not support learning transfer, report that here. Also explain that when it was recognized (through the evaluation process) that a problem was occurring (the support system was not helping), that action was taken by talking with those who might know or who might provide information about how things could be changed to support the training program next time.

Next, discuss Level 4, business impact, including how the sales training program positively influenced specific business outcomes. Reinforce the fact that the effects of the program were isolated; it must be clear to the audience that other influences that might have contributed to these outcomes were taken into account. Describe the options for isolation and explain why those options were chosen.

Then, report on Level 5, ROI. First, explain what is meant by ROI, clearly defining the ROI equation. Address the benefits of the program, the Level 4 measures, and how they were achieved. Explain how the data were converted to monetary value and detail the monetary benefits of the sales training program. Then, report the fully loaded costs. Recall that earlier in the evaluation methodology section of the report, the cost items were detailed, but a dollar value was not identified. It is here, after monetary benefits are reported, where the dollar values of the costs are outlined. The readers have already seen the benefits in dollar amounts; now provide the costs. If the benefits exceed the costs, then the pain of a very expensive sales training program is relieved because the audience can clearly see that the benefits outweigh the costs. Finally, provide the ROI calculation.

The last section in the detailed report concerns intangible benefits. Intangible benefits are those items that are not converted to monetary value. Highlight those intangible benefits and the unplanned benefits that came about through the sales training program. Reinforce their importance and the value they represent.

Conclusions and Next Steps

Develop and report the sales training program conclusions based on the evaluation, answering these questions:

- Was the sales training program successful?
- What needs to be improved?

Explain the next steps, clearly pointing out the next actions to be taken with regard to the program. Those actions could include continuing the sales training program, adding a different focus, removing elements of the program, changing the format, or developing a blended learning approach to reduce the costs while maintaining the benefits achieved. Clearly identify the next steps and set out the dates by which these steps will be completed.

Appendices

The appendices include exhibits, detailed tables that could not feasibly be included in the text, and raw data (keeping the data items confidential). The final report is a reference for readers as well as a story of success for others.

Throughout the report, incorporate quotes—positive and negative—from respondents. While it is tempting to leave out negative comments, ethically, they should not be omitted and including them enhances the credibility and respect for the report. By developing a detailed comprehensive report, there will be a backup for anything communicated during a presentation. When conducting a future ROI study on a similar sales training program, the road map is now clear. Table 4-2 presents a sample outline of a detailed report.

Executive Summary

Another important report is the executive summary. The executive summary follows the same outline as the detailed report although omits the appendices, and each section and subsection is not developed in such great detail. Clearly and concisely explain the need for the program, the need for the evaluation, and the evaluation methodology. Always include the ROI Methodology prior to the results so that the reader understands and appreciates the methodology. The understanding and appreciation build credibility and respect for the results. Report the data from Level 1 through Level 5 and include the sixth measure of success—the intangible benefits. The executive summary is usually 10–15 pages in length.

TABLE 4-2. Impact Study Outline for Detailed Report

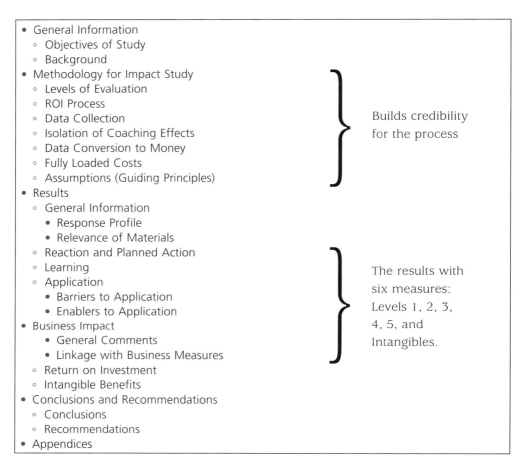

- General Information
  - Objectives of Study
  - Background
- Methodology for Impact Study
  - Levels of Evaluation
  - ROI Process
  - Data Collection
  - Isolation of Coaching Effects
  - Data Conversion to Money
  - Fully Loaded Costs
  - Assumptions (Guiding Principles)

  } Builds credibility for the process

- Results
  - General Information
    - Response Profile
    - Relevance of Materials
  - Reaction and Planned Action
  - Learning
  - Application
    - Barriers to Application
    - Enablers to Application
- Business Impact
  - General Comments
  - Linkage with Business Measures
  - Return on Investment
  - Intangible Benefits

  } The results with six measures: Levels 1, 2, 3, 4, 5, and Intangibles.

- Conclusions and Recommendations
  - Conclusions
  - Recommendations
- Appendices

General Audience Reports

General audience reports are a great way to describe the success of the sales training programs to the employees. General audience reports may be published in organization publications, like newsletters or in-house magazines; reported in management and team meetings, where a brief review of the report can be communicated in a meeting setting; and, finally, published as case studies. Case studies are published internally as well as externally. There are many opportunities to publish the case study outside of the organization, including trade or association publications or academic research publications. The key is to tell the story to show that the programs are working, and that when they don't work, steps are taken to improve them.

Single-Page Reports

A final micro-level report is a single-page report. Single-page reports are used with great care. Success of a sales training program should not be communicated using the single-page report until after the audience understands the methodology. If an audience sees the ROI of a sales training program without having an appreciation for the methodology used to arrive at the number, the audience will fixate on the ROI and never notice, much less form a regard for, information developed in the other levels of evaluation. Therefore, single-page reports are used with great care, but they are an easy way to communicate results to the appropriate audiences on a routine basis.

Macro-Level Scorecards

Macro-level scorecards can provide the results of the overall impact of learning and development programs, such as sales training programs.

These scorecards provide a macro-level perspective of success and serve as a brief description of sales training program evaluation as contrasted to the detailed report. They show the connection between the sales training program's contribution and the business objectives. The method of isolation is always included on the report to reinforce that credit is given where credit is due. The scorecard integrates a variety of types of data and demonstrates alignment between programs, such as sales training programs, strategic objectives, and operational goals.

EVALUATE RESULTS

A final step in the communication process is the evaluation of the results of your communication. While it is important to evaluate results of the sales training program, knowing how successful you are with the communication of those is just as important. Your training process may have been flawless, resulting in well over 100 percent ROI. But if the communication was poorly done, then your success may never be known.

So, how do you evaluate the success of your communication? Just like you evaluate your sales training. You observe reaction to the information and the communication process; ask participants if they know what the data mean and understand your evaluation process; follow up on actions taken as a result of the communication; observe subsequent impact (such as funding for the new training intervention); and, if you choose, calculate the ROI on your communication process. How you communicate, to whom you communicate, and when you communicate are critical elements to your overall evaluation strategy.

Remember, there are no perfect ROI studies—someone will find an improvement opportunity in everything you do. As long as you follow the process and the standards, keep your application of the ROI Methodology consistent, and clearly communicate your approach, your results are put into the context of methodology—credible and reliable. With that in mind, good decisions can be made about your sales training programs. The case studies in the following chapters provide examples of how the ROI Methodology has been used to evaluate sales training programs in various organizations.

DELIVERING BAD NEWS

One of the obstacles perhaps most difficult to overcome is receiving inadequate, insufficient, or disappointing news. Addressing a bad-news situation is an issue for most project leaders and other stakeholders involved in a project. Table 4-3 presents the guidelines to follow when addressing bad news. As the table makes clear, the time to think about bad news is early in the process, but without ever losing sight of the value of the bad news. In essence, bad news means that things can change—and need to change—and that the situation can improve. The team and others need to be convinced that good news can be found in a bad-news situation.

TABLE 4-3. Delivering Bad News

- Never fail to recognize the power to learn from and improve with a negative study.
- Look for red flags along the way.
- Lower outcome expectations with key stakeholders along the way.
- Look for data everywhere.
- Never alter the standards.
- Remain objective throughout the process.
- Prepare the team for the bad news.
- Consider different scenarios.
- Find out what went wrong.
- Adjust the story line to "Now we have data that show how to make this program more successful." In an odd way, this puts a positive spin on data that are less than positive.
- Drive improvement.

USING THE DATA

It is unfortunately too often the case that projects are evaluated and significant data are collected, but nothing is done with the data. Failure to use data is a tremendous obstacle because once the project has concluded, the team has a tendency to move on to the next project or issue and get on with other priorities. Table 4-4 shows how the different levels of data can be used to improve projects. It is critical that the data be used—the data were essentially the justification for undertaking the project evaluation in the first place. Failure to use the data may mean that the entire evaluation was a waste. As the table illustrates, many reasons exist for collecting the data and using them after collection. These can become action items for the team to ensure that changes and adjustments are made. Also, the client or sponsor must act to ensure that the uses of data are appropriately addressed.

TABLE 4-4. How Data Should be Used

Use of Evaluation Data	Appropriate Level of Data				
	1	2	3	4	5
Adjust project design.	✓	✓			
Improve implementation.			✓	✓	
Influence application and impact.			✓	✓	
Improve management support for the project.			✓	✓	✓
Improve stakeholder satisfaction.			✓	✓	✓
Recognize and reward participants.		✓	✓	✓	
Justify or enhance budget.				✓	✓
Reduce costs.		✓	✓	✓	✓
Market projects in the future.	✓		✓	✓	✓

FINAL THOUGHTS

This chapter discussed a crucial area of the ROI Methodology, reporting. When an ROI analysis has been completed successfully, the results must be communicated to various individuals with interest in the project. Proper communication of results is imperative for successful implementation of the ROI Methodology. The next section of the book is comprised of case studies where sales training has been measured in various types of organizations around the world.

Part II

Evaluation in Action

Case Studies Describing the Evaluation
of Sales Training Programs

5

Sales Training Program for Sales Executives

Multinational Automotive Company

Emma Weber

This case was prepared to serve as a basis for discussion rather than an illustration of either effective or ineffective administrative and management practices. All names, dates, places, and data may have been disguised at the request of the author or the organization.

Abstract

This case study describes how an automotive company evaluated a sales training process to demonstrate value, using data that were already available in the organization. This approach is powerful. The key to success was building trust in the process to enable a high level of response to the surveys. Multinational Automotive Company (MAC) had been operating a sales training program for at least five years. With the business becoming increasingly competitive and budgets for learning being squeezed, it was important to be able to demonstrate the ROI of the training program. The program was usually conducted five to six times per year and this evaluation runs for the total year. The programs included in the analysis were conducted in the period from May 2010 to May 2011, with each full program typically lasting 10 weeks. Lever Learning was contacted to perform an ROI analysis on the sales training program.

PROGRAM DESCRIPTION

A four-day sales training is run for MAC sales executives. It is essential for the skills to be transferred to the workplace, so the four-day training program is accompanied with a Turning Learning Into Action® program, which includes four 45-minute telephone coaching sessions to secure the learning transfer to the workplace. In total, the program and the telephone follow-up take place over a period of 10 to 12 weeks.

Why ROI?

For each program the Level 1, Level 2, and Level 3 data are already collected. The program receives good feedback and change occurs in the business consistently. However, to be able to show some financial benefit conclusively would be valuable for the training department to maintain support and funding.

PLANNING FOR ROI EVALUATION

Data Collection Plan

Figure 5-1 shows the completed data collection plan. It was decided that data would be leveraged that had already been collected by the business. Focus groups, interviews, and observation in the field were considered too expensive or inappropriate. Questionnaires at different stages of the program, including three months after the participants had completed the classroom element of the program, were used.

Access to sales data at a participant level was available, but because it was preferable to compare the before and after data and many of the participants were new to the business, a comparison could only be created for some of the attendees. For those that were new to the business it was impossible to isolate the data on the program.

ROI ANALYSIS PLAN

As data were collected, an ROI analysis plan was developed, as shown in Figure 5-2.

Levels 1 and 2 Data

Level 1 data (reaction) and Level 2 data (learning) are consistently collected for every program. A 100 percent response rate was achieved for the Level 1 survey, as this is completed at the end of the four-day training program before the participants leave the training venue.

The Level 2 data (knowledge and demonstration of new skills) are tested twice during the program, during role-plays observed by coaches. Coaches complete the Level 2 data forms. If a participant is not able to demonstrate the skills, he receives additional coaching to bring him up to the required standard. The role-play evaluation form is shown in Figure 5-3.

Figure 5-1. Data Collection Plan

Level	Broad Program Objectives	Measures	Data Collection Method/ Instruments	Data Sources	Timing	Responsibilities
1.	**Reaction, Satisfaction and Planned Action** • Positive reaction to the program • Recommend improvements collected	• Average rating of at least 4 on a 5-point scale • Percent of people who completed an action plan	• Reaction/feedback questionnaire • Action plan document	• Participants	• End of day 4 of the program	• Reaction/feedback questionnaire: Lead facilitator • Action plan: Consultant to collate
2.	**Learning** • Acquisition of skills including AUSS, WWW, using customer profiles	• Scale of 1 to 5 for each skill observed in live role-plays	• Coaches recording on an observation feedback form • Videos of role-play shared with participants to verify ratings	• Coaches observing participants	• During role-plays, days 2 and 4 of training	• Role-play coaches
3.	**Application/ Implementation** • Use of skills learned • Application of skills learned	• 4 telephone coaching conversations discussing progress, end valuation form collected 3-4 months after the 4-day program • Aim for 60% of participants to offer feedback	• Evaluation form including scale of meeting objectives, what changes have you made, what benefits have you made	• Participants	• After the final coaching call typically 2-3 months after the 4-day program	• Telephone coach to distribute • Consultant to collate info on to dashboard

Continued on next page.

Figure 5-1 continued.

4.	**Business Impact** • Sales increase • Changes made for business benefits	• Percent sales increase in units 6 months after the 4-day program compared to the 6 months before the 4-day program. Analysis completed for any participant who was in the business for 6 months before attending the program • Impact questions on evaluation form re: changes and benefits, estimated completed by 60% of people	• Sales taken from reports	• Reports	• 6 months after the end of the 4-day program	• Consultant to collate report on dashboard
5.	**ROI** • Target ROI	• Target ROI is greater than 20%	Baseline Data: Comments:			

Figure 5-2. ROI Analysis Plan

Data Items (Usually Level 4)	Methods for Isolating the Effects of the Program	Methods of Converting Data to Monetary Value	Cost Categories	Intangible Benefits	Communication Targets for Final Report	Other Influences/ Issues During Application	Comments
• Sales per participant • Questionnaire 3 months post program: "What benefits have the program brought for the business?"	• Trend-line analysis • Comparing pre-program and post-program uplift compared to companywide uplift	• Use an average gross per vehicle to convert sales to money. • Only convert if specific numbers are included by participant; otherwise move to intangible and show in word cloud.	• Facilitator costs • Turning learning into action costs • Travel costs (flights/ accommodation) • Administrative costs • Participant time	• Recorded through questions on questionnaire • Examples: NPS word clouds, changes in Level 3, and benefits in Level 4	• Create dashboard and distribute to senior teams • ROI figures to distribute to key stakeholders during stage 1	• Due to many of the participants having no historical sales, the pre- and post- program comparison cannot be made and therefore benefits are only available for some participants.	• Using the pre and post and comparing to overall business should discount seasonal changes.

Figure 5-3. Role-Play 2: Qualification/Objection Handling/Close

Name: _____ Coach: _____

Role-play: _____

Negative Behavior	Rating	Positive Behavior
Clearly unaware of customer pace/focus type. Does not change pace or focus to customer type. Continues "on a track" in spite of verbal/nonverbal signals. Speaks down to customer. Clear lack of 'customer type' understanding. Frequently uses 'motor trade' jargon.	Establishing pace and focus - - - + + +	Establishes customer pace/focus type. Demonstrates behavior appropriate to customer's pace/focus. Adapts qualification process to customer's stated needs. Speaks customer language. Avoids jargon.
Asks lots of closed, long, or assumptive questions. Does not probe when questioning. Changes subject abruptly. Never summarizes or paraphrases. Fails to record answers. Frequently asks for the same information. Clearly has no pattern or theme to questions.	Understanding needs - - - + + +	Seeks to obtain information at early stage of the process. Uses range of questions to establish need. Identifies key information, e.g., current vehicle, buying plans. Summarizes what customer has said to check understanding. Logically builds on line of questioning.
Stiff or stilted conversation. Disinterested or detached manner. Rambles; ignores questions; talks over customer. No indication of active listening. Poor body language and ignores nonverbal signals. Fails to indicate positive and personalized benefits. 'Feature dumps.'	Building rapport - - - + + +	Easy and natural conversation style. Attentive, calm, confident, and polite. Displays interest in customer. Observes and actively listens. Positive body language throughout. Matches benefits of product to customer need. Relates to customer's hobbies, interests, or family.
Unstructured in approach to objections. Shows a lack of sensitivity to points raised by the customer. Ignores/overrides objections. Does not establish cause of objection. Interrupts or contradicts the customer. Does not offer options. Leaves customer unhappy with outcome.	Handling objections - - - + + +	Effectively deals with customer objections. Uses a process. Always acknowledges objections. Asks probing questions. Paraphrases. Never directly disagrees/contradicts customer. Explores options. Seeks mutually agreeable outcome.

Fails to close or gain a commitment. Does not ask direct questions to close sale/gain commitment. Gets upset, irritated, or put off if rebuffed. Lacks variation in approach. Unclear on agreement/next steps. Makes excessive, unwise, or no concessions.	Gaining commitment - - - + + +	Attempts to close at an appropriate point in the conversation. Asks direct questions to close sale/gain commitment. Reacts calmly and confidently if rebuffed. Shows subtle persistence in rebuilding another closing opportunity. Precise and accurate about agreement reached. Acts commercially.
Customer feels uncomfortable/unwelcome. Salesperson clearly lacks basic knowledge of products and brand. Fails to summarize. Conversation finishes abruptly. Salesperson is not someone you would want to go back to or recommend to another person.	Overall - - - + + +	Helps customer feel relaxed and natural. Credible and knowledgeable about products. Summarizes agreed results. Ends on a positive note. Salesperson is someone you 'want to do business with.' You would recommend a friend to this salesperson.

☹   ☺

Fell below ☐   **Met** ☐   **Exceeded** ☐

Observations regarding attitude/behavior/representing the brand:

_____

_____

_____

_____

Continued on next page.

Figure 5-3 continued.

For Accreditation Summary:	
Role-play 2:	
☹	☺
Attitude/behavior/representing the brand:	
☹	☺
Delegate Action Plan	

Source: ©JBA Training Design Limited, www.jba.eu.com

The Level 1 data are collected, but are only used to highlight major challenges or disenchanted participants. On a regular basis, over 85 percent of responses to questions are at a five on a five-point scale. While this is rewarding for the trainer and the program content, it does not indicate business outcomes. It communicates that the program is of high quality, and that if a return is not realized, it is because of a problem further down the line, probably in the transfer of the learning. Figure 5-4 shows the questionnaire used for collecting data at Levels 1 and 2.

FIGURE 5-4. Level 1 and Level 2 Course Evaluation

Name: Dealership: Position:			Course Title: MAC Sales Training Instructor: Date:		

We would appreciate your evaluation of this course. Please tick the relevant rating boxes.

Objectives: As a result of this training course I am able to:	Strongly Disagree 1	Mostly Disagree 2	Neither Agree nor Disagree 3	Mostly Agree 4	Strongly Agree 5
Make a clear distinction between premium selling and other forms of selling.					
Describe the expectations of a customer buying a MAC brand.					
Explain the skills required by a successful sales consultant.					
Give and receive feedback and use feedback for self-development.					
Explain to others my personal strengths and development areas.					
Show how to make a good first impression and its importance in sales.					
Demonstrate the range of questions and techniques that can be used in sales.					
Explain the difference between emotional and rational focus of the customer.					
Practice active listening.					
Use positive body language and other nonverbal signals.					
Deliver a variety of closing techniques.					
Instructor Evaluation	**1**	**2**	**3**	**4**	**5**
The instructors demonstrated a thorough knowledge of the subject(s).					
The instructors' explanations were easy to understand.					
Course Evaluation	**1**	**2**	**3**	**4**	**5**
The course content was relevant to my role in the dealership.					
The course materials were easy to understand.					
The course provided me with adequate opportunity for involvement.					

Continued on next page.

Figure 5-4 Continued.

What changes, if any, should we make to this training course?
What did you find to be of the most value in this training course?
General comments:
Action Plan: When you return to the dealership, what initial steps will you take to apply your knowledge/skills?

Levels 3 and 4 Data

The Level 3 and Level 4 data are of most interest to the head office executives. These data describe the changes in terms of what participants have achieved after returning from the training program. Level 4 captures the impact this has had on the business. Specifically for this program, a sales increase is the goal, but the open questions on the survey will capture intangible benefits also. An 85 percent response rate for the survey was attained. The survey was conducted two to three months after the initial four-day training and at the end of the Turning Learning Into Action telephone coaching process.

This high response rate is achieved because the telephone coaching process is one-on-one and the coach builds rapport and trust with the participants and stresses the importance of responding. The script used for the phone conversation is as follows.

"Because everything that we have covered in the past four telephone coaching sessions is confidential, it is essential that the feedback forms are submitted to the automotive company. It is the only opportunity the automotive company has to know that you and I haven't just discussed the weather during our conversations. It should only take five minutes to complete and I will send it across to you by email this afternoon. It is an online form."

The survey is online and is created via a survey design program in our own bespoke system. It enables generation of Excel spreadsheets with the collected data for easy analysis. Also included are some Level 1 data on the coaching program itself and the NPS (Net Promoter Score), which is widely acknowledged to be useful in assessing client satisfaction, a Level 1 measure. This is interesting but does not contribute to the evaluation of program outcomes.

Information is collected on progress toward the goals that the participants have set at the end of training program and the level to which they have achieved them. In terms of commentary the following questions are asked:

* What changes have you put into place?
* What benefits or results have the changes created for the business?

IMPACT DASHBOARDS

Figure 5-5 illustrates an impact dashboard, which Lever Learning uses to display data at the impact level. The dashboard represents the program between May 2010 and May 2011 with 78 participants. It includes the detail of the sales; however, certain information was removed as it was too commercially sensitive to distribute across the business.

Clients enjoy the dashboards that are created. The dashboard gives them a tangible way to illustrate results even though it doesn't actually generate the results. Turning Learning Into Action, the learning transfer process, generates the results and the dashboard allows a manager, CEO, or learning and development professional to showcase the results. Until the creation of the impact dashboard, the person going through the changes knew how well the program worked, and sometimes the manager did as well, but results were not reported across the TLA program. When the dashboard was introduced, it gave the CEO or manager a birds-eye view of just how effective the program had been collectively. Figure 5-6 shows the questionnaire used for creation of the dashboard.

FIGURE 5-6. Questionnaire for Creation of Dashboard

<table>
<tr><td>

Name:
Program:
Date program completed:

</td></tr>
<tr><td>

1. Your calibration for goal 3 at the end of training program was:

2. For goal 3, where do you calibrate yourself now, at the end of the coaching? (Scale: 1 low—10 high)

3. Given your goals above—To what degree were your expectations of coaching as a transfer of training tool met? (1 low—5 high)

4. Given your goals above—To what degree have the objectives you set at the end of the training program been met? (1 low—5 high)

5. Given your goals above—To what degree, do you believe, would the objectives in your Action Plan have been met WITHOUT coaching? (1 not met—5 fully met without coaching)

6. Effectiveness of coaching—How useful was the coaching in ensuring that you followed through on your Action Plan? (1 not useful—5 essential)

7. What changes have you already made specifically as a result of the program and follow-up?

8. What benefits or results have these changes created for you or the business?

9. In an ideal world, what specifically would you like in the future to help you develop further in your role?

10. Any additional comments?

</td></tr>
</table>

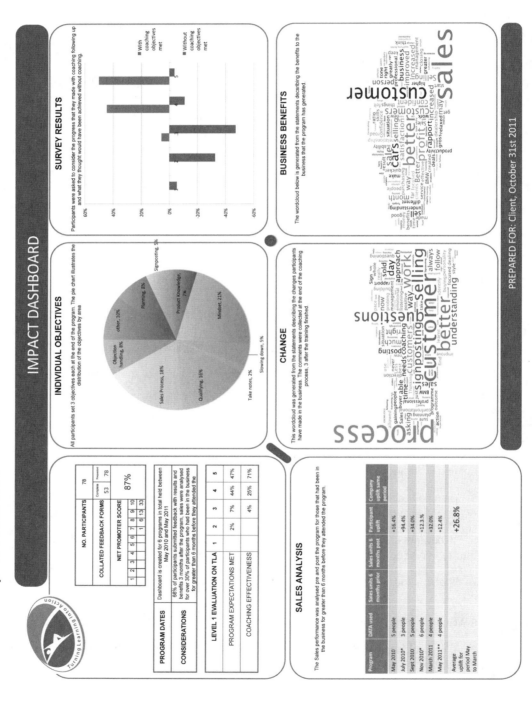

FIGURE 5-5. Impact Dashboard

Program Details

The program details box in the top left box of the dashboard offers the reader an immediate overview of the program the results relate to. As shown in Figure 5-5, 78 participants went through the TLA program and were asked to complete survey feedback. Of the 78 requested feedback forms, 53 people completed the feedback and the results in the impact dashboard relate to that feedback. Where the client is familiar with Net Promoter Score (NPS), the dashboard also includes this popular metric. The NPS is the score derived from asking customers one question: "How likely is it that you would recommend our company to a friend or colleague?" The theory is that the more "promoters" a company has, the greater the loyalty and impact and ultimately the greater the growth. It is a standardized way to gauge customer satisfaction.

The program details box also specifies the dates of the TLA programs and any considerations that need to be appreciated to interpret the dashboard effectively, such as people who have left the business or had extended leave.

This section also provides Level 1, reaction-based evaluation data. The data allow the reader of the dashboard to establish on a scale of 1–5 whether the participant's expectations of the program were met. It also demonstrates on the same scale of 1–5 whether participants considered the coaching effective in supporting their transfer of learning.

Remember, Level 1 evaluation is only interested in the reaction of participants to the process. While the most useful evaluations are Level 3 (application), Level 4 (impact), and Level 5 (ROI), this measure is a good indication to a manager what his or her people actually thought of the program. It gives a sense of participants' first impressions of the program and flushes out any major problems.

Individual Objectives

At the end of a training program everyone in the program commits to three actions that they detail in their TLA plan. The pie chart in the top middle box of the dashboard is a visual representation of the distribution of objectives by topic or area. Everyone's objectives are then grouped under relevant subheadings to create relevant categories. When this square is coupled with the top right box it becomes a Level 3 measure, as it captures what the participant puts into place back in the business by recording the goals set and the progress that they have made.

This offers managers a quick snapshot of the key themes or types of actions that participants have focused on during the change process, and most of the time these key themes will relate to the content of the training program. This is a quick way to see what issues were the most popular for participants to implement and work on during the TLA process.

Facilitators find this information useful because it tells them what parts of the training the participants think is most relevant to their daily job responsibilities. It offers insights about how to improve the training for maximum impact and it may even offer insights on how to create future training solutions. This information is also very useful for the head of learning and development for similar reasons. If this pie chart indicates that participants are using one topic or section of the training more than others, it may influence future content.

Survey Results

In the feedback process, all participants in the TLA program are asked to answer the following two questions:

1. On a scale of 1–5, to what level did you meet the objectives that you set at the end of the program?
2. On a scale of 1–5, what level do you think you would have met those objectives without coaching?

These questions allow participants to reflect on how far they have come in the TLA process and what they think would have happened had they not had that coaching support.

This box in the top right of the dashboard represents all actions for all participants, so it offers a big picture view of how effective participants have considered the process, and shows the manager how relevant the participant considers the TLA process to be. It has been determined over many years that when people are asked to self-score from 1–5, they view themselves in three ways:

- low level of objectives met (1–2)
- average level of objectives met (3)
- high level of objectives met (4–5).

If a participant gives herself a three, she is saying she is average, and we know that average in the context of learning transfer is about 20 percent implementation. If someone self-scores a one or a two, it means he is going to do nothing.

Around 10 percent of people believe they would have met their goals without coaching, which is generally true, as 10 percent of learners are typically focused enough to create their own change. This section in the impact dashboard provides the first Level 3 evaluation and indicates whether or not real behavioral change has occurred, if objectives have been met, and what knowledge people have applied.

Sales Analysis/Results Section

This is the box that is most tailored to each client, and the information that appears here will often depend on the type of training that was undertaken. In our example, it was sales training. This box details the results of the training and TLA program on sales uplift for each group of participants who went through the program.

For some clients, this dashboard results section looks at the individual goals set in the program and how far the participants have come in achieving those goals during the coaching. Participants are asked to rate themselves on a score of 1–10 on their objectives when they set that objective and then again after the coaching. For example, if a participant set a goal of generating more leads, he would be asked to rate himself on generating leads before the coaching and again after the coaching, and this results section would illustrate those improvements.

Much of the feedback displayed in this section of the impact dashboard is received from the TLA participants themselves. This is because it is the participant who knows her role best and therefore knows what she has achieved (or not). In Phillips' terms, we are using expert estimation, with the participant as the expert.

To add an additional level of validity to these results so that managers and leaders can be confident that they reflect real-world results and are not just wishful thinking by the participant, this section can include a manager's corroboration score. When the participants send the feedback on how they have done on the program and what changes they have made, the information is relayed to their manager, who is asked to verify their score. The manager is asked, "On a scale of 1–10 how confident are you that you have seen this level of change?" The answer is documented on the impact dashboard as the manager's corroboration score. The higher the score, the more the managers agree with the participants' assessments of their performance.

This section of the impact dashboard provides more in-depth Level 3 evaluation by exploring the real-world changes that have occurred in the business as a result of the training and TLA process.

Change

In the bottom middle section, the word cloud is generated around all the anecdotal information received in the feedback forms. Participants are asked, "What changes have you put into place?" and their responses generate the word cloud.

Word clouds or tag clouds were developed in the mid-1990s. They are a basic visualization method for text data; originally they were used to depict keyword metadata on websites. The importance of each "word" is shown in terms of size or color. Software developed in 2008 is used more widely to visualize word frequency in free-form natural language sets, which are great for analysis of individual changes made due to training. For purposes of creating the word cloud, www.wordle.net is used.

In the example shown, the words "process," "customer," "better," "questions," and "selling" are larger than "listening" or "positive" because the larger words appeared more often in the way the participants described the changes they had implemented following the TLA process.

This information can be useful to get a sense of what participants are really taking from the experience and what is actually changing. The larger words will reflect the content of the training and the genuine real-world changes that the participants have made in the workplace.

This section of the impact dashboard provides an additional perspective on Level 3 evaluation by describing the changes that have occurred as a result of the training and TLA process.

Business Benefits

The last section of the impact dashboard, the bottom right, contains another word cloud. This time it is generated using all the answers received from participants to the question, "What benefits have your changes created?"

Again, the larger words represent the words or descriptors most often used to describe the business benefits achieved as a result of the TLA process. This business benefits word cloud provides a Level 4 evaluation and explores the impact the training and TLA process has had on the business.

Intangible Benefits

Intangible benefits are those benefits that cannot be converted to monetary values credibly, with a reasonable amount of resources. Many intangibles were realized through the development of the word clouds such as better rapport with customers, improved customer satisfaction, better understanding, better focus and attitude, and enhanced knowledge.

COLLECTING THE LEVEL 4 SALES DATA

Seventy-eight participants completed the program between May 2010 and May 2011. The program was run six times with the average participants per program being 13. For each individual program, the sales history and data for the year, by month, needed to be collected.

When examining the participants' reasons that the data were not available or could not be used, explanations included:

- **Not in a sales role:** Some of the participants in the program were not in a direct sales role. They could have been sales managers who did not have sales directly attributed to themselves or they could have been cadets who were not yet fully selling but were being trained to sell. Their sales figures, therefore, had no pre- and post-sales and could not be used.
- **Left the business:** Likewise, sales managers who have left the business part of the way through the program cannot have the data included in the analysis.
- **No comparison data:** Those sales executives who had just joined the business before they attended the training program had no sales before the training

program and therefore could not be included in the analysis to create the business uplift comparison, or be included in the total benefits of the program.

- **Exceptions:** For some sales executives, even though they had been within the business for three months before and after the training program, their roles had significantly changed during the time period and they had not had an opportunity to use the new skills in their roles. The roles had changed to special vehicles in one case, and from used cars to new cars in the other case, where the volumes are completely different and therefore would skew the comparison.

Finally, the data were being collected from the incentive rewards program for the company. On investigation, one of the dealerships was not included in the incentive rewards program and therefore they had inaccurate data on the system. For the data from this particular dealership, the dealership was contacted directly and asked to manually collate the data for the two sales executives involved in the program.

Isolating the Benefits

To isolate the benefits of the program for each individual participant, we collected the total sales for the six months before the program and the total sales for the six months after.

Using the total number of people per sample, we calculated the average sales per consultant for six months before and then the six months after the program, enabling calculation of the additional cars sold per participant after the program. The company sales trend for the same period was then calculated for the six months before and six months after the program. For each program, those that had attended training had a higher uplift than the company average, as Table 5-1 shows. This difference illustrates a business benefit. The technique is often labeled control group analysis, where the trained group is the experimental group and the rest of the sales team is the control group.

TABLE 5-1. Participant and Company Sales Uplift

Program	Data Used	Sales Units 6 Months Prior	Sales Units 6 Months Post	Participant Uplift	Company Uplift Same Period
May 2010	5 people	176	205	+16.4%	+11.7%
July 2010	3 people	77	150	+94.4%	+7.8%
Sept. 2010	5 people	120	161	+34.0%	+3.6%
Nov. 2010	6 people	178	190	+12.3%	+3.2%
March 2011	4 people	107	142	+32.0%	+5.4%
May 2011	4 people	113	127	+12.4%	-32.7%

Having demonstrated business impact to create the ROI for the program it is important to convert the additional sales to money and then compare this to the cost of the program. This was accomplished by:

- Using the percentage uplift from the program, calculate this to the additional number of units sold.
- Using the percentage uplift from across the business at this time, calculate which of these sales were additional sales due to the sales training program.
- Using an average gross margin per unit, calculate the additional sales for the six months.

Tabulating the Costs

Fully loaded costs for the program were calculated by considering expenses for flights and accommodations, participants' salaries, trainer costs, administrative costs, and others, as shown in Table 5-2.

TABLE 5-2. Fully Loaded Costs

Category of Spend for Participants	Amount	For 13 Participants	% of Participants	Total Cost
Accommodation per person	$200	$2600	70%	$1820
Flights per person	$350	$4550	67%	$3048
Average wage package per	$2200 per person	$28,600	100%	$28,600
TLA cost per participant	$931	$12,103	100%	$12,103
Admin per participant	$50	$650	100%	$650
Other Categories of Spend				**Total Cost**
Cost for trainer		$2250 per day x 4 days		$9000
Program development costs*				
TOTAL				$55,221
Total cost for 6 programs				$331,326

*Program development costs were not included as the program was designed at least six years before. All development costs have by now been covered by previous programs.

Calculating ROI

$$\text{ROI (\%)} = \frac{\text{Monetary Benefits} - \text{Total Program Costs}}{\text{Total Program Costs}} \times 100$$

$$\text{ROI (\%)} = \frac{\$469,397 - \$331,326}{\$331,326} \quad .4167 \times 100 = 41.67\%$$

Remembering the 40.8 percent ROI is generated:

- only using the monetary benefits accrued in the six months immediately after the program, for each participant
- only 27 out of the 78 participants had data available to contribute to the ROI analysis.

From this, the business can easily see that the benefits from the program have been realized and the investment is worthwhile.

This can also be expressed as a benefit-cost ratio:

$$\text{BCR} = \frac{\text{Monetary Benefits}}{\text{Total Program Costs}}$$

$$\text{BCR} = \frac{\$469,397}{\$331,326} \quad = 1.417:1$$

COMMUNICATION STRATEGY

Due to an internal change in the head of the training department, it was important that ownership was taken for communicating the results to the business. The thoroughness and commitment of the training department to take the program to the level of ROI demonstrated that they were serious in wanting to make a real return to the business and were very conscious of business costs.

The department head communicated the results on a one-on-one basis to the key stakeholders involved and got their buy-in for the figures and the process. The report was received positively; but more importantly, the commitment to measurement set a new benchmark for the department.

POST-ROI ANALYSIS

Another automotive company department that is running a new recruitment process has asked for an ROI project to measure the effectiveness of the new process to be rolled out during the second half of 2012.

LESSONS LEARNED

The client was pleased with the study and outcome; however, with the benefit of hindsight two changes would be made for similar studies in future:

1. The comparison control group of the total company comparison wasn't ideal; for future programs we would try and isolate a smaller control group of a similar size and geographic location of the group attending the program. In addition, where sales consultants didn't have any sales history prior to attending the program, these participants would be matched with those of equal tenure in a control group.
2. In the costs section of the analysis, no costs were attributed to the ROI analysis itself; in future programs this would need to be budgeted for and included in the fully loaded costs.

QUESTIONS FOR DISCUSSION

1. What, if anything, could have been done to make the control group arrangement more reliable?
2. Telephone coaching was used in this study and helped achieve a high response rate. Could this be feasible in your organization? Why or why not?
3. Why do you think the clients had such a favorable reaction to the dashboards? To whom should these dashboards be presented?
4. Only six months of data were used in the analysis. Should a year of data be used? Why or why not?
5. Do you have enough data to fully understand the monetary benefits? If not, what do you need?

ABOUT THE AUTHOR

Emma Weber is the founder and director of Lever Learning. Prior to running her own business, she worked as a buying and merchandising specialist with leading U.K. retailers such as Next PLC and Debenhams, where she acted as a strategist and coach to her team. Under her leadership the team exceeded their performance expectations and achieved sales results well above their £10 million budget.

Since developing the Turning Learning Into Action coaching process, Emma has spoken internationally on the subject of learning transfer and is currently writing a book on Turning Learning Into Action and advanced coaching.

Lever Learning takes a unique approach to learning and business results. Cited as a training company that doesn't deliver any training, they focus solely on learning transfer and evaluation, ensuring that what is learned in a training environment or development program is transferred into behavioral change in the workplace. They then work with the client to evaluate the program to a level that meets the needs of the business, whether it is through a full ROI evaluation using the Phillips Methodology, or learning dashboards and supplementary case studies.

The company is based in Sydney, Australia but has an international team with Lever Learning, working on projects across Europe, Asia, and Australasia. Emma can be reached at emma@leverlearning.com.

6

Solution Selling for Sales Reps
Ricoh Production Print Solutions

David P. Cain

This case was prepared to serve as a basis for discussion rather than an illustration of either effective or ineffective administrative and management practices. All names, dates, places, and data may have been disguised at the request of the author or organization.

Abstract

Ricoh Production Print Solutions (RPPS), formerly known as InfoPrint Solutions Company, needed to improve solution selling skills for sales reps who sell monochrome continuous forms printers to increase revenue from this hardware category. RPPS offered a sales course entitled "Selling Monochrome Continuous Forms Solutions in the Production Print Market" twice to address this requirement. This course trained 17 sales reps in product information, competitive positioning, and sales methodology for the InfoPrint 4100 printer, a high-profile and strategically-important product in the RPPS hardware portfolio. We evaluated the courses using the Phillips ROI Methodology to guide the process. The program was a success: We met or exceeded our target metrics for student reaction, learning, and behavior change. In terms of the program's business impact, we attribute $96,533 of the overall monetary benefit and incremental profit gain in the year following the course, directly linked to the course experience; and this translates to a return on investment of 2.2 percent for the program.

THE CHALLENGE AND APPROACH

Introduction

Ricoh Production Print Solutions (RPPS), a privately-held international company based on a partnership between Ricoh & IBM, focuses on solving customers' print and output challenges through an industry-leading blend of consulting services, software, hardware, and maintenance offerings. This company was formed in April of 2011 and is based on the organization known as InfoPrint Solutions Company, which was founded in 2007 by IBM, and Ricoh and became a wholly-owned subsidiary of Ricoh in 2010.

RPPS offers approximately 20 to 30 face-to-face courses each year to a direct sales force of several hundred individuals, who are spread across 30 countries in four geographic regions. These courses cover such topics as: an overview of new products, competitive positioning, and sales tactics and strategies. These courses are designed to incorporate adult learning best practices. As such, they generally include a mixture of instructional strategies that are intended to reach individuals with a variety of learning styles and preferences. Typical activities include lecture, hands-on exercises with printer hardware or software, group discussion, role-playing, case studies, games, and a variety of other interactive activities.

Among the most strategic courses offered are those that cover continuous forms printing hardware. These machines are typically used to print high-volume monochrome applications including direct mail, customer statements and bills, brochures, and manuals by customers such as service bureaus, data centers, and corporate reprographics departments. These printers are large, fast, and can handle complex print jobs. They are strategically important in the RPPS portfolio because they often drive considerable additional revenue such as multi-year maintenance and supplies contracts, pre- and post-processing hardware, software, and consulting services. Therefore, courses that train RPPS salespeople on these products generally have attention from senior executives and are expected to directly result in substantial revenue.

The Program

The program manager in charge of continuous forms education conducted a needs assessment to determine whether sales reps had the skills necessary to successfully sell complex printing solutions that included a continuous forms hardware component. Through discussions with sales reps, sales managers, executives, and product marketing managers, it became apparent that there was a gap in the knowledge and skills needed to sell the InfoPrint 4100 printer, the primary printer hardware in the monochrome continuous forms category. Sales reps needed more information about the sales process, product information, and competitive positioning. Additionally, sales reps were unaware how to apply the InfoPrint solution selling methodology to the InfoPrint 4100, how to progress a monochrome continuous forms deal through the sales cycle, and how to close deals in a more timely manner. Finally, the business had a need to increase revenue from this product category.

To address these needs, the sales course entitled "Selling Monochrome Continuous Forms Solutions in the Production Print Market" was developed and offered at InfoPrint Solution Company's worldwide corporate headquarters in Boulder, Colorado. The course was run two times for 10 participants and seven participants, respectively. The course was advertised to sales reps with the following description:

InfoPrint will be offering a four and a half-day course on selling monochrome continuous forms solutions in InfoPrint's defined target market spaces. You know the products/features/marketplaces, but *how* do you put it all together to go from identifying an opportunity to closing it? Where do you find the information? How do you put it together? How do you progress to the next step? What are some steps to shortening the selling cycle and bringing in *more* revenue *quicker*?

The high-level program goals included the following. Solution consultants will be able to:

- connect their knowledge of InfoPrint's target markets and monochrome continuous form products to customers' needs to determine the best solution and close a deal
- demonstrate the ability to move a deal forward by practically applying InfoPrint's solution selling process tools
- use and apply various tools, techniques, deliverables, and resources at the appropriate times to keep a deal moving forward
- shorten the selling cycle and thereby bring in more monochrome continuous forms revenue more quickly.

This program was selected for an ROI study for several reasons. The InfoPrint 4100 printer is one of the strategic products in our continuous forms hardware lineup. As such, it has considerable management attention. The InfoPrint 4100 was also expected to generate tens of millions of dollars in revenue in the 12 months following the course, more than most other product categories. So, it was critical to not only deliver an effective educational experience for our sales reps, but also to measure the effect and convince all program stakeholders that the program had the desired results.

The Methodology

The methodology used for the impact study is based on the Phillips ROI Methodology. This framework is enumerated in numerous works by Jack Phillips, Patti Phillips, and their many co-authors, including *Beyond Learning Objectives: Develop Measurable Objectives That Link to the Bottom Line* (ASTD Press, 2008) and the six volumes that comprise *The Measurement and Evaluation Series* (Pfeiffer, 2008). Additionally training workshops are offered by the ROI Institute and the American Society for Training & Development (ASTD) for gaining expertise in developing and measuring programs that can demonstrate impact at each of five different levels, as defined by the framework of the Phillips ROI Methodology.

Objectives were developed with assistance from the education program manager at each of the five levels during course development. These objectives were created early during the course design process and were intended to comprehensively address all the needs identified earlier in the year. The objectives helped define the instructional strategies, content, facilitators and subject matter experts, as well as a variety of other considerations. This made evaluation and analysis of the course results much easier, since the foundation and all details of the course were intended to produce these results at each level. It was critical that we achieve objectives at each level, because all subsequent levels depended on success at preceding levels—this "chain of impact" was an expected result of designing a course to meet a series of linked objectives at the five levels of the Phillips ROI Methodology.

OBJECTIVES

Level 1 Reaction and Planned Action

At the end of this course, 80 percent or more of the participants will rate the course a 4 or higher on a 5-point Likert scale on the following statements:
- The facilitators/instructors were effective.
- I gained additional understanding of this material from the information presented.
- The material covered in this course is relevant to my job.
- I will use the concepts/advice from this course in my job.
- The course represented an excellent use of my time.
- I will recommend this education program to others.

Level 2 Learning

As measured via instructor observation and feedback during activities, discussion, and presentations, as well as via a student assessment (with a score of 80 percent or higher) administered within one week following the course, participants will be able to meet the following objectives.
- Identify the opportunities that are strong candidates for InfoPrint's CF monochrome production solutions and which are not.
- Ask appropriate questions to validate needs for an opportunity where they have stimulated interest.
- Identify and connect the needs of various customer decision makers/ stakeholders to InfoPrint's strengths and solutions.
- Create, find, and use the following tools, techniques, deliverables, and resources while proposing a solution:

- evaluation plan
- total cost of print analysis (TCOP)
- supplies cost of print analysis (SCOP) and supply business
- pricing/special bids
- proposal tools
- maintenance sales
- financing and purchase options
- contracts
- trials and proof of concepts
- briefings and customer visits
- solutions assurance
- techline
- print samples.
- Identify InfoPrint support team that is available to help progress an opportunity forward, and identify when and how to engage those individuals.
- Prepare for asking for their customer's business during the sales cycle, at the appropriate time.
- Describe InfoPrint's relative strengths and weaknesses.
  - Understand key competitor's relative strengths and weaknesses.
  - Respond to common messaging that key competitors use when selling against InfoPrint.
  - Understand appropriate messaging to use when selling against key competitors.
- Combine appropriate software and solution elements and services with InfoPrint CF hardware to package production solutions that solve customer pains.
- Identify the steps for the ordering process and be able to complete those steps for successful Firm Order Process.

Level 3 Application and Implementation

Within three months following the course, at least 80 percent of participants will:

- Progress at least three monochrome continuous forms opportunities past the "validation" stage.
- Complete the appropriate steps for successful Firm Order Process for every order during that period.
- Use at least six of the tools, techniques, deliverables, or resources listed above to progress the sell cycle of a solution to a potential client.
- Apply InfoPrint's solution selling process and related tools in at least one customer engagement.
- Engage in at least one deal that is positioned against key CF competitive offerings.

Level 4 Business Impact

Within six months following the course, at least 80 percent of participants will:

- Shorten the average selling cycle for monochrome continuous forms deals by at least two weeks.
- Increase the number of deals that include a monochrome continuous forms solution component by at least 10 percent.
- Increase revenue from deals that include a monochrome continuous forms solution component by at least 10 percent.

Level 5 Return on Investment

The two course offerings will achieve a positive return on investment in six months following the second offering of the course.

DATA COLLECTION STRATEGY

Several evaluation techniques were used as part of this study. An end-of-course survey was administered via a hard copy form to the participants in each course to measure reaction and learning. Behavior change and business impact were measured in a follow-up survey that was administered electronically six months after the second offering of the course. Figure 6-1 shows the completed data collection plan for the project.

Surveys were the primary data collection method—rather than face-to-face interviews, focus groups, or other more time-intensive methods—due to the ease of administration and low cost. In addition, our sales force was widely dispersed geographically, with a presence across the United States and in 36 other countries. The participants in these courses were from different parts of the country and a few were based outside of the United States, so we needed to collect information in a convenient manner, and surveys were the most expedient way to do this.

The information reported here was validated with key stakeholders to confirm that the sales and revenue information was in line with what others had seen, as well as compared with data in the InfoPrint customer relationship management sales database. The interval between the course and the final evaluation was sufficiently long enough, relative to the sales cycle of the product under focus, to allow for the desired business impact to occur.

FIGURE 6-1. Data Collection Plan

Program: Selling Monochrome Continuous Forms Solutions in the Production Print Market
Responsibility: David Cain (education evaluation specialist) & Sally Adams (education program manager)

Level	Broad Program Objective(s)	Measures	Data Collection Method/Instruments	Data Sources	Timing	Responsibilities
1	• The facilitators/instructors were effective. • I gained additional understanding of this material from the information presented. • The material covered in this course is relevant to my job. • I will use the concepts/advice from this course in my job. • The class represented an excellent use of my time. • I will recommend this education program to others.	• 80% or more of the participants will rate the course a 4 or higher on a 5-point Likert scale on the reaction objectives.	• Survey administered electronically on SurveyMonkey	• Students in class	• Final day of class	• David Cain (create survey) and Sally Adams (administer survey)

Continued on next page.

Figure 6-1 continued.

| 2 | • Identify the opportunities that are strong candidates for InfoPrint's CF monochrome Production solutions and which are not.
• Ask appropriate questions to validate needs for an opportunity where they have stimulated interest.
• Identify and connect the needs of various customer decision makers/stakeholders to InfoPrint's strengths and solutions.
• Create, find, and use the relevant tools, techniques, deliverables, and resources while proposing a solution.
• Identify InfoPrint support team members who are available to help progress an opportunity forward and when and how to engage those individuals.
• Prepare for asking for their customer's business during the sales cycle, at the appropriate time.
• Describe InfoPrint's relative strengths and weaknesses.
• Combine appropriate software and solution elements/services with InfoPrint CF hardware to package Production solutions that solve customer pains.
• Identify the steps for the ordering process and be able to complete those steps for successful Firm Order Process. | • Each Level 2 objective is achieved by at least 80% of students in class, and the average rating on a 5-point Likert scale is 3.5 or higher. | • Survey administered electronically on SurveyMonkey | • Students in class | • Final day of class | • David Cain (create survey) and Sally Adams (administer survey) |

#	Objective	Measure	Method	Audience	Timing	Responsible
3	• Progress at least three monochrome continuous forms opportunities past the "validation" stage. • Complete the appropriate steps for successful Firm Order Process for every order during that period. • Use at least six of the tools, techniques, deliverables, or resources listed in item #4 in the above list to progress the sell cycle of a solution to a potential client. • Apply InfoPrint's solution selling process and related tools in at least one customer engagement. • Engage in at least one deal that is positioned against key CF competitive offerings.	• Each Level 3 objective is achieved by at least 80% of students in class.	• Survey administered electronically on SurveyMonkey	• Students in class	• 3 months after class	• David Cain (create and administer survey and conduct interviews)
4	• Shorten the average selling cycle for monochrome continuous forms deals by at least two weeks. • Increase the number of deals that include a monochrome continuous forms solution component by at least 10%. • Increase revenue from deals that include a monochrome continuous forms solution component by at least 10%.	• Each Level 4 objective is achieved by at least 80% of students in class.	• Survey administered electronically on SurveyMonkey	• Students in class	• 6 months after class	• David Cain (create and administer survey and conduct interviews)
5	Baseline Data: Investment threshold for projects at InfoPrint is 20%, so ROI in excess of this amount is desirable. ROI will be measured against profit generated from monochrome continuous forms deals.					
	Comments: Specific objective for the two courses is to achieve a positive return on investment in six months following the second course.					

THE RESULTS

Level 1 Reaction and Satisfaction

Level 1 feedback was measured at the end of the course to determine how the participants reacted to the course. Six standard questions are asked for each face-to-face course to enable comparison within the course. The participants are asked to rate each questions on a five-item Likert scale: 5 (strongly agree), 4 (agree), 3 (neutral), 2 (disagree), and 1 (strongly disagree). We received feedback from all 17 participants in the two courses at this first level of evaluation. Table 6-1 shows the results for each course.

TABLE 6-1. Level 1 Course Evaluation Results

Metric	Course 1	Course 2	Mean
Facilitators	4.80	4.71	4.76
New information	4.50	5.00	4.71
Relevance to job	4.60	4.86	4.71
Usefulness	4.80	4.86	4.82
Good use of time	4.40	5.00	4.65
Recommend to colleagues	4.80	5.00	4.88
Mean	4.65	4.91	4.76

Based on results from other face-to-face courses at InfoPrint, the expected target on these objectives was a score of 4.0 or higher on the 5-point Likert scale. Therefore, we exceeded our goal on all six objectives for both courses. This indicates that participants generally had a very favorable reaction to the course, especially related to the novelty, usefulness, and relevance of the content.

Level 2 Learning

Level 2 feedback was measured at the end of the course to determine how much the participants learned during the course, relative to 10 specific learning objectives that were defined early in the course development process. Nine of these objectives applied to the first course and eight applied to the second course. Again, feedback was received from all 17 participants in the two courses at this second level of evaluation.

Participants were asked to rate each questions on a seven-item Likert scale: N/A (not applicable to my job or already knew how to do prior to course), 5 (greatly improved my ability), 4 (slightly improved my ability), 3 (no change in my ability), 2 (more confused now than I was prior to course), and 1 (no value provided in this area).

The learning results for each course are shown in Table 6-2. The score for each objective is the average of the 1–5 ratings from all participants in each cohort who provided a numerical rating for that objective.

TABLE 6-2. Level 2 Course Evaluation Results

Learning Objective	Course 1	Course 2	Mean
Identify the opportunities that are strong candidates for InfoPrint's CF monochrome production solutions and which are not.	3.38	4.20	3.72
Ask appropriate questions to validate needs for an opportunity where you have stimulated interest.	3.63	N/A	3.63
Appropriately use the Fluency/Development Prompter in preparing questions to validate needs with sponsors for opportunities.	N/A	4.33	4.33
Identify and connect the needs of various customer decision makers/stakeholders to InfoPrint's strengths and solutions.	3.25	4.17	3.63
Create, find, and use the tools, techniques, deliverables, and resources we discussed in class while proposing a solution.	3.67	5.00	4.22
Identify InfoPrint support team members who are available to help progress an opportunity forward and when and how to engage those individuals.	3.56	4.86	4.10
Prepare for asking for your customer's business during the sales cycle, at the appropriate time.	3.11	N/A	3.11

Based on results from other face-to-face sales education courses at InfoPrint, the target we were expecting to achieve on these objectives was a score of 3.0 or higher on the 5-point Likert scale. Therefore, we exceeded our goal on all nine objectives for the first course, and all eight objectives for the second course. This indicates that participants generally learned everything that the courses were intended to teach. These results were validated in conversations with sales managers, who confirmed that their teams now possessed all the necessary knowledge to perform their sales activities.

One caveat for the learning results is that the second course showed substantially higher average scores than the first course on predominantly the same learning objectives. This is likely due to a combination of several different factors:

- improvements made to the course content and instructional strategies based on observation from sales education team members and program stakeholders as well as student feedback from the first course
- a different average profile and experience level for participants in the second course versus the first course
- several international participants were in the first course (for whom English-only instruction may have presented some slight challenges), versus a student population in the second course that was entirely from the United States.

Level 3 Application and Implementation

The sales education team, in collaboration with the various program stakeholders, identified five key behaviors that the sales reps were not currently exhibiting, but needed to exhibit on the job following the course. Due to the length of the InfoPrint 4100 sales cycle and the complexity of customer engagements, we waited to evaluate whether these behaviors were being performed until 12 months had elapsed following the course.

Due to a variety of circumstances, seven of the original 17 sales reps who completed the course had left the company. Therefore, there were only 10 participants remaining from these two courses, and we were able to solicit feedback from nine of them. Although nine out of 17 is a disappointing response rate, we did not assume any business impact from the sales reps who had left the business. We did not extrapolate any results to the participants who were no longer available for our study. The behavior change and business impact data for the entire cohort was therefore dependent on results from those nine individuals.

Participants were asked to rate each of the questions on a six-item Likert scale: 5 (very significant change), 4 (significant change), 3 (moderate change), 2 (some change), 1 (no change), and 0 (no opportunity to apply). The application results for each course are shown in Table 6-3.

There was not a predefined expectation of what an acceptable average score would be for these five objectives. Since the behaviors were not being performed at all prior to the course, any demonstration of these skills on the job would be an improvement. As such, the scores for both courses showed that all of the behaviors were being implemented on the job, especially for the participants who were in the first course. It was surprising that these participants showed a greater application of learning, because they had lower scores on the learning objectives than the participants in the second course. Additional research will be required to uncover the reason for this unexpected relationship between Level 2 and Level 3 results.

TABLE 6-3. Level 3 Course Evaluation Results

Objective	First Course	Second Course
Progress monochrome continuous forms opportunities past the "validation" stage.	3.67	2.50
Complete the appropriate steps for successful Firm Order Process.	3.33	3.00
Use the tools, techniques, deliverables, and resources discussed during the class to progress the sell cycle of a solution to a potential client.	3.67	3.50
Apply InfoPrint's solution selling process and related tools in customer engagements.	3.33	3.00
Engage in deals that are positioned against key continuous forms competitive offerings.	3.67	2.50
Mean	3.53	2.89

Level 4 Business Impact

Once again, the length of the InfoPrint 4100 sales cycle and the complexity of customer engagements indicated that we wait an appropriate interval before measuring whether the skills learned in the course translated into real business results. Therefore, we waited to evaluate business impact until 12 months had elapsed following the course.

An online survey was administered for participants to report on their sales activity in the year prior to the course, as well as the year following the course. These data were clarified through discussions with each sales rep where necessary, and validated with other key stakeholders to ensure that the reported figures were in line with other observations.

Because this was a sales course, it was not difficult to convert the business impact into a dollar amount. In fact, the primary impact measurement used was profit, so the impact was already stated in the metric in which executives are most interested. The profit margins for monochrome continuous forms deals (that include hardware, software, and services components) range from 20 percent to 50 percent. For the purposes of this study, I used the average margin of 35 percent, which is a typical result for deals closed with this population of sales reps.

Participants reported that the number of InfoPrint 4100 deals, the total revenue, and profit related to these deals increased in the year following the course, as shown in Table 6-4.

TABLE 6-4. Non-Isolated Business Impact From Courses

		12 Months Prior to Course	12 Months Following Course	Change
First Course	# of deals	5.66	7.33+	+1.66
	Value of deals ($USD revenue)	$1.60 million	$3.68 million	+$2.08 million
	Profit ($USD)	$560,000	$1.288 million	+$728,000
Second Course	# of deals	4.00	6.00	+2.00
	Value of deals ($USD revenue)	$600,000	$720,000	+$120,000
	Profit ($USD)	$210,000	$252,000	+42,000
	Additional benefits from one-time revenue	N/A	$100,000	+$100,000
	Additional benefits adjusted for profit margins	N/A	$35,000	+$35,000
	Profit + additional benefit ($USD)	$210,000	$287,000	+$77,000

The difference in these measurements is the maximum business impact that could be attributed to what the participants learned in the course. The first course showed an increase in revenue of $2.08 million following the course and an increase in profit of $728,000. The second course showed a total benefit of $220,000 (comprised of both a revenue increase and an additional one-time revenue monetary benefit). The profit increase for this course was $77,000, comprised of $42,000 in profit from sales gain plus the $35,000 profit from additional monetary benefit. A post-class survey administered the following year, when enough time had elapsed for the students to incorporate their new sales skills into their job activities, indicated that one participant estimated an additional $100,000 in sales as a result of the course which, adjusted for profit margin, equals $35,000.

Specifically, the participant indicated that the benefit was related to "TCOP for proposals." This is in reference to "Total Cost of Print," a sales technique that was covered in class that tabulates the fully loaded cost per page of printing that incorporates the cost of the hardware, software, maintenance, and supplies. Though the up-front hardware cost might be higher for InfoPrint products, when you consider maintenance and supplies costs and other customer expenditures, the product actually comes at a lower cost to the customer per page printed, than a less expensive or discounted hardware alternative from a different company. This technique taught in the course armed participants with a new strategy for selling the products to customers.

Isolating the Effects of the Program

Of course, many other factors contributed to successful sales activities, and it is absolutely critical to isolate the effects of the course versus other variables. To this end, the participants were asked which factors had an influence on their sales activity in the year following the course. The options presented to the participants were all the factors that sales managers and executives believed could have played a role in encouraging sales activity for the InfoPrint 4100.

The participants themselves were asked to estimate the effects of the program versus other factors for several reasons. This was the most expedient and least costly method of performing this analysis. In some ways, this is among the most accurate methods, because the participants themselves are closest to the sales activity and are therefore best able to identify how much the course or any other factor helped them close a sale. Other methods of isolating the effects of the course were not feasible: control groups, trend-line analyses, and forecasting would not have resulted in usable data. The geographic dispersal of the sales force (and resultant lack of an appropriate control group cohort), uncertainty around sales expectations, and lack of historical sales data for the participants (some of whom were new to this product category) would have resulted in less precise estimates of the importance of the course against other factors in the business that all contributed to the sales activities following the course. Results are shown in Table 6-5.

It was gratifying to learn that for both student cohorts, the face-to-face course was cited as being among the most important factor in improving the sales activity following the course. For the first course, the course experience was the single most important factor, and for the second course, the course was the third largest influence on the participants' subsequent sales success.

These results were used to isolate the effect of the course against all other factors that contributed to the increased sales activity following the course. Those results were isolated by looking at the dollar amount of sales during the period following the course, multiplied by the percentage of that sales success that the participants attribute to the course itself, multiplied by their confidence in their estimate of that impact. This methodology not only isolates the effects of the course against all the other factors that contributed to the sales results, but it also results in the most conservative estimates of the business impact of this course since the uncertainty of the estimate is taken into consideration. As a result, the calculation of the business impact of the course is easily defensible and we do not overstate our results.

TABLE 6-5. Isolating the Effects of the Program

	First Course		Second Course	
FACTOR	Weight	Confidence	Weight	Confidence
"Selling Monochrome Continuous Forms Solutions" class	19.05%	63.33%	12.92%	87.50%
Other educational offerings (webinars, CBTs, etc.)	13.92%	50.00%	11.24%	87.50%
Management focus on monochrome continuous forms	17.58%	60.00%	11.24%	70.00%
New product or solution offerings	17.58%	56.67%	13.48%	72.50%
Marketing campaigns (internal, .com, or solutions partner campaigns)	5.13%	51.67%	12.92%	70.00%
Incentives	13.19%	36.67%	14.61%	80.00%
Sales plan	12.45%	30.00%	12.36%	45.00%
Other factor(s)	1.10%	20.00%	11.24%	70.00%
TOTAL	100%		100%	

Table 6-6 shows the business impact results for each course (with the effects of the course versus other factors identified). See Table 6-4 for non-isolated business impact amounts and Table 6-5 for weight and confidence measures.

TABLE 6-6. Isolated Business Impact From Program

Program	Sales Success Due to Class	Confidence in That Estimate	Total Profit Increase + Additional Monetary Benefit	Profit Increase Attributable to Class
First Course	19.05%	63.33%	$728,000	$87,829
Second Course	12.92%	87.5%	$77,000	$8,704
TOTAL			$805,000	$96,533

Program Costs

An aggregate business impact of $96,533 has been determined. It was isolated from other factors in the business that may also have driven additional profit for the first and second courses. It is now important to consider whether the expense of developing and delivering this program on two occasions was a good investment. This determination hinges on how much was spent on the program.

In order to be as accurate and complete as possible, every cost of the program was tabulated, those incurred directly as well as indirectly. The categories we included, and the amounts spent in each category, are shown in Table 6-7.

TABLE 6-7. Program Costs

Cost Category	First Course	Second Course	TOTAL
Travel			
• Airfare	$8,300	$4,000	$12,300
• Car rental	$3,650	$2,555	$6,205
• Lodging	$7,440	$4,800	$12,240
• Meals	$2,520	$1,470	$3,990
Time			
• Course development, preparation, and logistics—sales education team	$14,436	$4,852	$19,288
• Content development and preparation by subject matter experts	$5,655	$4,025	$9,680
• Student time, instruction, facilitation, and evaluation activities by sales education staff and SMEs	$19,168	$10,734	$29,902
Logistics			
• Program materials (hard and soft copies)	$220	$154	$374
• Candy and other giveaways	$10	$10	$20
• Facilities cost	$0	$0	$0
• Facilities fees (rental, A/V service, setup, etc.)	$0	$0	$0
• Guest speaker fees	$0	$0	$0
• Teleconference/webinar charges	$0	$14	$14
• Coffee and water service	$37	$31	$68
• Snacks	$125	$100	$225
• Catering for working lunches	$0	$105	$105
TOTAL	**$61,561**	**$32,850**	**$94,411**

The costs for travel were calculated based on the average airfare, hotel rates, and car rental fees rather than tabulating every participant's actual expense report. The value of time for the participants, instructors, and subject matter experts (for course development activities, time in course, and work on post-course evaluation activities) was calculated using the average burden rate, including salary plus benefits, for a population of about 750 employees, rather than using actual compensation information for each person, which is considered confidential.

A number of assumptions went into each calculation. In every case where there might be multiple ways to calculate or estimate a cost, the more conservative method was chosen so that the costs were stated as the higher of the possibilities. This is intended to make the cost estimates as defensible as possible, should any stakeholders challenge the ROI calculation.

ROI and Its Meaning

The benefits from these courses were outstanding, but the costs were significant as well. In order to evaluate whether the courses were a cost-effective way to address the skills gaps and sales challenges, it is important to compare the costs with the benefits, as shown in Table 6-8.

TABLE 6-8. Return on Program Investment

	First Course	Second Course	TOTAL
Total revenue increase	$2,080,000	$220,000	$2,300,000
Revenue from class	$250,939	$24,871	$275,810
Profit from class (at 35% margin)	$87,829	$8,704	$96,533
Costs (direct + indirect)	$61,561	$32,850	$94,411
Benefit-cost ratio (BCR)	1.43:1	0.26:1	1.02:1
Return on investment (ROI)	42.67%	-73.50%	2.2%

Two measurements were taken: return on investment (ROI) and benefit-cost ratio (BCR). The first course had a BCR of 1.43:1, meaning that for every dollar spent on the course, the business realized $1.43 in new profit. This translates to an ROI of 42.67 percent. The second course resulted in a negative return on our investment due to the much lower revenue increase in the year following the course. It showed a BCR of 0.26:1, indicating a revenue increase of $0.26 for every dollar we spent on the course. This translates to an ROI of –73.50 percent.

At first glance, it appears that the first delivery of this program was a good investment of limited company resources and the second was not. However, it is also useful to view the program as a single entity, and to aggregate the costs and benefits. Indeed, the program went through a single design phase and the objectives were largely identical between the two deliveries. In this case, the program as a whole showed positive results. The BCR was 1.02:1, indicating that for every dollar of expense the business realized $1.02 in new benefits. This translates to an ROI of 2.2 percent.

There are several different thresholds to which these figures can be compared. Of course, any program with a positive ROI is desirable. However, it is also important to consider the relative merits of the many possible programs that compete for limited funding. At RPPS, programs must generally meet the expectation of a 20 percent or greater return to be eligible for funding consideration. The 42.67 percent ROI for the first course exceeds this threshold by a comfortable margin, although the second course had a negative ROI. As an integrated whole, the monochrome continuous forms education program had a positive ROI of 2.2 percent, falling below the 20 percent funding threshold at RPPS but an encouraging sign for future deliveries of this program—which will continue to generate additional profit at very reduced incremental course development costs.

Intangible Benefits

For the purposes of this study, "intangible benefits" are all positive outcomes of the course experience that were not converted to a monetary value, and therefore are not part of the business impact and return on investment calculations. There were a number of ancillary benefits that resulted from these courses. These include:

- improved relationships in the geographically-dispersed sales force through the networking made possible by coming together for a face-to-face event
- better teamwork, cooperation, and communication among sales reps
- better sales support from product marketing managers and technical support personnel, due to the relationships forged or strengthened with the sales reps during course
- improved employee morale
- improved employee engagement
- higher customer satisfaction rates resulting from a more skilled sales force.

All of these benefits undoubtedly will contribute to RPPS being a more successful company with happier and more productive employees, but these benefits are not included in the business impact or ROI calculations. The rationale for this decision was that although real, these benefits are much harder to quantify in terms of dollars or a contribution to the bottom line than the revenue figures that were the centerpiece of this study. Rather than weakening our argument by including some of these less-verifiable measures, we left business impact as a purely profit-related calculation. This should make the study easier to explain and defend to other stakeholders or executives at RPPS.

RECOMMENDATIONS

Barriers and Enablers

Many other factors besides the course enabled the sales reps to more effectively sell InfoPrint 4100 printers. These factors, and the relative contribution to incremental revenue in the year following the course, are listed in Table 6-5.

Likewise, there are a number of factors that are barriers to success for sales reps, things that prevent them from applying what they learned in course in their day-to-day activities, or that counteract the positive behaviors that they demonstrate and serve to inhibit the likelihood of sales success. We inquired about these factors during our final follow-up survey so that we could bring them to the attention of sales management.

These factors include:

- competing job responsibilities that make it difficult to focus enough time on continuous forms hardware sales
- requirements from the sales plan to sell other product categories instead of continuous forms hardware
- incentives in the compensation plan to focus attention on other product categories instead of continuous forms hardware
- management direction to spend time on other duties or product areas.

Because RPPS sells so many product categories to so many different types of customers, these challenges continue to be a struggle for the sales force in terms of focusing on one particular product set, no matter how strategically important to the overall portfolio. Sales managers and executives are aware of these challenges and continue to refine the strategy, sales methodology, routes to market, sales plan, and sales incentives.

Suggestions for Improvement

The educational efforts directed toward improving skills to enable more effective selling of RPPS monochrome continuous forms hardware can always be strengthened.

Specific student feedback from these courses indicates the following changes should be considered for future monochrome continuous forms hardware courses:

- condense agenda from five to four days
- offer separate versions of course for newer and more experienced reps
- eliminate hands-on time with the printers at the Boulder InfoPrint Center for advanced reps
- include more discussion of software
- include more discussion of competitive offerings from other companies.

Other changes recommended by education staff, sales managers, and executive stakeholders include the following:

- perform additional analysis of learner needs during process of developing learning and behavioral objectives
- continue to refine instructional strategies to maximize student engagement and learning
- as time permits, validate sales data reported by sales reps and managers by cross-referencing with information from our customer resource management system
- when possible, isolate the effects of the course against other factors by comparing student population with a control group that did not participate in education during the same period.

As we implement as many of these improvements as possible for future courses and program evaluation projects, we will see more effective education programs that result in a greater level of behavior change, business impact, and return on our educational investment.

Conclusions

The two "Selling Monochrome Continuous Forms Solutions in the Production Print Market" courses proved to be an excellent case study for a deep examination of whether all objectives for a high-profile, strategically important program could be achieved. In this case, we were pleased to realize a positive return on investment for the overall program, and to exceed the standard investment threshold with the ROI from the initial course delivery. We have been able to apply the lessons learned here to our other education programs, and continue to reap the benefits of a better-prepared and more skillful sales force.

Recommendations

Now that the evaluation of this education program is complete, "next steps" for the sales education team include disseminating the results of this study throughout the organization, so that our management structure is aware of the contribution that effective education can have on the company's bottom line. These results can also be used to help clarify what direction the company should head in the future, as we prepare the sales plan, incentive structure, marketing strategy, and future education programs.

These actions include:

- reviewing course results with the general managers in each RPPS geography
- using results to improve future offerings in other parts of the business
- incorporating education development and assessment methodologies with courses that cover the other main continuous forms printer hardware product (InfoPrint 5000)
- using evaluation data to inform what is included in the final business plan for future years.

These actions will ensure that we are able to leverage all the lessons we learned from these courses and improve our education, sales, and marketing management activities.

QUESTIONS FOR DISCUSSION

1. Critique the evaluation design and methods of data collection.
2. Discuss the impact on the study of having only 10 respondents out of the original 17 participants available for the Level 3-5 evaluation.
3. What other strategies for isolating the impact of the sales education program would have credibility here?
4. Discuss the approach of combining the costs and benefits of the two courses in order to calculate an overall program ROI.
5. When this course is offered again, would it be a good use of resources to perform a full evaluation study on that delivery?
6. What aspects of this methodology could you apply to your own sales training programs?
7. What are your thoughts about the $100,000 additional one-time revenue benefits?
8. What makes this study credible?

ABOUT THE AUTHOR

David P. Cain has worked in corporate training for six years, with diverse responsibilities including instructional design, program delivery, and evaluation. He has experience in the technology industry at IBM, InfoPrint Solutions Company, and Ricoh, and the pharmaceutical industry at Sandoz. He has a BA from Yale University as well as an MS and MBA from the University of Colorado at Boulder. Additionally, he has achieved the CTT+ certification (certified technical trainer) from CompTIA and the CRP certification (certified ROI Professional) from the ROI Institute. He lives in Lafayette, Colorado and enjoys swimming, hiking, and spending time with his wife Christina.

7

Account Manager Development for a Technical Training Center
Financial Services Firm

Marwa Hassan

T his case was prepared to serve as a basis for discussion rather than an illustration of either effective or ineffective administrative and management practices. All names, dates, places, and data may have been disguised at the request of the author or organization.

Abstract

The Technical Center for Training (TCT) used to have a unique status as a technical training center until many players started to enter the market and target its main customers. Seeing the changes taking place in the market, and as a step to better tune its performance to clients' needs, TCT started a new initiative, Account Management (AM), whereby a special team of qualified training professionals would be trained on selling skills and assigned the responsibility of following up on a number of clients.

Evaluation data were collected at all levels using different tools. As for Level 4 evaluation data (impact), it was found that the two set objectives were fully achieved: 1) increase the revenue generated from tailored programs; and 2) increase the number of training hours in tailored programs to cover the canceled public ones. At Level 5, the ROI value was very large, exceeding expectations. Also, there were other intangible benefits that were not converted to monetary values.

Based on the results of the study, some measures were recommended, notably to remove the AMs to an independent department and provide them with more product awareness concerning technical programs. In addition, the most important point was to adjust internal procedures pertaining to issuing and signing agreements to avoid conflict and assign accountability.

BACKGROUND

The Technical Center for Training is a small company that once enjoyed an extensive net of clients, but it started to face fierce competition caused by:

- emergence of other entities that provide the same type of programs, with equal quality and competitive prices
- changes that took place in the management of most of their clients, where long standing relationships had already been established, with a new set of training managers who have different mindsets with diverse needs and new requirements
- Emergence of new trends in the customers' needs that showed preference to specific types of training programs that are especially tailored for their needs.

TCT provides a comprehensive range of quality programs that target professionals working in the different technical areas at all levels, from fresh graduates to experienced professionals.

TCT provides different forms of training products such as:

- Public programs: Off-the-shelf products that are public, for which clients can nominate people to attend.
- Tailored programs: Programs designed based on a specific client's needs in which the target audience comes from this client only.

For the past 15 years the main focus of operations was the public programs with some tailored programs sporadically appearing in recent years. However, the demand for the public programs started to decrease at an alarming rate, with some increased demand for the tailored ones.

Need for the Program

TCT decided to dedicate part of its training staff to the program, and enhance their skills with training in sales techniques to make them the main point of contact with clients. TCT opted for this solution rather than using a seasoned sales staff, due to the importance of being very well-oriented with TCT products, in addition to being aware of the internal policies and procedures. Furthermore, TCT products tend to be a complicated mix, rendering it difficult for any salesperson to grasp its benefits and features in a short time. The decision to form this team was seen as the best alternative after reviewing the analysis done for the following data:

- public programs performance over 24-month duration
- tailored programs performance over 24-month duration

- client satisfaction surveys for two years.
  Analysis of the above data resulted in the following facts:
- The cancelation rate among public programs is increasing even though the original number of public programs is decreasing, with a noticeable increase in the tailored programs.
- Customers indicated that communication with TCT was difficult and it took them a long time to reach the correct person to get their needs met. Additionally, they are dissatisfied with the quality of public programs compared to the quality of tailored ones.

Based on the above, the management team took effective steps to form a team of account managers, whereby they will keep direct contact with clients with the following goals in mind:

- Enhance communication with clients by having an account manager that focuses on a limited number of clients to cater to their specific needs. This technique will be a change from the sporadic methodology previously followed where any department head may set occasional meetings with clients and will focus on presenting his or her products only.
- Select the team members from people already working in the training departments and accordingly they will have a profound understanding of the products they are to sell to meet specific client needs.
- Each account manager will be responsible for selling different types of programs in order to create a proper training mix that better serves the clients' needs based on consultative selling techniques.

The new initiative was announced and employees were left the choice to volunteer for that position with a guarantee that they would still have the option to return back to their normal jobs if they did not feel comfortable after a six-month period. A screening process was used to select the proper candidates from those who applied. Originally, 11 applied to join the sales team, of which six were accepted.

The training program was designed by a former salesperson with 15 years of experience in the field in addition to being a trainer at TCT. He built the program around "consultative selling" methods, where focus is given to identifying clients' needs and tailoring training programs that meet these needs. The program lasted for 50 hours over seven days, and included knowledge introduction (since participants had no previous idea about any selling techniques) as well as skill practice. This covered four learning objectives that participants should master in order to be able to carry their work successfully. By the end of the program, participants should know how to:

- report on account coverage (dealing with all stakeholders within the account)
- gather information and uncover needs (questioning and probing techniques)

- present solutions to clients (promoting products)
- get the deal (closing techniques).

The implementation of the AM initiative started with a training program that was conducted for the selected group of six participants. In the first two weeks, participants took their time running desk research on the clients they would be assigned to in order to get acquainted with the accounts they would be responsible for in terms of their training needs and consumer behavior. Then, in the following two weeks, they started running sales visits for clients in order to introduce themselves and get acquainted.

Objectives of the Study

The aim of this study was to measure the impact of the account management initiative on TCT performance. The main objectives were:

- Increase the revenue generated from tailored programs.
- Increase the number of training hours in tailored programs to cover the gap of the cancelled public ones.

Due to the high visibility of the program and its importance to realizing TCT objectives, there were many stakeholders interested in evaluating the program at different levels, such as:

- chairman and management team
- evaluation department
- trainer
- participants' direct managers
- participants.

The need for evaluation arose from the high interest of the management team due to the intention to enlarge the circle of application in the future, with a possibility to create a separate department dedicated to this operation. In addition, the success of the program will lead to gaining the lost market share and thus, help realize TCT operational goals related to increasing the number of training hours across the board. There was a need to apply the ROI Methodology with its five levels, especially with the presence of different stakeholders, each requiring a specific type of data to address their concerns and validate the success of the training. The evaluation department will benefit from collecting data at all levels as it needs to fully incorporate the ROI Methodology into its evaluation system, which usually stops at the application level. The importance of objectives at each level is outlined in Table 7-1.

TABLE 7-1. Objectives at Each Level

Evaluation Level	Objective of Evaluation
Level 1: Reaction & Planned Action	It is important to receive positive feedback from participants in terms of their reaction to the program to measure the intention to go ahead with the application phase; otherwise they will not be able to achieve the future assigned tasks. In addition, the trainer will benefit from Level 1 data by realizing the limitations of the program (if any) that can be avoided upon program repetition in case the decision for such a step is taken.
Level 2: Learning	Participants will be interested in knowing the level of progress they had achieved throughout the program. Meanwhile, the points that need improvement will be highlighted to them by the trainer to take notice of during application when they start visiting clients.
Level 3: Application & Implementation	Application of the skills taught will be of interest to all stakeholders, especially the management team, as it will give indications of the problems that might negatively affect the set business measures, or help in promoting them. The stakeholders may manage to solve such problems on time, especially in the work flow process.
Level 4: Impact	Impact of the skills application will be of great benefit to all since it will mean measuring where we stand from realizing TCT business goals, and where we stand from the set business measures.
Level 5: ROI	Knowing about the final return on investment will be of importance to the management team as it will affect the decision of generalizing the initiative, in addition to determining the monetary value of the initiative.

EVALUATION PLANNING

Levels of Evaluation

To evaluate the new initiative, the Phillips ROI Methodology was put into practice; using its 12 guiding principles for implementing the evaluation process. TCT has adopted the ROI Methodology to measure its programs at different levels to comply with international best practices. All programs conducted at TCT are subject to Level 1 evaluation. All programs with learning objectives that are knowledge/comprehension based are carried up to Level 2. Programs that are skill-based are evaluated at Level 3, mostly through questionnaires.

Following Guiding Principal 1: "When conducting a higher level evaluation, collect data at lower levels," all levels of evaluation were put into effect, each targeting a different audience as each tackled the program from a different perspective. To guarantee support for the project from different stakeholders, the evaluation specialist held meetings to introduce the idea, set clear expectations for the evaluation process, and gain buy-in.

The ROI Methodology

Implementing the ROI Methodology required gathering different types of data using different tools subject to the type of information needed and the participating stakeholder. Since the full methodology will be put into effect, evaluation at Levels 1 and 2 was performed using the simplest and most cost-effective tools. This option was preferred following Guiding Principle 2, "When planning a higher level evaluation, the previous level of evaluation is not required to be comprehensive." Level 3 was measured using three different tools, which might be viewed as excessive, but the case here was different since two of these tools were set to measure different learning objectives, and the third was used to validate them.

Data Collection and ROI Analysis Plan

A comprehensive data collection plan was designed in accordance with the ROI Methodology including the type of tools to be used, when they will be administered, and whose responsibility it will be to collect the data. The data collection plan can be seen in Figure 7-1.

After the data items were identified at Level 4 (business impact), an ROI analysis plan was developed, detailing costs, methods of converting data to money, methods of isolating the impact of the program, and possible intangible benefits. The ROI analysis plan can be seen in Figure 7-2.

Isolation Technique

In compliance with the ROI Methodology, in order to decide on the impact of training on the percentage of sales achieved for tailored programs within the first six months after the program, it was important to isolate other effects and establish a direct relationship between the training and the increase in sales. Due to the limited number of participants, the control group technique was cancelled. Forecasting was not an option due to the lack of knowledge of any other factors that could be directly connected to the increase in sales of tailored programs.

At first, SME estimate was considered as a reliable source, however, the SMEs available could not be depended upon since it required the involvement of managers that have a direct interest in the results and might provide subjective opinions.

Ultimately, the decision was to use two techniques: participants' estimates and trend-line analysis. Participants' estimates were used because the participants were in the field and were in the best position to tell how each deal went and why they succeeded. Their success in selling the programs was the final criteria for evaluating their performance by the HR department, rather than being tied to the means by which they achieved the deal.

FIGURE 7-1. Data Collection Plan

Program: <u>Consultative Selling Program (Account Management Initiative)</u> Responsibility: <u>Marwa Hassan</u>

Level	Program Objective(s)	Measures	Data Collection Method/ Instruments	Data Sources	Timing	Responsibilities
1	Satisfaction/ Planned Action	• Achieving a score of 4 or above on a 5-point scale	• Reaction questionnaire	• Participants	• At the end of the program	• Evaluation Specialist
2	Learning	• 90% of participants able to perform minimum of 5 skills out of the 9 introduced	• Role-play (assessment sheet)	• Trainer	• At the end of the program	• Trainer
3	Application/	• 80% of AMs able to achieve the status of "no further monitoring will be required during visits" within the first 6 weeks • Applying the 4 skill areas taught in the program scoring above 3 [limited success] in each on a 5-point scale • Applying the 4 learning objectives learned in the program	• Observation checklist • Application questionnaire • Financial report	• Trainer • Participants • Participants	• 6 weeks after program ends • 3-4 months after program ends • 1 month after program ends and ongoing until end of project	• Trainer • Evaluation Specialist • Trainer and Evaluation Specialist
4	Business Impact	• Increase the revenue generated from tailored programs. • Increase the number of training hours in tailored programs to cover the cancelled public hours.	• Standard reports	• Accounting department • Training records • System	• 6 months after program ends	• Evaluation Specialist
5	ROI—Break even					

FIGURE 7-2. ROI Analysis Plan

Data Items (Usually Level 4)	Methods for Isolating the Effects of the Program/ Process	Methods of Converting Data to Monetary Values	Cost Categories	Intangible Benefits	Communication Targets for Final Report	Other Influences/ Issues During Application	Comments
• Increase the revenue generated from tailored programs. • Increase the number of training hours in tailored programs.	• Trend line • Participant estimates • Trend line • Participant estimates	• Standard value for revenue generated • Data will be reported, but conversion will not be conducted since item #1 will be the only measure used for ROI calculation	• Selection process • Program design and delivery • Program administration • Participants' time out of work • Evaluation process	• Increase diversification in programs conducted • Activate business with clients that do not utilize TCT services on tailored basis	• Chairman • Management team • Participants (account managers) • Evaluation team	• Resistance from managers and other staff members	• This is the first impact/ROI study to be conducted by TCT, accordingly business measures to be converted to monetary data were restricted to the simplest and most important ones

In order to validate the estimates, trend-line analysis was also used. This technique was thought of as both valid and reliable, since TCT owns a great deal of historical data, enabling the company to run such an analysis to establish a historical trend. Considering that the use of tailored programs was already increasing, the trend had already been established. No other influences were available to affect this trend.

Data Conversion

Guiding Principal 4, "When analyzing data, select the most conservative alternative for calculation," was not an issue in this study since data were based on actual value of training programs produced by the sales team. The main business measure to be converted to money in this study was the revenue generated from tailored programs, so no conversion was needed. The figures were available from the accounting department, which is considered as a reliable and conservative source, since the amounts retrieved from it are based on net revenues registered in TCT's annual balance sheet, after deducting other costs associated to the programs.

Intangible Benefits

Besides the two main business measurements that were the focal point of this initiative, there were some intangible benefits that were expected as a by-product. Following Guiding Principal 11, "Intangible measures are defined as measures that are purposely not converted to monetary values," the following two benefits were realized but not converted to monetary value:

- There was an increase in the diversification in programs conducted, since the sales team was able to bundle different topics and offer them as a comprehensive training solution rather than stand-alone programs.
- Activated performance of some clients who do not usually cooperate with TCT.

These two benefits did not need to be turned into monetary value since other values were already set for this category. In addition, the first intangible identified was not expected to have major impact on TCT business, since during the first six months of the sales force the focus was more on familiarizing themselves with different products and how to blend them into attractive mixes. The second measure should take place because each AM will be responsible for a limited number of clients and certain sales achievements should occur. These two points were included as intangible benefits due to lack of any urgent or immediate need to turn them into a monetary value.

Costs

The AM initiative involved various costs that could be detailed in the following items:

- **Analysis process:** The analysis depended on three sources to reach a solution. However, no cost for the analysis process will be included since all the steps were done as part of routine work conducted by the departments and was not conducted just for the initiative purpose.

- **Selection process:** The selection process of participants included running a "sales assessment" interview for each. The time spent in each interview was included in the program costs that covered the fees paid to the interviewer, as well as the hourly rate of participants during the time they spent in the interview.
- **Program design and delivery:** The training program was already available as part of TCT training material, which was previously designed by the trainer. The trainer depended on his own experience and knowledge of TCT needs to develop exercises that meet participants' needs. Only the cost of the time he consumed in such work was included. There was no direct delivery cost since the trainer was part of TCT staff and was paid a monthly salary. However, he was hired to deliver programs to TCT clients and not staff, so his hourly wage was included to cover both delivery and coaching of AMs.
- **Program administration:** Running the program incurred the following administrative costs:
  - The training room used was owned by TCT so no rental fees were paid. Only utilization cost price was included.
  - Breaks (two coffee breaks and one lunch daily) for participants and trainer.
  - Material printing: presentation and handouts.
  - Stationery.
- **Participants' time out of work:** The cost of the time consumed by the six participants who sat for the program was included, along with the time they spent answering the application survey.
- **Evaluation process:** Costs for time for designing the evaluation plan, working with the trainer on the assessment tools to be used, designing the data collection tools, and analysis of data were all included in the study based on the hourly rate of the evaluation specialist. In addition, the hourly rate of the coach was also included for the observations he conducted for the team.

Other Influences/Issues

A point worth mentioning is that comparisons and figures across the study are provided in terms of number of programs and number of hours. That is mainly due to the diversity of programs offered by TCT. For example, one training program may last for eight hours, while another one might consume 40 hours. An increase in the number of programs does not necessarily correspond to an increase in the hours. Since program prices depend mainly on the number of hours, the ROI value was calculated according to the hourly revenues and not program revenues.

DATA COLLECTION

Satisfaction and Planned Action

Level 1 data were collected through a simple questionnaire. The first eight questions used a 5-point scale with a focus on measuring participant reaction to the knowledge introduced and skills acquired, and whether they were comfortable with performing them. Participants were also asked about their ability to implement the skills later in actual work settings and to give an assessment of the trainer performance. Two additional questions were included. The first was qualitative where participants were asked to list any expected difficulties they might face during the implementation of the new initiative, and the second was a checklist to rate the level of effect that the initiative might have on TCT's performance. Response rate was 83 percent.

Learning

Learning data were collected directly from the trainer at the end of the program. Each participant was assessed through an observation checklist with recommendations for performance improvement during a later stage of coaching. This method was used because sales are a skill gained rather than knowledge acquired. It was best to test this skill through a role-play to assess any shortcomings in each participant's performance and work on monitoring his or her progress in future checks during actual visits. The exception from this assessment was the skill related to "report on account coverage (dealing with all stakeholders within the account)," since this one needed more desk research and office work. The trainer ensured participants' full understanding of this skill through in-class participation to be measured in full during the application phase. Based on the level of performance demonstrated during the role-play, the trainer should provide his recommendation for future monitoring of the AM performance. An assessment of learning for 100 percent of the participants was provided.

Application of Skills/Knowledge

Three different data collection tools were used to validate findings and ensure participants' success in applying the new techniques. The first occurred one to two months after the program, in which the trainer ran random observation during actual sales calls that he attended with each of the sales team. The assessment was based on monitoring participants' (AMs) performance during a real visit to one of the clients and evaluating whether they were actually applying the skills covered during the training or not.

The trainer used the same "observation checklist" used to measure at Level 2. At the end of the observation, he assigned the level of progress achieved by the AMs after having practiced the skills for some time and provided recommendations on future observation. This method was used for the following reasons:

- Sales techniques are skills gained and picked up by practice, it was best to test through a real case situation and role-plays.
- It had the same set of assessment criteria used by the same observer.
- The observation could be conducted for each salesperson individually.
- Since the observer is a TCT employee who is known to clients, it was convenient to have him present in some of the visits conducted.

It is worth noting that participants were not aware during which sales calls they would be observed, to decrease the element of nervousness during the calls. Although the trainer/coach might be subjective in the assessment, the data of this phase were mainly required to measure the progress participants achieved throughout the visits conducted and to coach participants accordingly. This method was helpful for monitoring any progress achieved by each AM and deciding on the ability of each to continue with the initiative. The data provided by the coach was compared to the data provided by the participants at this level to make sure the transfer of learning to workplace has taken place. All of the participants (100 percent) were observed during actual visits.

For the second collection tool, participants were requested to provide weekly reports summarizing their visits to clients. There were two types of reports, aiming to help each AM to fully understand the nature of the clients assigned to him or her and be fully aware of their behaviour and needs. The two reports were the activity planner and weekly progress report. The first was designed to encourage AMs to plan for their visits, define what targets they are trying to achieve from the visits, and collect needed information pertaining to the client they intend to visit. The second report was designed to report any data or information collected about the client to achieve the market coverage, mainly the deals they succeeded in concluding and potential business opportunities. All of the participants submitted the required reports.

And finally, three to four months after the program, participants were asked to complete an application questionnaire. The questionnaire had nine questions; the purpose of the first one was to detect how far the participants succeeded in applying the skills. In questions two and three, participants were asked to rank the skills they learned in terms of which ones they started to immediately apply and which of them were used the most. The three questions used a 5-point scale technique in measuring how far the participants succeeded, with the target to achieve a minimum score of 3 (limited success) in each skill area. Questions four and five were qualitative and left a free space for participants to mention the type of barriers they faced during application of the skills and the factors that enabled better application.

Questions six and seven asked about how many deals were closed and how much of the success could be attributed to the acquired skills. Question eight was a repetition of question 10 in the Level 1 questionnaire, which asked which areas of the initiative the participants think had a higher impact on TCT's overall performance. The objective of this question was to check if participants' perception toward this initiative had undergone any change. Although this was an application survey, these questions (seven and eight) were important since "participants' estimates" will be used as an isolation technique at a later stage, while their "perceived impact" will be used as part of measuring the impact. In question nine, participants were given a free space to indicate any concerns they had and how TCT management could help them to make this initiative a success.

The questionnaire was very short and focused more on application with only two questions related to measuring impact. The main objective of it was to compare the results yielded from participants' points of view to those to be provided by the trainer. The questionnaire also assessed participants' perceptions of the effect of the program on their performance and TCT's overall business operations. Most (83 percent) of the participants responded to the questionnaire.

Business Impact

Measuring impact started six months after the end of the program, and included collecting data from two sources that were used for their credibility, following Guiding Principle 3, "When collecting and analyzing data, use only the most credible source."

- The accounting department provided reports containing revenues generated by the sales team through the six months.
- The training records, which included all the hours conducted during the set duration, and historical data were required for isolating effects.

In order to isolate the effects of the program, two methods were used in accordance with Guiding Principle 5, "Use at least one method to isolate the effects of a project":

- trend-line analysis
- participants' estimates.

In question number seven of the application questionnaires, participants were given three reasons that might have contributed to the expected increase in sales. The options were:

- The selling skills I have learned during the course.
- The deal was concluded due to pushing from another person within TCT.
- The deal was a continuation from previous dealings.

The above options were given possibilities affecting the conclusion of deals. The first one was the target of this study, the second considered that some people still maintain direct relations with clients, and the third was because some clients were already working with TCT in ongoing projects. It was realistic to assume that some of the tailored hours achieved would be a continuation of ongoing projects that the AM did not exert any additional effort in obtaining. Participants were also given a free space to provide more reasons that might have assisted them in concluding deals but were overlooked by the evaluator.

DATA ANALYSIS

Since the ROI Methodology was used to measure the impact of training, all steps of the process were followed. The main target of the study was to measure the impact of having such a practice introduced to TCT and its clients. Account management through a trained team of salespeople was new to the organization, and there were many reservations toward its implementation and success. However, since the success of the process will lead to decisions that might affect the organization, it was important to decide on the level of impact achieved with a recommendation to calculate the ROI.

Isolating the Effects of Training

In order to determine the actual effects of the training and the initiative itself, there was a need to isolate the other factors that might have affected the increase in TCT activities. Two tools were selected: trend-line analysis and participants' estimates.

Isolation of other effects on the following measures was an important step, followed by converting only the first to monetary value. The second measure was not converted due to being both related and linked to the first measure.

- Increase the revenue generated from tailored programs.
- Increase the number of training hours in tailored programs to cover the canceled public hours.

Results yielded by each were somewhat different, as participants' estimates attributed a higher percentage than from the trend-line analysis. To be conservative, the lower figure was used to calculate the ROI.

Trend-Line Analysis

The original plan was to use trend-line analysis in order to isolate program effects from results. However, the historical data collected showed a great fluctuation in the programs as well as hours achieved across different years and months. Figures 7-3 and 7-4 show the results achieved over 10 years with peaks and major drops in the numbers registered. Although this does not indicate a steady increase, it clarifies that there is a tendency toward increase across years.

The data show a fluctuation across programs and hours depending on the month, which is considered normal since the training market fluctuates and is affected by many cultural factors.

FIGURE 7-3. Programs Hours Trend

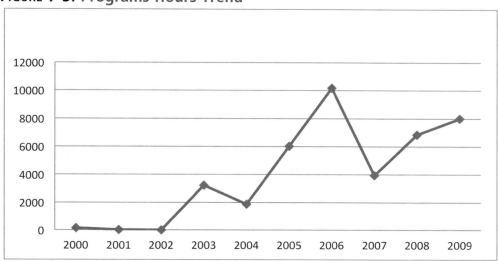

FIGURE 7-4. Programs Trend

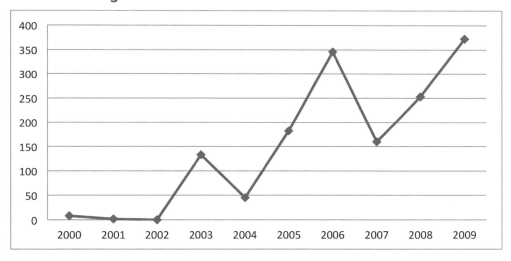

In order to isolate the impact of the AM initiative, the following points were considered:

● Average increase in the number of hours and number of programs across 10-year duration (from 2000 to 2009) was calculated at 23 percent for programs and 10 percent for hours.

- Since the trend increased more in the last five years, the increase from years 2005 to 2009 was calculated and revealed an average of 36 percent for programs and 24 percent for hours in terms of yearly increase.
- In order to calculate the expected increase in 2010 if no intervention was introduced, the actual numbers achieved in 2009 (during the first six months) were used with the supplement of the average increase mentioned above to calculate the expected increase to take place in the similar duration of 2010.

Figures 7-5 and 7-6 show a comparison between actual figures achieved and expected results if normal numbers of hours and programs took place. Both figures clarify that the actual achieved was higher across the six months with the exception of the month of May, which is a normal fluctuation given that this is the normal trend of TCT performance across the months.

FIGURE 7-5. Expected vs. Actual Programs Implemented

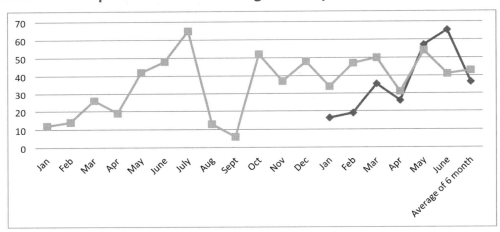

FIGURE 7-6. Expected vs. Actual Hours Achieved

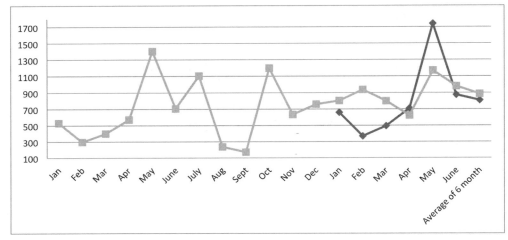

For further clarification, Table 7-2 shows the variance between expected numbers and actual numbers for 2010 based on per month average.

TABLE 7-2. Forecasted vs. Actual Hours and Programs

Per Month	Forecasted	Actual	Variance	Percentage
Hours	807	885	78	9%
Programs	36	43	6	15%

Participants' Estimates

In the application questionnaire, participants were asked to provide an estimate of the impact of selling skills applied during visits on the actual products sold. Although the questionnaire was conducted four months after the program rather than waiting until the end of the six-month duration, the estimate was considered effective for usage since participants' confidence in their ability at this stage was mature enough and could be used as a reliable data. This was also clear in the changes they had in their perceptions of their ability to contribute effectively to boosting TCT's performance as explained in the questionnaire analysis.

Following Guiding Principle 7, "Adjust estimates of improvement for potential errors of estimation," the percentages given were adjusted by asking participants about their confidence level in them, thus minimizing the possible margin for errors. Table 7-3 shows the results of the questionnaire.

TABLE 7-3. Participants' Estimates Adjusted for Confidence

Reasons for Success	Average Percentage (%)	Confidence Level (%)	Estimated Effect (%)
Selling skills I have learned during the course	57	79.8	45.5
Deal was concluded due to pushing from another person	34	52.5	17.9
Deal was a continuation from previous dealings	17	10	1.7
Other	30	99	29.7

The data in Table 7-3 indicate that 45.5 percent of the revenue generated and hours achieved in the area of tailored programs can be attributed to the sales skills they have learned during the training, since they did not have enough sales experience prior to the training program.

Converting Data to Monetary Value

After isolating the other effects on the achieved results, and in order to calculate the ROI, the net amount gained from this initiative must be determined. Since the standard value will be used in calculation, no data conversion is required; and as there were two impact measures, only one will be used in calculating the final ROI.

Cost of the Intervention

Following Guiding Principal 10, "Fully load all costs of a solution, project, or program, when analyzing ROI," careful measures were taken to include all costs incurred during the project implementation, as shown in Table 7-4 in Egyptian monetary units.

TABLE 7-4. Total Program Costs

Item	Total Cost
Selection process	LE1,274
Program design and delivery	LE4,785
Program administration	LE9,420
Participants' time out of work	LE6,300
Evaluation process	LE4,832
Total costs	**LE26,612**

RESULTS

Level 1, Reaction

Reaction to the program indicated high satisfaction from participants with all items. Based on TCT benchmarking standards, the target was to achieve a minimum score of 4 out of 5 in each skill area, and the data indicate that six items out of eight received above benchmark scores, with one item just meeting the standards, and only one item scoring below standards. Scores are reported in Figure 7-7.

In a trial to predict the concerns of participants on the success of this endeavour, an open space was left to them to express the barriers that might hinder them from the application of learned skills. From their feedback the following points were detected:

- Clients have had unsatisfactory past experiences.
- TCT complicated process and procedures.
- Lack of cooperation and support from other staff members.

FIGURE 7-7. Participants' Reaction to the Program

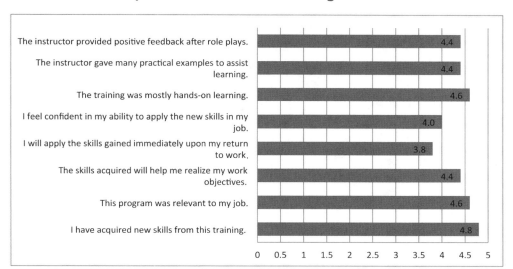

Level 2, Learning

The trainer provided five checklists, each representing the performance of participants' role-play individually. The trainer was then asked to provide a recommendation based on that performance, which had to be one of the following:

- No further monitoring will be required during visits; ongoing coaching only will be needed.
- Minor monitoring will be required during visits along with ongoing coaching.
- Needs constant monitoring during visits along with ongoing coaching.

Results show that 100 percent of participants were able to demonstrate a minimum of five skill areas. Figure 7-8 shows the classification of participants' status according to coach observation.

FIGURE 7-8. Trainer Recommendations

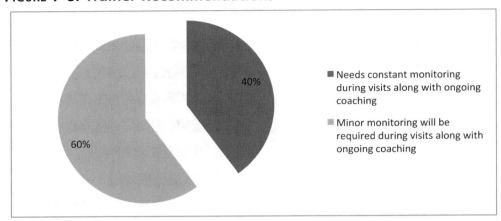

- Needs constant monitoring during visits along with ongoing coaching
- Minor monitoring will be required during visits along with ongoing coaching

Level 3, Application and Implementation

Following Guiding Principle 6, "If no improvement data are available for a population or from a specific source, assume that little or no improvement has occurred," data at this level were collected from five participants only, since the sixth participant did not provide any data.

Coach assessment started three weeks after the program and ran sporadically to monitor the progress of each AM. There were no common pitfalls among participants, and they mostly progressed in accordance with the coaching provided. The coach commented on their performance, indicating that although there was room for improvement, which was normal in this stage, overall demonstration of the skills learnt was satisfactory, with the target of 80 percent of AMs (total of four) achieving the status of "no further monitoring will be required during visits" within the first six weeks.

Participants were requested to provide weekly reports summarizing their visits to clients.

The main objective of collecting these data was to measure participants' ability to master the "reporting on account coverage." The first reports indicated that the focus was given to establishing a positive relationship with clients, the aim of these visits was to introduce oneself and build rapport with the clients. This went on for approximately the first two or three weeks of application. After that, more valuable data about clients started to show, with considerable improvement toward the end of the six months.

Participants provided feedback on the application questionnaire. The main objectives of this questionnaire were to measure how successful participants were in making the skill transfer on sales calls, and to identify the barriers and enablers for applications. Based on their feedback, and compared to the original study objectives, three of the skills achieved a score above 3 (limited success). Table 7-5 shows the degree of success to which the participants implemented the skills.

TABLE 7-5. Degree of Success With Implementation

Skill	Degree of Success in Implementation	Average Score
Report on account coverage	5 were generally successful	4.0
Gather information and uncover client needs	4 were generally successful 1 had limited success	3.8
Present solution to the client	3 were generally successful 2 had limited success	3.6
Close the deal	3 had limited success 2 had very limited success	2.6

The data in Table 7-5 indicate that:
- All participants assigned the highest success rates to the skill "report on market coverage."
- Most participants felt confident about their success in "gathering information."
- Almost half of the participants felt confident about their success in "presenting solutions."
- All participants still feel unconfident in their ability to "close the deal" compared to the other skills they earned.

When asked to rank the skills in terms of "immediate application" when they returned back to work, participants indicated that the most used skill was "gathering information and uncovering client needs," followed by "reporting on account coverage," "presenting the solution to clients," and "getting the deal."

Barriers to Implementation

Through the questionnaire, participants reported the following barriers that they faced during their visits to clients that created obstacles against performing all the skills gained, especially "getting the deal":
- Clients' perceptions toward TCT and their unsatisfactory past occurrences.
- The clients they met were not the real decision makers.
- The long and complicated process and procedures makes it difficult to present timely solutions to clients.

It is worth adding that the first and last points were future concerns expressed by participants while collecting Level 1 data.

Enablers to Implementation

Participants felt that the main thing that enabled them to implement the skills effectively was the training, in addition to the continuous coaching after the program. Another enabler was the wealth of information available at TCT about each client's historical performance and past relationships.

Conclusion From Data Levels 1–3

- Participants have gained more confidence in their ability to have a positive impact on TCT performance compared to their initial feedback in Level 1.
- All participants assigned the highest success rates to the skill related to "report on market coverage," which complies with their ability to master this skill within the first two months as indicated in their weekly reports.
- All participants still feel the least confident in their ability to "get the deal" compared to the other skills they learnt, which coincided with the coach tips in terms of the need to focus more on the closing techniques in the role-play and in most of the observations conducted afterwards.
- When comparing the points of views in Level 1 to those in Level 3, it was found that some perceptions have changed. The difference between their perception during collection of Level 1 and Level 3 data is shown in Figure 7-9.

FIGURE 7-9. Participants' Differences in Perspective

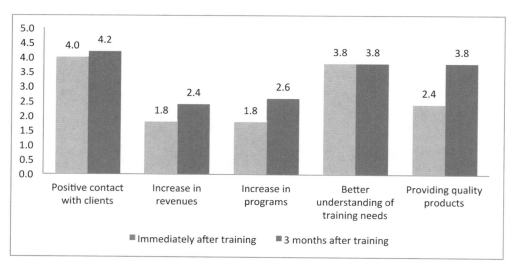

Level 4, Impact

The target of the whole project was to:

- Increase the revenue generated from tailored programs. Net revenues after deducting program costs were LE3,317,196 in the first 6 months of 2009 compared to a net revenue of LE4,478,665 achieved in 2010.
- Increase the number of tailored programs to cover the gap of the canceled public ones. Table 7-6 shows the figures in detail.

TABLE 7-6. Increase in Tailored Training Programs

	2009	2010
Public programs	351	222
Canceled programs	185	148
Tailored programs	161	257

Table 7-6 shows that in 2009, the number of tailored programs did not cover those lost in the public ones, contrary to 2010 when the number of tailored programs covered and far exceeded the cancelled ones. However, it is important to measure this as a percentage since the number of public programs as well as those cancelled in 2010 is less than those registered in 2009.

It is worth highlighting that the number of programs is not the only criterion for measuring success. Equally important is the number of hours generated as a result of these programs. Table 7-7 shows the results in terms of hours.

TABLE 7-7. Increase In Hours of Tailored Training Programs

	2009	2010
Public programs	6,923	4,676
Canceled programs	3,212	3,021
Tailored programs	3,903	5,308

Table 7-7 shows that the number of tailored hours covered the canceled ones with an increase of 22 percent, which is much less compared to the percentage achieved in 2010, 76 percent.

Aside from these data, in a trial to gauge participants' thoughts about the impact of the AM initiative on TCT general performance, participants were given a list of possible impact measures and asked to advise which ones will be of "significant effect," "high effect," "moderate effect," "minor effect," or "no effect." When asked about how far they thought TCT's performance was affected by the AM initiative their answers show that they still think that the highest benefit is that of establishing "positive contact with clients," followed by a "better understanding of clients' training needs," and "providing quality products." Meanwhile, they still think that "increasing the number of training hours" and "increasing the revenue" are the lowest in terms of gaining direct and immediate benefits.

Level 5, ROI Calculation

After isolating the effects of the training, which was 45 percent based on participants' estimates and 12 percent based on the trend-line analysis, the more conservative 12 percent was used to calculate the ROI. Net revenue achieved in the first six months of 2010 was LE4,478,655.00 with an increase of LE1,161,469.00, compared to 2009 net revenues of the same duration.

Following Guiding Principle 9, "Use only the first year of annual benefits in ROI analysis of short-term solutions," the number was annualized based on a total of 10 months calculation rather than 12. This was because two months of the projected year are not suitable for any training, which is a yearly trend because of summer vacations and the holy month of Ramadan. To be on the conservative side, August and September 2010 were excluded from the calculation of the annualized revenue. Total revenue expected for the whole year would be LE1,935,782.00.

Taking 12 percent of this amount, which is the average of the impact on hourly increase and programs increase attributed to the AM efforts, the total benefits are LE232,294.00.

Benefit-Cost Analysis

$$\text{Benefit-Cost Ratio (BCR)} = \frac{\text{Monetary Benefits}}{\text{Program Costs}} \quad \frac{232,294.00}{26,612.00} = 8.73{:}1$$

Return on Investment

$$\text{ROI (\%)} = \frac{\text{Net Monetary Benefits}}{\text{Program Costs}} \quad \frac{232,294.00 - 26,612.00}{26,612.00} \times 100 = 773\%$$

Intangible Benefits

Diversification of programs conducted to clients (cross selling) increased. The trend at TCT was that each training manager usually sold his or her own programs without trying to promote any other products. With the new AM initiative, the focus was different. The diversification of products for each bank was encouraged. The plan is not to sell short-term programs, but rather to secure and maintain long relationships with clients.

The data collected show that although this mix was not achieved, new product lines started to show as part of the promotable products. In addition, other clients started to ask for soft skills programs when the usual trend was using them for technical training only.

Some of the dormant accounts were activated. In this area, great improvement was achieved where six clients were successfully reactivated by the AM team.

COMMUNICATION OF RESULTS

Following Guiding Principle 12, "Communicate the results of ROI Methodology to all key stakeholders," an executive brief was provided to the chairman, while the management team were given a complete presentation. The trainer and participants were given access to the full study. A copy of the study was posted to TCT's portal for reading and review by different stakeholders.

CONCLUSIONS

The amount of revenue generated as a result of the AM initiative was not high, still the initiative was not a failure; on the contrary it achieved a positive ROI and met the set target of covering its costs. In addition, the positive relations established with clients at different levels, especially juniors, and the stream of data provided through the team was of impressive value, especially in the areas related to complaints and internal information, which led to perceiving the AM team as performing a sort of "market intelligence."

Although the initiative originally started in January 2010 it was not expected that the trained participants would succeed from the first month in achieving any special deals. Accordingly, the trial was perceived as a success due to the expectation to increase returns with the more experience participants gain over a longer time span. Building on that, the second half of the year may well yield better results than those calculated at present.

RECOMMENDATIONS

At the end of the project the following points were recommended to maximize the AM initiative:

- Move the AMs to be an independent department.
- Provide the sales team with awareness training about different technical topics.
- Adjust the internal procedures pertaining to issuing and signing agreements to facilitate the flow of work.

LESSONS LEARNED

Running this evaluation study was not an easy task to accomplish. Although the training itself was simple and linking it to business measures was not a complicated issue, collecting data and convincing some stakeholders of the need to have specific and reliable information was not a smooth process and was not always viewed as a priority. By managing to run this study internally, it was proved beyond doubt that such a calculation is possible, which will certainly strengthen the evaluation processes within the company and add to its credibility.

It is worth highlighting here that there were some lessons learned for me personally as an evaluator:

- One of the major benefits I had from the study was the ability to read and refer back to the books I had from the ROI Certification workshop. They proved to be a very effective as a guiding tool throughout the study.
- The planning phase is a very integral and vital step in any evaluation project.
- Through this study, I benefited a lot from experimenting with forms until reaching the final format that I felt would provide me with the required data and be user-friendly enough for recipients to complete easily. I also learned how to construct questionnaires in a way that echoes previous ones in order to build on the data.
- On the other hand, there were some setbacks that I encountered while working:
  - The participants' estimates used to measure the level of impact were disconcerting as they were unusually high and thus deemed unfit for usage.
  - The method selected for isolation of impact, trend-line analysis, was dependent on the previous 12 months of data to build a trend. When the data proved to be very fluctuating, I used the five-year data, but that too proved to be very erratic. Hence came the idea of using TCT performance for the 10-year duration to forecast what monthly increase could take place.

I realized through the study that the role of the evaluator depends a lot on his or her ability to establish open and trustworthy communication channels with all involved parties, otherwise, getting data will prove next to impossible. This is especially true in a culture like Egypt's where people tend to feel more comfortable talking than writing; accordingly, many of the comments mentioned in their written feedback had to be verified through one-to-one meetings.

QUESTIONS FOR DISCUSSION

1. Is using 10 years' worth of data feasible in your organization? Why or why not?
2. Could any other methods have been used to isolate the effects of the training?
3. Is a volunteer-basis training program feasible for evaluation, or should participants have been selected? Why?
4. Should the two "dormant" months have affected the ROI calculation?
5. Should the revenue be adjusted for the profit margin?

ABOUT THE AUTHOR

Ms. M.M. Hassan is an experienced trainer in the soft skills area, in addition to being experienced in specialized training domains like needs analysis and evaluation. She has assumed different managerial and administrative posts in the tourism industry where part of her responsibilities included conducting staff training needs analysis and setting training plans as well as carrying them out. Upon leaving the hotel industry she worked as a freelance trainer and participated in many training projects including designing, delivering, and evaluating training programs at different levels. She became a Certified ROI Professional in 2010.

8

Simulation-Based Sales Training at a Telecom Company

Future-Tel

Claude MacDonald, CRP
Louis Larochelle, CRP

Abstract

Future-Tel, a national telecom company in Canada, invited TalentPlus, a professional services firm specializing in business development, to develop and deploy a unique simulation-based training program. The one-day training activity, called The Solution Challenge, was aimed at enhancing the way Future-Tel's 560 sales professionals go about selling solutions to their clients. Specifically the training program had to enhance three key competencies: 1) the ability to create value through skillful questioning; 2) the ability to qualify major opportunities and decide if they are worth pursuing; and 3) the ability to build strong business proposals.

The training program was also aimed at testing, honing, and developing people's knowledge of Future-Tel's solution portfolio as well as the key vertical markets their clients evolve in.

To evaluate the effect and profitability of the project, Future-Tel asked TalentPlus to conduct a Level 5 ROI study. Therefore, data on reaction, learning, application, business impact, as well as intangible benefits were collected during and after the training activities. After isolation of the effects and conversion of data to monetary value, the ROI study showed that each dollar invested in the training program brought back $1.42 in sales revenues for Future-Tel.

BACKGROUND

Future-Tel is a major Canadian telecommunications company offering a wide variety of IT and telecom solutions to private and public organizations across the country. Future-Tel has also developed industry-leading telecom consulting expertise and has adopted industry-recognized assessment tools in order to measure, understand, refine, and fully implement "best practices."

Thirty years of experience has enabled Future-Tel to build strong alliances with all major hardware and software manufacturers, including IBM, HP, Cisco, and Microsoft. The company has also forged partnerships with smaller, more specialized IT companies. Those partnerships allow Future-Tel to offer a broad solutions portfolio through its sales force.

Program Description

After observing a decline in sales results, Future-Tel initiated a major reorganization that led to the creation of a new entity: The Future-Tel Business Market Group. The strategic objective of this new group was to improve operational efficiency and enhance customer intimacy.

As part of the overall strategy to accomplish this goal, Future-Tel decided to enhance the competencies of its sales professionals. In this context it was decided to provide all sales professionals with a Solution Selling Training Program.

A survey was conducted by the sales effectiveness team to understand what Solution Selling meant for Future-Tel's professionals. Most expressed the importance of understanding and meeting the requirements in their specific vertical markets, such as health, government, financial services, retail, and others. The data from this survey allowed the sales effectiveness team to identify the following key learning objectives with regards to the training program:

- Improve teamwork among sales representatives.
- Develop people's business acumen.
- Develop and refine vertical market knowledge.
- Improve knowledge of the Future-Tel solutions portfolio.
- Develop skills to understand the client's business challenges.
- Develop skills regarding the design and delivery of complex solutions.

In light of Future-Tel's requirements and challenges, TalentPlus was chosen to develop a one-day program, called The Solution Challenge Sales Simulator, a game-based approach that allows acceleration of learning and increases the retention rate of participants.

Three hundred twenty-one (321) individuals, including 308 sales professionals, took part in the program. The training was structured as follows:

Part 1 (2 hours):
- Vertical forum:
  - most important drivers (four or five) of the vertical markets clients evolve in
  - identification of current projects that focus on such drivers
  - presentation by each team.

Part 2 (5.5 hours):
- The Solution Challenge Sales Simulator, as shown in Figure 8-1.

FIGURE 8-1. The Solution Challenge Sales Simulator

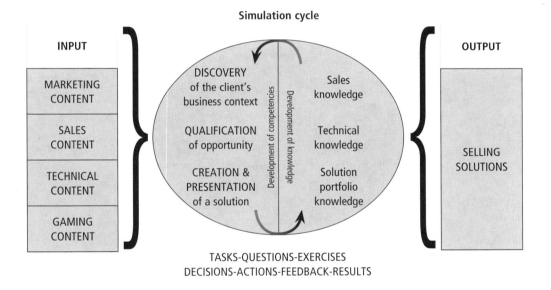

EVALUATION METHODOLOGY

In order to validate the relevance and profitability of the training program offered to Future-Tel's sales representatives and solutions specialists, TalentPlus suggested conducting an impact study.

The Phillips ROI Methodology was selected due to its proven and documented use. This approach produces six types of data: reaction, learning, application, business impact, ROI, and intangible benefits.

Also, the Methodology uses a systematic logic model to collect, analyze, and report data. Along the way, the process is guided by 12 conservative standards.

The levels of data captured by the ROI Methodology are listed in Table 8-1.

TABLE 8-1. Levels of Data

Level 1: Reaction	• Measures the participants' reactions to training. • Data captured at the end of the session.
Level 2: Learning	• Measures the participants' level of retention. • Data captured at the end of the session and validated in the application survey.
Level 3: Application	• Assesses the frequency of use of what was learned. • Data captured via an online survey, 60 to 90 days after the training.
Level 4: Impact	• Measures variations on KPIs (revenues, margins, etc.) • Data captured via an online survey and through client database, 120 to 180 days after the training.
Level 5: ROI	• Measures the actual ROI, by comparing the net monetary contribution of the training program against its fully loaded costs.

General Description of Approach

Figure 8-2 shows that the ROI Methodology was integrated into the entire training project.

Before starting the design of the training content, a meeting took place between TalentPlus CRP's and Future-Tel's stakeholders in order to align (phase 1) the client business objectives and the evaluation objectives. Following the alignment meeting, a data collection plan and an ROI analysis plan were produced and then validated by Future-Tel. Table 8-2 describes the assessment levels.

FIGURE 8-2. Evaluation Methodology

TABLE 8-2. Desired Outcomes

Level 5	Desired ROI	What kind of ROI is required from this project?
Level 4	Desired business impact	To achieve the ROI target, what business impact is required?
Level 3	Behaviour outcomes	To get business impact, what kind of behaviours need to change?
Level 2	Learning outcomes	To change those behaviours, what must people learn?
Level 1	Reaction outcomes	To drive learning, what kind of reactions must we provoke?

During the skill-building phase, 24 training sessions (one day) took place. At the end of each training session, the participants, the most credible source of data, had to complete two questionnaires to assess Levels 1 and 2.

Sixty days after the completion of data collection at Levels 1 and 2, each sales professional who attended the one-day training session had to complete a Level 3 survey. The collected data allowed assessment of what extent the salespeople were using the knowledge acquired during their one-day training session.

In addition, after 120 days, the sales professionals were given a business impact questionnaire (Level 4) to verify if the changes in terms of attitude and behaviour were maintained. This questionnaire also allowed collection of information on predefined key performance indices (KPI).

At the end of the training program, Future-Tel granted TalentPlus access to its business results database. Performance indicators such as average revenue per closed sale, number of opportunities closed with their dollar amounts, and sales cycle duration were observed.

To calculate a conservative and precise ROI, one KPI was selected: revenue increase. It was decided to measure the difference between the total sales revenues won by Future-Tel nine months before the training sessions and nine months after the training program.

In order to isolate the effects of the program, the participants were asked to estimate in percentage the actual impact of the training on their sales results as well as their level of confidence in their evaluation. This provides the actual contribution of the program.

The revenue increase measured was then multiplied by the actual contribution to assess the portion of revenue increase which could be associated to the training program.

Finally, in order to be as conservative as possible, the ROI was measured by comparing the costs of the program to the net profit generated through the revenue increase. The net profit considered in this study was chosen based on the lowest net margins observed in Future-Tel's annual reports over the last three years.

DATA COLLECTION STRATEGY

The data collection plan was developed following the alignment meeting between TalentPlus CRP's and Future-Tel stakeholders. Table 8-3 shows an abstract of the data collection plan, which details objectives at all levels, the measures, source, and collection method of data, as well as the timeline and responsibility for collection.

Level 1 data were captured through a satisfaction questionnaire completed at the end of the training session. Figure 8-3 shows an example of the questionnaire. Participants were asked to rate each statement from one to four, with one being "strongly disagree" and four being "strongly agree."

TABLE 8-3. Data Collection Plan

Level	Program Objectives	Measures	Data Collection Method	Data Source	Calendar	Responsibility
1	**Reaction and Perceived Value**					
	• Check whether the participants said they gained additional knowledge and information through the training program (target = 80%).	• Percentage of participants who report having gained new knowledge. Scale of 0 to 100%.	• Satisfaction questionnaire	• Participants	• End of each training session	• TalentPlus
	• Estimate the number of participants intending to use the knowledge gained (target = 80%).	• Percentage of participants who said they plan to use the knowledge gained (target = 0 to 100%.	• Satisfaction questionnaire	• Participants	• End of each training session	• TalentPlus
	• Assess how many participants intend to recommend the activity to others.	• Percentage of participants who intend to recommend the activity. Scale of 0 to 100%.	• Satisfaction questionnaire	• Participants	• End of each training session	• TalentPlus
	• Identify elements that could prevent participants from implementing the objectives of the activity.	• Percentage of participants who indicate that the activity is highly relevant. Scale of 0 to 100%.	• Satisfaction questionnaire	• Participants	• End of each training session	• TalentPlus
2	**Learning and Confidence**					
	• Assess whether the participants know how to apply what they learned (target = 80%).	• Percentage of participants who know how to apply what they learned. Scale of 0 to 100%.	• Satisfaction questionnaire	• Participants	• End of each training session	• TalentPlus
	• Evaluate the level of retention of key concepts by participants (target = average results of 80%).	• 5 questions measuring the level of understanding of 5 key concepts.	• Learning questionnaire	• Participants	• End of each training session	• TalentPlus
	• Evaluate the level of retention of key concepts by participants (target = average results of 80%).	• 3 questions measuring the level of retention about 3 key concepts.	• Application questionnaire	• Participants	• 45-60 days after the training session	• TalentPlus

Continued on next page.

Table 8-3 continued.

3	**Application and Implementation**			
	• Check if participants use recently learned techniques such as 6P methodology, the 5 strategies and the MARS methodology (target = 80%).	• The percentage of participants who use techniques they learned. Likert scale going from strongly agree to strongly disagree.	• Participants	• 45-60 days after the training session	• TalentPlus
	• Evaluate to what extent the training has helped develop the participants' skills to hold professional conversations that enhance their business acumen and their industry knowledge (target = 80% agreeing).	• Percentage of participants who say that the training helped develop this skill. Likert scale going from strongly agree to strongly disagree.	• Participants	• 45-60 days after the training session	• TalentPlus
	• Evaluate to what extent the training has prompted the participants to offer comprehensive solutions (multiple products or services) to their customers (target = 80% agreeing).	• The percentage of participants who say that the training prompted them. Likert scale going from strongly agree to strongly disagree.	• Participants	• 45-60 days after the training session	• TalentPlus
	• Identify which training content has the greatest impact on the respondents' ability to hold quality business conversations, to qualify opportunities and to prepare high-quality business presentations.	• Multiple choices related to key training concepts.	• Participants	• 45-60 days after the training session	• TalentPlus
	• Identify the factors that could prevent the implementation of knowledge and skills acquired during the training activity.	• Multiple choices, with "other" option.	• Participants	• 45-60 days after the training session	• TalentPlus

	• Identify the factors that could facilitate the implementation of knowledge and skills acquired during the training activity.	• Multiple choices, with "other" option.	• Application questionnaire	• Participants	• 45-60 days after the training session	• TalentPlus
	• Assess the frequency of use of the newly acquired knowledge (at least few times a month = 80%).	• The frequency of use of the new knowledge. Likert scale: never; once per month; a few times per month; multiple times per week.	• Impact questionnaire	• Participants	• 90 days after the training session	• TalentPlus
4	**Impacts and Consequences** • Assess the variation of sales revenues before and after the training program.	• $ values	• CRM	• Finance department	• Monthly reports for 2009 and 2010	• Future-Tel: Steve Thomas
5	**ROI** 25% ROI					

FIGURE 8-3. Satisfaction Questionnaire

Trainer:_____   Date:_____

Name (Optional):_____

Title (Optional):_____

Thank you for taking the time to complete this questionnaire. The information we collect will enable us to assess the real impact of this training activity on the business objectives.

Your reactions:
Indicate on a scale of 1 to 4 if you agree with the following statements
(4=Strongly Agree, 3=Agree, 2= Disagree, 1= Strongly Disagree)

	Statement	Score			
		4	3	2	1
1	I have acquired new knowledge or additional information in this training activity.				
2	I intend to use what I learned in this training activity.				
3	I would recommend this training activity to my colleagues.				
4	I will be able to apply what I learned in this training activity.				

Enablers
Among the following, identify at least three elements that could facilitate or help you with the implementation of the knowledge and skills acquired during the training activity.
• Support from my supervisor to sustain the implementation of knowledge
• Additional training on the same subjects
• Coaching
• Increased support from the specialist in charge of my vertical
• Better teamwork

• Other: _____

_____

_____

Your comments and suggestions are appreciated: _____

_____

_____

ROI ANALYSIS STRATEGY

Table 8-4 shows the ROI analysis plan for the project, which gives a guideline for measuring ROI. It features the Level 4 Impact measures, the method used to isolate the effect on the data, the method of converting the data to monetary values, categories of costs, intangible benefits, and the targets for communication of results.

TABLE 8-4. ROI Analysis Plan

Data Element	Isolation Method	Conversion Method	Costs Categories	Intangible Benefits	Communica-tion Target	Other Influence or Problem
Sales revenues	1. Participants' estimate: • A. How much impact did the Solution Challenge training activity have on your sales funnel since the training activity? (Scale 0 to 100%) • B. How much confidence (in %) do you have in your estimate? Average of A x B = Project's Level of Impact 2. Seasonality: Historic of variation of sales per month in percentage	• Standard Value – profit margin • Internal experts	• External services • Salaries and benefits of the project team, participants, and other employees • Introduction video • Printing and reproduction	• Better preparation for business presentation • Better team work • Greater capability to discover client's concerns	• Project team • Executives	N/A

OBSERVATIONS AND CAPTURED DATA

Reaction (Level 1) Data

Reaction and learning data were captured immediately following each training session. The participants were first given a satisfaction questionnaire. The overall results obtained for all 312 participants (sales representatives) are shown in Table 8-5. The reaction results from the 312 participants surpassed expectations. The objective had been set for each question at 80 percent.

TABLE 8-5. Reaction Data: Percentage of Participants Who Agree or Strongly Agree

Questions	Score
I have acquired new knowledge or additional information in this training activity.	98%
I intend to use what I learned in this training activity.	98%
I would recommend this training activity to my colleagues.	96%
I will be able to apply what I learned in this training activity.	98%

Here are a few examples of comments received during the reaction level evaluation:

- "The course was challenging and exceeded expectations. We were challenged to think on our feet and provide responses to situations in 10 or 15 minutes. That was a great way to make the course relevant to real life."
- "I believe the 6Ps can be an effective tool for pre-call planning."
- "Great training session! I really enjoyed the 6P approach—very thorough and applicable."

Learning (Level 2) Data

As shown in Table 8-6, a knowledge assessment questionnaire was used immediately following the training to measure the participants' level of retention of the key concepts.

TABLE 8-6. Learning Data (Immediately Following the Training)

Number of Questions Answered Correctly	% of Teams that Answered Adequately
5/5	93%
4/5	7%
3/5	
2/5	
1/5	

In order to verify the participants' retention of the key concepts 60 days after the training, three knowledge assessment questions were included in the application questionnaire. Note that 312 questionnaires were sent and 164 of them were completed. Table 8-7 presents the overall results obtained from the respondents in percentage.

TABLE 8-7. Learning Data (60 Days After the Training)

Questions	Results
Name at least 4 key drivers related to your market that have been presented during the Sales Simulator training session.	79% of respondents gave 4 good answers out of 4 for this question.
Name the 5 strategies that can be adopted to push forward an opportunity.	89% of respondents gave 5 good answers out of 5 for this question.
Name the 4 components of the MARS method that allow preparing a strong business presentation.	92% of respondents gave 4 good answers out 4 for this question.

Application (Level 3) Data

As shown in Table 8-8, the application level data were gathered 60 days after each training session. The questions asked were identical for all respondents.

TABLE 8-8. Application Questionnaire

Questions	Results
The Sales Simulator training activity has helped develop my skills to hold professional conversations that show my business acumen and my industry knowledge.	24% Strongly agreed 64% Agreed **Total in agreement 88%**
The Sales Simulator training activity prompted me to offer comprehensive solutions (multiple products or services) to my customers.	17% Strongly agreed 56% Agreed **Total in agreement 73%**
I have used or I intend to use in the near future the 6P Methodology (Perspective and Planning, Projects and Preoccupation, etc.) to improve the way I uncover my clients' business concerns and expectations.	15% Strongly agreed 61% Agreed **Total in agreement 76%**
I have used or I intend to use in the near future one or several of the 5 strategies (frontal, lateral, etc.) to move forward one or many opportunities.	24% Strongly agreed 52% Agreed **Total in agreement 76%**
I have used or I intend to use in the near future the MARS Methodology (Message, Audience, etc.) to prepare one or more business presentations.	29% Strongly agreed 49% Agreed **Total in agreement 78%**

The application questionnaire also identified which key concepts taught to participants had the most impact on their ability to hold quality business conversations, to qualify opportunities, and to prepare high quality business presentations, as shown in Table 8-9.

TABLE 8-9. Key Concepts With the Most Impact

Rank	Content
1	Increased knowledge of my vertical market's key drivers
2	Opportunity qualification evaluation grid
3 - Tie	5 strategies related to the pursuit of opportunities
3 - Tie	6P Methodology
5	MARS Methodology
6	VCC principle (Value Creation Capability)

Barriers and Enablers

The application questionnaire also captured potential barriers that could hinder the use of the training content. Multiple answers were allowed. Note that 96 people out of 185 respondents to this precise question gave the answer "none" (meaning no barrier) (see Figure 8-4).

FIGURE 8-4. Barriers to Implementation

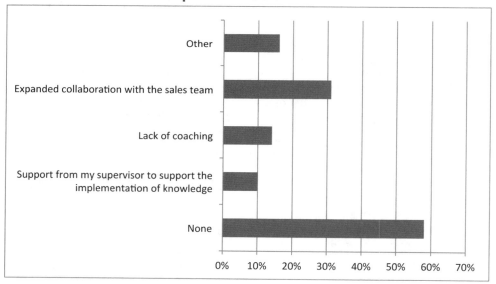

Potential enablers were also captured, such as elements that could facilitate the implementation of knowledge and skills acquired during the training activity. Multiple answers were allowed. Note that 216 people out of 312 participants gave the answer "better teamwork" (see Figure 8-5).

FIGURE 8-5. Enablers to Success

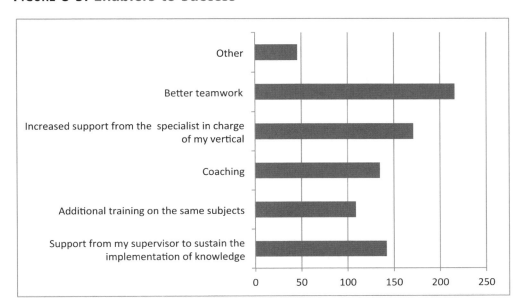

Business Impact (Level 4) Data

The business impact of the project was measured using three methods:
- a questionnaire to isolate the effects of the training solution
- a questionnaire on actual usage of the training content
- an in-depth study of Future-Tel's customer relationship management (CRM) database.

Isolating the Effects of the Program

To assess the contribution the program had on sales revenue, each respondent had to answer two questions:
- How much impact did the Sales Simulator training activity have on your sales since the session (e.g., 20%)?
- How much confidence do you have in your estimate (e.g., 60%)?

Both answers were multiplied (20% x 60% = 12%) for each participant and then an average was calculated using the results from all participants. This approach is recognised by the ROI Institute as an effective method to isolate the effects of a training solution. Overall, 312 questionnaires were sent and 227 were returned, representing a 65 percent response rate.

The collected data shows that participants who confirm the program significantly contributed to their sales are those who most often use the techniques learned. Figure

8-6 shows that the more a sales representative uses the techniques, the higher the contribution percentage was.

Figure 8-6. Content Usage Frequency

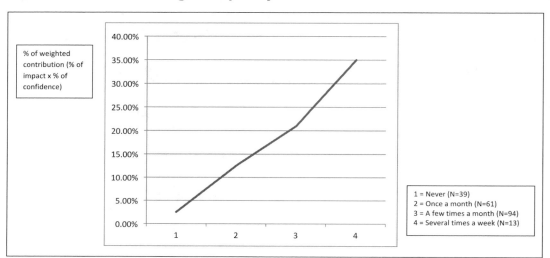

After the calculation of the contribution given by each participant, it appeared that the average contribution was 15.6 percent.

The application/impact questionnaire shown in Table 8-10 was used to obtain each participant's estimate regarding the contribution of the Sales Simulator program to their sales. It also assessed the usage frequency of specific techniques taught during the training. Please note that 312 questionnaires were sent and 204 of them were completed.

The CRM database was analyzed using the following methodology:
- Sales volume (opportunities closed and won revenues) analysis according to Table 8-11.
- Investigation of the seasonality in the sales cycle over the course of a complete year and reduction of the contribution accordingly.

Since the actual contribution of the Sales Simulator training program on revenue is 15.6 percent, the actual contribution of the Sales Simulator training program is:

$$\$39,870,785.68 \times 15.6\% = \$6,299,584$$
in additional revenue attributed to the program.

TABLE 8-10. Application/Impact Data Questionnaire (120 Days After the Training)

Questions	Results
How often have you used the 6P Methodology (Power and People, Projects and Preoccupation, etc.) to uncover your clients' concerns and expectations?	80% of respondents use the 6P Methodology at least once a month to discover their customers' requirements and challenges.
How often have you used the MARS Methodology (Message, Audience, etc.) to prepare a business presentation?	79% of respondents use the MARS Methodology at least once a month to prepare a business presentation.
How often have you used the 5 commercial strategies (frontal, lateral, etc.) to move an opportunity forward?	78% of respondents use the 5 commercial strategies at least once a month to move opportunities forward.

TABLE 8-11. Won Revenues: Before vs. After (from CRM Database)

Director of Sales	CRM Closed Won Revenues Before	CRM Closed Won Revenues After	Variation
Director 1	$26,868,761.85	$15,377,730.51	($11,491,031.34)
Director 2	$13,747,394.63	$28,988,430.62	$15,241,035.99
Director 3	$13,900,757.10	$15,333,933.34	$1,433,176.24
Director 4	$22,071,110.74	$20,908,274.90	($1,162,835.83)
Director 5	$18,118,868.35	$18,497,932.45	$379,064.10
Director 6	$15,172,906.14	$30,115,566.87	$14,942,660.74
Director 7	$6,816,578.26	$10,948,935.45	$4,132,357.19
Director 8	$22,068,795.45	$33,949,732.24	$11,880,936.79
Director 9	$17,142,327.16	$23,464,606.08	$6,322,278.91
Director 10	$9,887,337.21	$7,528,824.48	($2,358,512.73)
Director 11	$19,220,684.40	$31,978,905.88	$12,758,221.48
Director 12	$17,425,731.21	$20,029,077.99	$2,603,346.78
Director 13	$10,938,664.41	$12,620,177.63	$1,681,513.23
Director 14	$40,183,349.32	$22,054,822.13	($18,128,527.19)
Director 15	$10,082,033.32	$11,719,134.64	$1,637,101.33
TOTAL	**$263,645,299.53**	**$303,516,085.21**	**$39,870,785.68**

Conversion Methodology

In order to be as conservative as possible, it was decided with Future-Tel's CFO to use the net contribution of the project as the number to be compared to costs.

Using Future-Tel annual reports of the last three years, the lowest net profit over the three years was 9.8 percent.

- 2009 Operating Revenues: $17.735 million
- 2009 Net Earnings: $1.738 million
- 2009 Net Profit Margin: 9.8 percent

Therefore the real contribution of the Sales Simulator program is:

additional revenues attributed to the program x net profit margin
$$\$6,299,584 \times 9.8\% = \$617,359$$

Fully Loaded Costs

In order to calculate a credible ROI, all costs associated to the program were calculated. Table 8-12 provides a detailed description of these costs.

TABLE 8-12. Fully Loaded Costs of the Sales Simulator Program

Analysis Cost	$4,125
Salaries and benefits – Future-Tel team members	
Total Analysis Cost	$4,125
Development Cost	
Salaries and benefits – Future-Tel team members	$8,000
Salaries and benefits – Other Future-Tel employees	$10,000
Printing and reproduction	$200
Introduction video	$5,300
Total Development Cost	**$23,500**
Delivery Cost	
Salaries and benefits – Future-Tel team members	$30,000
Salaries and benefits – Participants	$150,000
Salaries and benefits – Other Future-Tel employees	$800
Meals, travel, and incidental expenses – Participants	$15,125
External services	$160,000
Facility costs	$4,500
Total Delivery Cost	**$360,425**
Evaluation Cost	
Salaries and benefits – Future-Tel team members	$4,125
Printing and reproduction	$50
Total Evaluation Cost	**$4,175**
Total Program Cost	**$392,225**

The fully loaded cost that will be used to calculate the ROI of the program will therefore be $392,225.

ROI CALCULATION

The ROI calculation requires several data. Here are the different variables calculated until now:

- Total variation (before and after) of opportunities closed and won revenue = $39,870,785.68
- Estimated contribution by participants = 15.6%
- Additional revenues attributed to the program = $39,870,785.68 x 15.6% = $6,299,584
- Profit added = $6,299,584 x 9.8% = $617,359
- Fully loaded cost of the Sales Simulator training program = $392,225

ROI calculation based on real monetary benefits and fully loaded cost:

$$\text{BCR (Benefit-Cost Ratio)} = \frac{\text{Benefits}}{\text{Costs}} \quad \frac{\$617,359}{\$392,225} = 1.57:1$$

$$\text{ROI (Return on Investment) \%} = \frac{\$617,359 - \$392,225}{\$392,225} \times 100\% = 57.4\%$$

Consequently, each $1 invested in the Sales Simulator program created a return on investment (ROI) of $1.57.

To compensate for seasonal variations in sales, we also calculated the ROI based on adjusted revenues. Using financial data provided by Future-Tel's CFO, a negative variation rate of 9.7 percent was calculated. Consequently, the real contribution of the Sales Simulator program becomes: $617,359 x (1 – 0.097) = $557,475

ROI calculation with adjusted revenue according to sales seasonality:

$$\text{BCR (Benefit-Cost Ratio)} = \frac{\text{Benefits}}{\text{Costs}} \quad \frac{\$557,475}{\$392,225} = 1.42:1$$

$$\text{ROI (Return on Investment) \%} = \frac{\$557,475 - \$392,225}{\$392,225} \times 100\% = 42.1\%$$

Consequently, each $1 invested in the Sales Simulator program created a return on investment (ROI) of $1.42 (adjusted for seasonal variations).

INTANGIBLE BENEFITS

The intangible benefits were also captured throughout the impact study. Figure 8-7 presents the intangible benefits identified by the participants (multiple answers were allowed).

Note that four of the intangible benefits obtained over 40 percent of support. They are:

- better preparation for business presentation
- better teamwork
- greater capability to discover clients' concerns
- higher capacity to create value for clients.

FIGURE 8-7. Intangible Benefits

LESSONS LEARNED

A High Retention Level Yields a High Impact on Sales

Some learning level questions were included in the application level questionnaire, in order to verify the participants' level of retention regarding specific concepts. The results obtained were very revealing. As proof, it appears that the questions that received the highest scores overall were about market knowledge and business opportunity development strategies.

In addition, the same application questionnaire revealed that both of these concepts were identified by the respondents as having had the greatest impact on their work. As shown in Table 8-13, it can be concluded that there is a strong correlation between the elements that had the greatest level of retention and those that had the most impact on business development.

TABLE 8-13. Retention of Key Concepts

Rank	Key Concepts With Highest Impact	% of Retention About Key Concepts
1	Increased knowledge of my vertical market's key drivers	79% of sales representatives gave 4 over 4 good answers regarding 4 key drivers related to the vertical market
2	Opportunity qualification evaluation grid	N/A
3 - Tie	5 strategies related to the pursuit of opportunities	89% of sales representatives gave 5 over 5 good answers regarding 5 strategies to push an opportunity
3 - Tie	6P Methodology	N/A
4	MARS Methodology	92% of sales representatives gave 4 over 4 good answers regarding 4 MARSs communication method components allowing to prepare a business presentation
5	VCC principle (Value Creation Capability)	N/A

This shows the importance of measuring the retention level immediately after the training sessions as well as other amounts of time after. Both sets of data show a strong correlation with the content elements that have the most impact for the participants.

A Strong Correlation Exists Between Actual Usage and Contribution to Sales

The application level questions verified to what extent the participants had used or planned to use the key techniques and strategies taught during the training session. It appears that more than three fourths (75 percent) of the respondents confirm they use or plan to use these techniques.

In addition, the objective of the impact level questionnaire was to assess the usage frequency of the same techniques found in the application questionnaire. The analysis results indicate that more than 50 percent of respondents confirm that they use these techniques at least once a month.

As demonstrated in Figure 8-8, there is a strong correlation between the use of acquired knowledge and usage frequency.

FIGURE 8-8. Content Usage Frequency

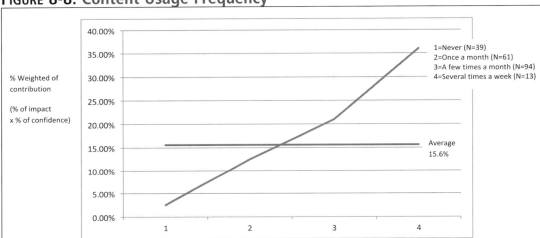

Several Teams Have Taken Ownership of the Content Elements

The results of the Level 4 questionnaire show that the Sales Simulator program contributed a 15.6 percent increase in sales. A more in-depth analysis of the contribution percentage for each director of sales reveals that the contribution percentage varies greatly among them. The assumption can therefore be made that certain senior managers have assumed ownership of key techniques and strategies taught and have integrated them in their business processes more than others.

The assumption can also be made that certain groups felt that the contents of the program were more applicable to their situation (specifically when all the participants were from the same vertical market and worked only in this vertical market).

The Data Show a Clear Chain of Impact

The analysis carried out on the Sales Simulator program has a very clear chain of impact between the reaction, application, and impact levels.

- The results from the reaction questionnaire revealed that 98 percent of the participants confirm having the intention of using the knowledge acquired during the training in conjunction with their work.
- The results from the application level questionnaire indicate that a high proportion (about 78 percent) of the participants use or plan to use three of the most important techniques taught during Sales Simulator.
- The results from the impact level questionnaire reveal that the majority of respondents confirm they use these same techniques at least once per month (79 percent).

In spite of a high usage rate for the concepts taught, the chain of impact shows a gradual decrease in enthusiasm among the people trained regarding the training contents. It would therefore be important to examine the ways of maintaining momentum and encouraging the use of the training's contents.

The Absence of Barriers Correlates With Greater Use

The application level questionnaire reveals that 52 percent of respondents do not see any barriers to implementation of the knowledge acquired during Sales Simulator. Moreover, the impact level questionnaire shows that more than 79 percent of respondents use the key techniques taught during the training at least once a month. It is therefore very probable that those who do not see any barriers to implementation are those who actually use the knowledge acquired and who grant a higher percentage of contribution.

Teamwork: Mission Accomplished

One of the Sales Simulator program's objectives was to encourage teamwork. Consequently, multidisciplinary teams across specific vertical markets were formed in order to achieve this objective. The importance of teamwork was also answered in various questionnaires. The results obtained are quite revealing:

- The reaction level questionnaire reveals that 67 percent of the participants say that teamwork is a major facilitating element with respect to the implementation of the knowledge acquired.
- The results from the application questionnaire show that teamwork is the second highest intangible benefit (48 percent) resulting from the Sales Simulator training.

These two observations confirm the initial strategy regarding the formation of groups was good. Furthermore, should other similar business transformation projects be initiated, in our opinion Future-Tel would benefit, from repeating this strategy.

The Content Was Not Only Useful but Very Relevant

The analysis of results from the application rates reveals that 78 percent of respondents say they use or plan to use the 6P and MARS techniques. A few eloquent testimonials prove the usefulness of these techniques. In fact, the use of the MARS technique helped to reactivate and conclude an important multimillion project with a major account. According to the testimonial, the project had been dragging for a while and the MARS technique enabled implementation of the strategy needed to provoke action from the client. This kind of data shows the relevance and effectiveness of the techniques and strategies taught during the Sales Simulator program.

Application of Content Yields Business Results

The majority of participants confirm having acquired useful knowledge. This correlates with the application data which shows usage rates of up to 78 percent. When asked how much the program contributed to their sales results, overall contribution is 15.6 percent, which is considered very good for a one-day training program. Moreover, the 42 percent ROI shows that the techniques used contributed to improving sales within the Future-Tel business market group.

Finally, 73 percent confirm that it did contribute to increasing the number of offers of more complex solutions. Please note that the initial objective was set at 80 percent. It would therefore be important to offer effective means of encouraging the use of the techniques taught and of convincing the participants of their effectiveness.

QUESTIONS FOR DISCUSSION

1. Should all training programs related to business development or sales be submitted to an ROI study?
2. To what extent is it important to adjust revenue variation according to seasonality of the business?
3. What is the actual impact on the study when scorecards are created and presented to senior management on a regular basis?
4. What is the correlation between the size of a company and the need to measure the outcome of projects?

RESOURCES

Phillips, Jack J., and Patricia Pulliam Phillips. (2007). *The Value of Learning: How Organizations Capture Value and ROI and Translate it into Support, Improvement, and Funds*. San Diego: Pfeiffer.

Phillips, Jack J., and Patricia Pulliam Phillips. (2007). *Show Me the Money: How to Determine ROI in People, Projects, and Programs*. San Francisco: Berrett-Koehler.

ABOUT THE AUTHORS

Claude MacDonald, a graduate from the McGill Executive Institute, is president and founder of Talentuum, a Canadian leader in sales culture enhancement. Over the last 23 years he has trained over 25,000 managers, professionals, and employees from various prominent organizations in Canada. In business since 1996, he has held management positions both in training and business development. Recognized as a true innovator and a business development specialist, Mr. MacDonald is also the author of many training programs and conferences offered by Talentuum.

Louis Larochelle. Over the last 20 years, Mr. Larochelle has held key business development positions: consultant, sales and marketing executive, project manager, product manager, and sales representative in the software and telecom industry. He has a deep understanding of many business segments which allows him to offer high level expertise on the improvement of business processes and the ROI assessment of any project or program. Mr. Larochelle is the vice-president, professional services of Talentuum.

9

Trustworthy Selling for
Commissioned Sales Representatives
Independent Financial Services Agency

Delores Freitag and Nancy Murphy

T his case was prepared to serve as a basis for discussion rather than an
illustration of either effective or ineffective administrative and management practices. Names, dates, places, and data may have been disguised at
the request of the author or organization.

Abstract

A group of 23 sales reps that attended the Trustworthy Selling training program in the fall of 2011 registered a 27 percent increase in policies, a 31 percent increase in new clients, and an 18 percent increase in premiums written
in the three months after training compared with the three months prior to
training. During the same time period, a group of 113 sales reps from the
company that did not attend the training program registered a 3 percent
increase in policies, a 1 percent increase in new clients, and a 2 percent increase
in premiums written. This company realized a 165 percent return on its investment in training.

PROGRAM BACKGROUND

The company represented in this case study is an independent financial services
agency with a sales force of 150 commissioned sales representatives affiliated with a
large national life insurance company. A small group of sales reps from the company
attended the Trustworthy Selling training program, which is designed to provide financial services organizations a new approach to increasing productivity and retention
through 10 facilitator-led modules that form a holistic development process. The

171

objective of the program is to equip producers with skills needed to break down the barriers that consumers have built as a result of preoccupation and lack of trust. The program was piloted on a small group within the agency with the expectation of conducting a thorough productivity and ROI analysis; depending on performance results and the outcome of the ROI analysis, the company would enroll additional sales reps in the training program.

EVALUATION METHODOLOGY

The Trustworthy Selling training program was evaluated at five different levels using the ROI Methodology. The Level 1 evaluation was conducted by the program facilitator at the conclusion of the four-day program. The program facilitator gave the attendees paper questionnaires on which they rated their reaction to 15 elements of the program using a 10-point scale, where "10" was the highest rating. Average ratings were calculated for all 15 elements. In addition, the 15 elements were organized into three general topics; average ratings were derived for facilitation, program content and materials, and the program overall, including investment of time.

The Level 2 evaluation was conducted by the program facilitator through the Capstone and Action Planner module at the conclusion of the program. The overall objective for the attendees was to summarize, evaluate, and integrate the principles and practices learned during the program. As course review, the facilitator led a brief discussion, where attendees were asked to identify key points from the foundational, tactical, and seller psychology modules. The facilitator listened for 12 specific points to be mentioned as means of evaluating whether the material had been learned.

Next, attendees took part in a fast-paced group review quiz consisting of 20 multiple-choice questions led by the facilitator. No official scores or grades were recorded.

Finally, working in triads, participants role-played two case studies, with each member playing the role of financial professional, prospect or client, or observer. In each case, the "observer" evaluated the "financial professional" on how effectively he or she interacted with the "prospect or client." Skills and concepts being observed and evaluated included best practices, skillful language, effective questions, and use of processes and tactics presented in the program. The facilitator as well as the "observer" and the "prospect or client" provided feedback to the "financial professional."

As a final step, participants identified three skills or concepts within each of the six tactical modules that they would commit to incorporating regularly into their work practices over the next 30 days, and to which they would hold themselves accountable to their named accountability partner (an in-house trainer, coach, other sales rep within the company, or someone else outside the company, such as a spouse or professional mentor).

The Level 3 evaluation was conducted by the program developers one month after the conclusion of the program. Program developers emailed an online survey to the attendees asking them to indicate the extent to which they use 50 techniques presented in the program. Their self-reported responses were on a 4-point scale ranging from:

- Didn't used to do this and still don't (response value = 0).
- Used to do this and still do (response value = 1).
- Didn't used to do this but do now as a result of training (response value = 2).
- Used to do this but do now even more as a result of training (response value = 3).

Responses "didn't used to do this and still don't" and "used to do this and still do" were combined to create a "no change in behavior" response category. Similarly, responses "didn't used to do this but do now as a result of training" and "used to do this but do now even more as a result of training" were combined to create a "change in behavior" response category. For each technique an average score was calculated, as well as the percentage of respondents indicating that they had changed their behavior.

The Level 4 evaluation was conducted by the program developers three months after the conclusion of the program. The participating company was accustomed to systematically tracking and monitoring the monthly production for all of its financial sales representatives; company-generated monthly production reports for each of the three months prior to training and each of the three months post-training were submitted for analysis. Production measures included number of policies, number of new clients, and premium written. Production information was provided not only for the 23 representatives who attended training but also for 113 who did not attend training but who would otherwise have experienced similar sales opportunities, market conditions, management styles, sales support, and office morale. As such, the non-attendees served as a control group for the analysis to isolate the effects of the training. Only those sales reps for which a complete set of production data was provided for both the pre- and post-time periods were included in the analysis.

The Level 5 evaluation was conducted by the program developers along with the Level 4 evaluation. Using the production measure of premium converted to profit, the ROI was derived by calculating the difference between the total profit of the premium actually written by the attendees in the three months post training and what they might have written assuming they had not attended training, divided by the total cost of the training program. The "assumed" post-training production for the attendees was derived by applying the percent change in premium for the non-attendees to the pre-training premium for the attendees. The total cost of the program included fees paid to the facilitator plus the costs of coordinating the program, program materials, and meals and refreshments. Figure 9-1 shows the ROI analysis plan for the program.

FIGURE **9-1.** ROI Analysis Plan

Data Items	Methods of Isolating the Effects of the Program	Methods of Converting Data	Cost Categories	Intangible Benefits	Communication Targets	Other Influences and Issues
• Number of policies • Number of new clients • Premium	• Control group analysis	• N/A • N/A • Standard value—profit margin	• Facilitation fees • Program materials • Meals and refreshments • Cost of coordination	• N/A	• Key personnel at company • Program implementation staff	• N/A

A formal written report that included a detailed comparison between the attendees and the non-attendees and the results of the ROI analysis was shared with key personnel at the company as well as with program developers and facilitators.

EVALUATION RESULTS

Reaction

Attendees were asked to complete an evaluation of the training program at the conclusion of the program. Sixteen of the 23 attendees completed an evaluation (70 percent response rate). Using a 10-point scale, with "10" being the highest rating, attendees rated their reaction to 15 elements of the program. Overall, the attendees were highly satisfied with the facilitation, the program content and materials, and the program in general. Results of the Level 1 evaluation are shown in Table 9-1.

Learning

The Level 2 evaluation was conducted by the program facilitator at the conclusion of the program. The evaluation began with a brief discussion and review quiz, and then concentrated on the attendees demonstrating their understanding of the essential techniques and best practices presented in the program through role-play in two master case studies. No grades or scores were calculated, but participants received both verbal and written feedback from their peers and the program facilitator.

TABLE 9-1. Level 1 Evaluation Summary

1. How would you evaluate the facilitator's ability to reinforce the subject matter presented in the videos?	9.4
2. How would you rate the facilitator's style of delivery?	9.5
3. How much participation was encouraged by the facilitator?	9.4
4. How would you evaluate the facilitator's treatment of differing needs and viewpoints?	9.1
5. How well did the facilitator keep the program on track?	9.5
FACILITATION	**9.4**
6. How clearly were the concepts, principles, and techniques explained in the videos?	9.5
7. How well did the program modules and ideas move from one to the next?	9.1
8. How useful were the participant materials and tools/resources contained in the binder?	9.4
9. How valuable did you find the website to be as part of your learning experience?	7.6
10. How often could you relate the situations in the case studies and/or role-plays to your own practice?	9.6
11. How useful did you find the exercises and activities?	9.4
PROGRAM CONTENT AND MATERIALS	**9.1**
12. To what degree did the program challenge your thinking and present you with new ideas?	8.6
13. How much do you think you will be able to apply what you learned in this program to your job situation?	9.1
14. How confident do you feel about putting the skills and techniques into practice as a result of the program?	8.6
15. As an investment of your time, how would you rate this program?	8.8
PROGRAM OVERALL	**8.8**

Application

The Level 3 evaluation was conducted by program developers one month after the completion of the program. Program developers asked attendees to complete an online survey designed to gauge their application of the strategies, language, and techniques presented in the program as well as the progress they had made on their action commitment. Thirteen of the 23 attendees completed the online survey (57 percent response rate). Sixty percent or more of the respondents reported making changes in their behavior in 22 of the 50 significant on-the-job activities presented in the program. Results of the Level 3 evaluation are shown in Table 9-2.

TABLE 9.2 Level 3 Evaluation Summary

How Consumers Think and Feel	Average Rating	Change in Behavior
1. I recognize when my prospects and clients are motivated by the avoidance of pain or the desire to gain something.	1.50	46%
2. I connect our products and services to the six emotional drivers that motivate all human behavior (e.g. the need for certainty, the need for variety, etc.).	1.64	69%
3. I actively incorporate relevant LIMRA statistics into my conversations with prospects and clients.	1.86	77%
4. I recognize and identify the preferred communication style (such as dynamic, interpersonal, or analytic) of my prospects and clients.	1.36	54%
5. I am aware of my selling style and proactively adapt my style to that which is preferred by my prospects and clients.	1.50	54%
Average	1.57	60%
Business Development Techniques		
1. I ask for favorable introductions each and every time I interact with prospects and clients.	1.86	54%
2. I use an Ideal Client Profile during my prospecting process in order to help those from whom I am asking for favorable introductions to better understand my target clients.	1.00	31%
3. I have identified and nest within at least one organization or industry.	1.50	54%
4. I have fully internalized and consistently use the new business development language I learned in Trustworthy Selling.	1.93	92%
5. I regularly attend networking events and incorporate the best practices I learn in order to build my business.	0.43	15%
6. I have fully internalized the business development objection-handling language I learned in Trustworthy Selling.	1.21	38%
7. I develop and regularly use my LinkedIn profile to identify potential prospects to feed when asking for favorable introductions.	1.36	31%
Average	1.33	46%
Engagement Techniques		
1. I increase my competence and credibility by reading books, articles, etc. on topics relevant to my business.	1.57	54%
2. I use well-designed telephone scripts to increase my effectiveness in reducing resistance and setting appointments.	1.21	23%
3. When on the telephone, I actively overcome objections for every call and I track my effectiveness.	1.50	38%
4. I eliminate prospects' preoccupation and gain their interest when first speaking with them.	1.71	46%

5. I engage prospects upon initial contact by using a fully-developed Defining Identity Statement.	1.21	46%
6. I utilize power phrases in conversations with prospects.	2.00	77%
Average	1.54	48%
Collaborate Discovery Techniques		
1. I assess my Trustworthy Listening skills regularly, and work on improving by adding one to two best practices each week.	1.07	46%
2. I regularly paraphrase throughout the discovery process including a comprehensive paraphrase at the conclusion of the process.	2.14	85%
3. I develop RPM questions for a certain area of planning (e.g. life insurance, long-term care, retirement planning) and incorporate them into my collaborative discovery process.	1.64	62%
4. I keep a weekly "Courageous Conversations" journal to capture each time I step out of my comfort zone.	0.43	15%
5. I assess my Collaborative Discovery skills regularly, and work on improving by adding one to two best practices each week. (n=12)	0.85	25%
6. I strive to obtain an advance at the conclusion of each collaborative discovery meeting as a way to test for commitment from the prospect (e.g. budget commitment, scheduling the closing appointment, obtaining referrals).	2.00	62%
7. I regularly send a follow-up discovery letter after each meeting to recap items discussed and to ensure alignment between myself and the prospect.	1.71	54%
Average	1.41	51%
Gain Commitment Techniques		
1. I assess my ability to Gain Commitment regularly, and work on improving by adding one to two best practices each week. (n=12)	1.25	42%
a. I use personal stories to overcome irrational optimism.	2.38	85%
b. I use heuristics or rules of thumb.	2.54	85%
c. I avoid ambiguity, using simple language and checking for understanding.	2.54	85%
d. I help prospects visualize the personalized benefits of owning products I present.	2.07	69%
e. I demonstrate fairness by involving my prospects in the decision making process.	2.29	77%
f. I help prospects recognize the present value of my financial solutions.	2.14	69%
g. I assist prospects with budgeting for my solutions by appealing to their mental accounts.	2.14	69%
3. I regularly complete a Case Preparation worksheet (i.e. Case Preparation Questions) while preparing for my closing presentations.	1.14	38%

Continued on next page.

Table 9.2 continued.

4. I use an agenda for all my closing presentations and meetings.	1.14	31%
5. I share at least one personal story with potential clients during my presentations.	2.07	62%
6. I regularly use features/advantages/benefits language for products I am presenting each week.	2.00	69%
7. I have fully internalized the language that creates a sense of urgency in my prospects.	1.36	38%
Average	1.93	62%
Deepen Client Relationships Techniques		
1. I segment my clients based on the criteria I learned in Trustworthy Selling.	1.64	69%
2. I work collaboratively with my staff/associates in order to provide quality service to each segment of my client base.	1.57	54%
3. I develop a marketing plan that outlines how many times I will "touch" each client based on their segment.	1.36	54%
4. I analyze the amount of effort I am expending on each client segment.	1.36	54%
5. I develop an activity plan to ensure I am spending the majority of my time with my top client segments.	0.79	31%
6. I analyze my client segments to identify cross-selling opportunities based on each client's life stage.	1.43	46%
7. I develop a client service model that identifies the frequency, the type of service (face-to-face, telephone, email) and who is responsible (staff, associate, myself) for each task.	0.79	31%
Average	1.28	48%
Achieve Peak Performance Techniques		
1. I regularly work on and revisit my vision for the future, describing where I want my business to be in the next three to five years.	1.93	69%
2. I evaluate any self-limiting beliefs I currently have that are preventing me from soaring in this business.	2.21	92%
3. I use a positive affirmation to support my vision and goals. (n=12)	2.08	92%
4. I spend time thinking about what goals to set and how to hold myself accountable to them.	2.29	77%
5. I evaluate how I spend my time, looking for ways to spend more time in "the green."	2.43	92%
Average	2.20	81%

Impact

The Level 4 evaluation was conducted by the program developers three months after the completion of the program. The program developers analyzed the participating company's productivity reports for each of the three months prior to training and for each of the three months after training. These monthly reports included three measures of production for all sales reps in the agency; for those that attended training as well as for those that did not attend training. The evaluation included calculating average monthly performance measures for the pre- and post-training time periods for the group of attendees and for the group of non-attendees (control group), deriving the percentage of change in the three performance measures for each group, and comparing the productivity between the two groups.

Level 4 evaluation results show that attendees registered a 27 percent increase in policies, a 31 percent increase in new clients, and an 18 percent increase in premiums written in the three months after training compared with the three months prior to training. During the same time period, non-attendees from the same agency registered a 3 percent increase in policies, a 1 percent increase in new clients, and a 2 percent increase in premiums written. It is reasonable to conclude that the improvement in production for the attendees is a result of their attending the training program. Results of the Level 4 evaluation are shown in Table 9-3.

TABLE 9-3. Level 4 Evaluation Summary

Policies				
	n	Pre-Training Monthly Average	Post-Training Monthly Average	% Change
Attendees	23	7.65	9.72	27%
Non-attendees	113	4.44	4.58	3%
New Clients				
	n	Pre-Training Monthly Average	Post-Training Monthly Average	% Change
Attendees	23	3.43	4.50	31%
Non-attendees	113	2.03	2.05	1%
Premium				
	n	Pre-Training Monthly Average	Post-Training Monthly Average	% Change
Attendees	23	$9,193	$10,877	18%
Non-attendees	113	$11,773	$11,969	2%

Intangible Benefits

In a paper-based survey administered at the conclusion of the program, intangible benefits such as increased productivity, increased levels of employee confidence, existing program enhancement, and provision of new ideas were reported by participants.

ROI

A Level 5 (ROI) evaluation was conducted by the program developers three months after the conclusion of the program to complete the assessment of the value of the training program. The data are annualized to show first year monetary values. Also, a 25 percent profit margin (net premium revenue) was used to arrive at the earnings generated by this program. The company realized a 165 percent return on its investment in training. Table 9-4 shows the steps taken to calculate the ROI.

TABLE 9-4. ROI Calculation

Pre-Training				
	Average Monthly Premium	Number of Months	Number of Sales Reps	Total Premium
Attendees	$9,193	3	23	$634,317
Non-attendees	$11,773	3	113	$3,991,047
Post-Training				
	Average Monthly Premium	Number of Months	Number of Sales Reps	Total Premium
Attendees	$10,877	3	23	$750,513
Non-attendees	$11,969	3	113	$4,057,491
% Change in Total Premium				
Attendees	($750,513 – $634,317)/$634,317			18%
Non-attendees	($4,057,491 – $3,991,047)/$3,991,047			2%
Estimated Post-Training Total Premium (assuming no training)				
Attendees	$634,317 x 1.02			$647,003
Program Benefits Attributed to Training for 3 Months				
Attendees	$750,513 – $647,003			$103,510
Annualized Monetary Benefits				
Attendees	$103,510 x 4 Quarters			$414,040
Converting Data to Money for ROI Calculation				
Attendees	$414,040 x 25% Profit Margin			$103,510
Cost of Program				
Facilitator fees	$2,500 per day (4 days)			$10,000
Program materials	$1,195* per participant (23 participants)			$27,485
Meals and refreshments	$12 per day (4 days, 23 participants + 1 facilitator)			$1,152
Facilities	N/A (in house)			
Salaries and benefits	N/A (commissioned sales reps)			

Cost of coordination	$100 per day (4 days)	$400
Evaluation	N/A	
Total cost		$39,037
ROI	($103,510 − $39,037)/$39,037	165%

*Program costs vary by class size. The highest per participant fee was used in the calculation.

COMMUNICATION STRATEGY

Formal written results from the Level 1, Level 3, Level 4, and ROI evaluations were shared in a face-to-face meeting with key members of management within the participating company at both the agency level and the enterprise level. The "stellar" results of this pilot group were used by the agency to market the training to additional experienced agents for a second program in 2012. The enterprise is using the data to market the training to additional agencies as part of their growth strategy addressing sales effectiveness in 2012 and 2013. The reaction to the course has been positive, increasing confidence and interest among experienced sales representatives to attend "training" and encouraging the company to move forward with its investment in quality training. The word on the street is, "When is the next program?"

Results were also shared with the program developers and facilitators whose reaction was a combination of renewed appreciation for the value of the program and commitment to continual improvement to the curriculum and its delivery.

LESSONS LEARNED

The Level 3 evaluation was valuable in two ways. Not only did it provide an effective means of measuring the extent to which the attendees were applying the strategies and techniques presented in the program, it also provided a critical snapshot of elements of the curriculum that might warrant more attention during the training. To maximize the benefits of this evaluation we would want to find ways to achieve a higher response rate, perhaps even 100 percent!

RESOURCES

Phillips, J.J. (2003). *Return on Investment in Training and Performance Improvement Programs* (2nd ed.). Woburn, MA: Butterworth-Heinemann.

Kirkpatrick, D.J. (1994). *Evaluating Training Programs: The Four Levels.* San Francisco, CA; Berrett-Koehler.

Johnson, J., Catania, M., Freitag, D., Gmach, M., Hamstra, B., McLaughlin, D., and Williamson, F. (2005). *Evaluating Field Development Activities: A Practical Road Map to ROI.* LIMRA's MarketFacts Quarterly, 24, 30-33.

QUESTIONS FOR DISCUSSION

1. Are the data and results credible?
2. Should the company enroll additional sales reps in the training program?
3. How can you apply this process in your company?
4. What would happen if we could prove that training makes a difference?
5. What obstacles do we face in getting "clean" credible data?
6. For new clients generated, could the lifetime value of a new client be used in the analysis?

ABOUT THE AUTHORS

Delores Freitag, Assistant Vice President, Talent Development, LIMRA. Delores has more than 25 years of experience in sales management and training for the financial services industry. Over the course of her career, she has interviewed and trained thousands of producers, managers, and wholesalers.

Delores began her career with Prudential, where she served as internal consultant for Prudential Securities Retail Division and director of training for Prudential Mutual Funds. She developed the firm's first competency-based assessment tool for selection of stockbrokers and advised directors on selection, development, and retention issues. She also provided initial training for new recruits and advanced training to experienced managers from all functions within the company. In addition to these accomplishments, Delores launched dedicated wholesaler training for Prudential's asset management unit.

In her current role, Delores designs and delivers customized training programs for agents, advisors, managers, and field support staff of client companies. She is credited with developing LIMRA's Recruiting and Selection in the 21st Century program, LIMRA's Sales Leadership Development System, and LIMRA's Sales Effectiveness Programs, including Trustworthy Selling, Selling with Style, Managing with Style, and Sales Booster.

Delores can be reached at dfreitag@limra.com or (860) 298-3821.

Nancy Murphy, B.A. Mathematics, Associate Research Consultant, Assessment and Development Solutions Group, LIMRA. Nancy is responsible for conducting industry-wide and company-specific validation studies for LIMRA's sales and management assessment products as well as its training and development programs. She can be contacted at nmurphy@limra.com or (860) 298-3911.

10

Coaching Training for
First-Level Sales Managers
National ABC Homebuilding

Gwendolyn Brown

The his case was prepared to serve as a basis for discussion rather than an illustration of either effective or ineffective administrative and management practices. All names, dates, places, and data may have been disguised at the request of the author or the organization.

Abstract

National ABC is an organization of dedicated professionals, building fine homes for single family and townhome dwelling customers. As a result of an organizational employee satisfaction survey, performance indicators showed that 51 percent of associates expressed that sales managers were not appropriately assisting with the utilization of Individual Development Plans (IDP) in lieu of identifying actions that could be taken to improve the performance of the sales consultants. A sales manager coaching training workshop intervention was developed and implemented to improve performance to effectively coach sales consultants. As a result of the coaching training workshop, each sales manager developed an action plan that was conducive to discussions with sales consultants that enhanced communication during one-on-one meetings and performance reviews.

BACKGROUND INFORMATION

National ABC is a homebuilding organization of dedicated professionals, continuing an American tradition that began in Chicago in 1939. Building fine homes of enduring value first in greater Chicago, and since 1989 across the country, National ABC has helped thousands of families achieve the American dream of home ownership. A sense of service continues to be a trademark of each of National ABC's 1100 associates. Dedication has enabled the company to reach from Naples, Florida to Portland, Oregon and from Cleveland, Ohio to Houston, Texas. National ABC has grown to be one of the nation's 25 largest homebuilders. The organization averages about 3,000 home sales per year in a difficult market. Revenue is down 20 percent year-over-year.

Performance Issues of the Organization

Various problems within National ABC have been highlighted and require improvement in the manner in which the organization manages its resources. Operations, finance, and human resources management have been identified as the three strategic partners who map and align the goals and objectives of the organization. Human resource development (HRD) has been identified as one of the three areas that will be critical to improving individual and organizational performance as it relates to developing knowledge, skills, and abilities (KSAs). Sales revenue growth is declining due to various factors centered on the KSAs of the sales consultants. The organization has recently eliminated 15 percent of the workforce due to economic market conditions. Analysis showed that the turnover rate for the organization was recorded at 40 percent, and the rate at which voluntary and non-voluntary terminations are occurring is past the point of using existing associates to pick up the slack. The desired turnover rate is 20 percent or less.

An employee satisfaction survey conducted within the last 12 months showed that performance management was identified as a dimension and an area of improvement for National ABC. Focus group interviews were conducted to understand the root causes of the identified problem. The design and development of a coaching training workshop will prepare each manager to effectively understand the role of a coach and how to effectively communicate with employees.

The Performance Gap

As a result of the employee satisfaction survey, 51 percent of associates expressed that sales managers were not appropriately assisting with utilizing Individual Development Plans (IDP) for the purpose of identifying actions that could be taken to improve the performance of the sales consultants. Mercer Consulting (2006), suggested that the normative comparison for this ranking is –10 percent above the normative average. An improvement in this area will validate that sales managers are providing associates with sufficient direction, clearer goals, and will show that mangers have successfully obtained a clearer understanding of the associates' needs to improve individual performance.

The Root Causes of the Performance Gap

Based on the recent associate satisfaction survey, the identified performance gap is not isolated within one group and the performance management problem is common throughout the organization. Existing data had been gathered thus far as it relates to job descriptions, exit interviews, sales reports, and customer service reports. Observations, surveys, one-on-one interviews, and focus group interviews have been obtained that offer valuable information to the research process and thereby have contributed to the overall process of understanding the problem at hand. The root cause analysis showed that 1) sales managers have not demonstrated the effective skills in resolving conflict and communication issues to effectively develop each subordinate; 2) sales managers provide inadequate feedback as it relates to explaining to each subordinate how he or she must improve individual performance; and 3) critical skills are needed for the sales manager to effectively perform the job. According to World at Work (2007), increasing the ability of sales managers to effectively develop subordinates affects the ability to improve employee satisfaction scores for performance management and is a top driver of retention.

TRAINING INTERVENTION

The design and development of a coaching training workshop will prepare each sales manager to effectively understand the role of a coach and how to effectively counsel employees. The goal within the organization is to develop current sales associates through proper coaching that is received from sales managers. The objectives of the Coaching Training Workshop are to provide National ABC sales managers with 1) skills, knowledge, and abilities to be more effective in the job; 2) tips and techniques that will be helpful as managers; 3) skills assessment; and 4) the ability to utilize systematic, practical, and theoretical information to effectively develop direct reports.

The argument exists that many companies lack a disciplined approach to managing the coaching process and measuring outcomes, often lacking a precise understanding of the benefits of coaching or even what to expect from a coaching assignment (Management-Issues, 2007). Sales managers are unapprised of the advantages to themselves, the associates, and the organization for becoming successful coaches. As a result, sales managers are uncomfortable with the entire scheme of discussing performance problems with an associate. Attempts to ignore the problem or assume that the situation is hopeless often result in sales managers terminating associates as the only way to resolve the issue. Ignoring the problem nearly always leads to failure in effectively coaching subordinates.

Performance issues are centered on creating learning programs specifically focused on areas that are critical to organizational success such as: 1) the redesign of business processes to increase effectiveness and efficiency; 2) focusing on individual accomplishments as it relates to "soft" skills; 3) delivery of exceptional customer service, teambuilding, and conflict resolution through team dynamics, development, and improvement of general critical analysis and management skills; and 4) the fostering of individualized development plans and career paths to promote and support organizational succession planning.

As a part of the synchronous training, the participants were assessed on initial pretest scores by utilizing an 18-item Coaching Skills Inventory® questionnaire and were required to score an overall effectiveness score of +33 (most effective being +36) or above, which will serve to measure how well he or she has the ability to conduct effective coaching meetings. Sales managers developed an action plan and will participate in a Coaching Skills Follow-up Session three months after the training has been implemented.

Before the ROI evaluation begins, the program objectives must be identified or developed. The objectives form the basis for determining the depth of the evaluation; this, in effect will determine what level of evaluation will take place for a National ABC (Phillips, 2003).

PROGRAM OBJECTIVES

Objectives for the training program were set at all five levels, according to the ROI Methodology.

Reaction

Involvement in the Coaching Training Workshop (CTW) should lead program participants to have:
- opportunity to succeed at coaching
- new or enhanced information
- balance between theory and practice
- satisfaction in the program in order to achieve performance effectiveness.

Learning

From ongoing participation in the CTW program, participants should:
- have awareness of the action plans
- retain new learning and skills based on utilization of interactive practice exercises
- have realized learning transfer by utilizing tests, skill practices, role-plays, simulations, group evaluations, and other assessment tools during the CTW training program
- be able to conduct one-to-one sessions with each employee
- have attained confidence in using coaching training workshop applications.

Application/Implementation

At the end of the program, participants should be able to continue to:

- implement action plans and conduct effective coaching meetings
- achieve a minimum goal of conducting one monthly one-to-one meeting with the sales consultants
- use the overall effectiveness score to measure success conducting effective coaching meetings.

Business Impact

Business impact objectives for the Coaching Training Workshop were defined as follows:

- increase associate satisfaction by 10 percent in six months
- increase the sales inventory for new homes from one unit per month to two home sales per month for sales consultant's year-over-year growth in six months
- reduce employee turnover to at least 32 percent during first six months.

ROI

The ROI objective was set at 25%.

DATA COLLECTION

The tools used for purposes of data collection were focus groups and surveys (secondary data were also analyzed to be used as a point of comparison in conjunction with the focus groups and surveys). Various stakeholders were represented through these tools, along with varying timetables so that pre-intervention, "during" intervention, and post-intervention data could be gathered.

The coaching training workshop intervention was evaluated using the five levels of evaluation: Level 1 reaction, Level 2 learning, Level 3 application, Level 4 business results were for aligned with the objectives of the intervention, and Level 5 ROI. A needs assessment was conducted to collect baseline data, as well as the development of an evaluation plan and a data collection plan. Pre- and post-program data were compared based on the collection of data from the CTW intervention. A strategy was developed to isolate the effects of the Coaching Training Workshop intervention by using techniques to identify factors related to performance improvement that can be linked to the interventions and deemed as a program benefit.

The data collection consisted of surveys and focus group interviews. The utilization of derivative data such as action plans were evaluated and used in contrast with the proposed tools. A variety of participants were represented as it related to the proposed tools in conjunction with timetables to illustrate use of control, comparison measures, and the process of continuous evaluation for the ongoing non-training and training interventions. Table 10-1 illustrates detailed aspects of the program objectives, measures, data collection methods and instruments, data sources, timing, and responsibilities of HRD staff.

TABLE 10-1. Data Collection Plan

Evaluation Purpose: Determine the impact and ROI of the leadership development program for performance management

Program: Coaching Training Workshop   Responsibility: Training Manager   Date: July 29

Level	Broad Program Objective(s)	Measures	Data Collection Method/ Instruments	Data Sources	Timing	Responsibilities
1	REACTION and PLANNED ACTIONS • Positive associate response to the Performance Management Coaching Process Model	• Positive reaction from managers	• Feedback questionnaire	• Participants	• At the end of managers' CTW	• Facilitator
2	LEARNING • Manager understanding of the model • Identify a minimum of one coaching strength and a minimum of one coaching improvement need	• Score on post assessment, at least an overall effectiveness score of +33	• Assessment of CSI	• Participants	• At the end of managers' CTW	• Facilitator

3	APPLICATION/ IMPLEMENTATION				
	• Effective and consistent implementation and enforcement of the coaching skills program	• Manager's response to program	• Individual action plan to track and measure the extent of applications among the managers	• Managers	• Following CTW sessions, sample 1 group at 3 months and another group at 6 months	• HR Program Coordinator
	• Positive reaction from current associates regarding the Coaching One-to-One process	• Associate's response on program's influence	• Follow-up questionnaire to managers (2 sample groups)	• Associates	• Following CTW sessions, conduct at 3 months	
	• After the completion of the CSI self-assessment, mangers will complete individual development plans (IDP)	• Completion of IDP with 100% of the associates within 3 months.	• Follow-up questionnaire to associates (2 sample groups) and focus group sessions with 8-12 managers	• Managers		

Continued on next page.

Table 10-1 continued.

4	**BUSINESS IMPACT** • Increase associate satisfaction by 10% in 6 months	• Associate Satisfaction	• Follow-up questionnaire to managers and associates	• Company records	• 6 months after completion of CTW	• HR Program Coordinator
	• Increase the sales inventory for new homes from 1 unit per month to 2 home sales per month for sales consultant's year-over-year growth in 6 months	• Sales Increase	• Monitor daily/ monthly sales	• Company records	• Monthly	• Nat'l Training & Dev. Mgr.
	• Reduce employee turnover to at least 32% during first 6 months	• Turnover	• Monitor turnover	• Company records	• Monitor monthly and analyze at 6 months post-implementation	• HR Program Coordinator
5	**ROI** • Target ROI: 25%					
	Baseline Data: Turnover, Sales, and Associate Satisfaction					
	Comments:					

DATA ANALYSIS AND RESULTS

Favorable results were indicated at all five levels of evaluation.

Reaction and Satisfaction

End-of-course evaluations were collected from each of the CTW sessions. The participant response rate was an impressive 98 percent. The rankings from the evaluations showed that:

- 97 percent of the participants felt that the CTW sessions would help him or her to be more effective in the job.
- The reaction and overall satisfaction were positive for the CTW sessions and participants provided written comments noting that the group interaction, role-plays, and presentation were well received.

Learning

As it relates to measuring learning:

- 100 percent of the managers reported that the tips and techniques introduced during the training session would be helpful in his or her job.
- 96.9 percent agreed that the exercises and role plays helped to understand the key learning points of the CTW sessions.

Application and Implementation

The CTW sessions were implemented over a six-month timeframe. After the training sessions, each sales manager had an opportunity to identify one of seven skills that needed to be developed as a result of completing the Coaching Skills Inventory (CSI) assessment. The seven areas assessed are as follows: 1) opening the meeting, 2) getting agreement, 3) exploring alternatives, 4) getting a commitment, 5) handling excuses, 6) closing the meeting, and 7) overall effectiveness.

- Each sales manager completed a development action plan based on one of the seven skills that required improvement and was instructed to practice improving that skill over a three-month timeframe.
- Focus groups and CTW follow-up sessions were conducted throughout each region. As it relates to the success with the application of new skills, the sales managers reported that more effort is needed to reduce the number of disruptions when conducting one-to-one meetings.
- A reduced amount of paperwork occurs as ongoing sessions take place monthly.

Barriers and Enablers to Successful Implementation

Participant estimation derived from a force field analysis focus group meeting conducted with 12 sales managers provided information regarding barriers and enablers to successful implementation. The meeting generated discussions about the improvement in performance of the CTW and the contributing factors (the one-to-one meeting process, retention rate, management emphasis, and job satisfaction) that influenced the overall improvement, as noted in Table 10-2.

TABLE 10-2. Barriers and Enablers to Successful Implementation

Barriers	Enablers
Restraining Force A: Low Employee Satisfaction Surveys What can be done to reduce the effect of this force? • Improve the lack of motivation of managers. • Address the lack of environmental and economic resources. • Increase cultural sensitivity and support of senior management. **Restraining Force B: Barriers to Effective Coaching of Employees: 1) too busy, 2) too many interruptions, and 3) inexperienced in handling and reacting to conflict.** What can be done to reduce the effect of this force? Too busy: • Must be committed to coaching. • Must delegate. • Must set expectations regarding priorities. Too many interruptions: • Block time. • Create the environment. • Be fully present. Inexperienced in handling and reacting to conflict: • Continue learning. • Practice role-plays. • Know the employee and situation.	**Driving Force A: Effective Coaching of Employees** What can be done to increase the effect of this force? • Increase the willingness of the sales managers to change. • Increase need for consistency and awareness of coaching and development process. • Raise awareness of accountability of sales managers to provide coaching and development to sales consultants. **Driving Force B: Effective use of coaching process** What can be done to increase the effect of this force? • Design new performance management process for sales consultants. • Improve the coaching skills of managers through coaching training workshops. • Apply new coaching skills to address high felt need of the sales consultants.

Adapted from Hustedde, R., and M. Score. (1995). *Force Field Analysis: Incorporating Critical Thinking in Goal Setting*. Milwaukee, WI: Community Development Society. (ERIC Document Reproduction Service No. ED384712).

Business Impact

The objectives for conducting the CTW were positively realized from the standpoint that the baseline of turnover improved.

- The initial turnover was 40 percent at the onset of the CTW sessions; six months after the CTW sessions the post-training turnover was 20 percent.
- Monthly homes sales were captured slightly above projections based on year-over-year figures, as shown in Table 10-3.
- Associates satisfaction survey results increased from –10 to +3 percent above the normative average for the organization.

TABLE 10-3. Monetary Benefits

Location of Participants (A)	Annual Improvement (Profits from Sales) (B)	Measure (C)	Converting Data to Monetary Values (D)	Contribution of The Program % (E)	Other Factors (F)	Confidence Estimate % (G)	Adjusted Value (H)
Chicago	$135,000	Sales	Standard	60	3	80	$64,800
Chicago	$115,000	Sales	Standard	80	3	70	$64,400
NCAL	$100,000	Sales	Standard	85	2	90	$76,500
Houston	$70,000	Sales	Standard	60	1	80	$33,600
Dallas	$74,000	Sales	Standard	50	1	75	$27,750
San Antonio	$65,000	Sales	Standard	60	2	75	$29,250
Las Vegas	$61,000	Sales	Standard	80	3	70	$34,160
Tampa	$78,000	Sales	Standard	50	2	90	$35,100
	$698,000						
Total Monetary Benefits B x E x G						Total Benefits	$365,560

Isolation of the Effects of Training

The effects of the implementation of the coaching training workshop (CTW) were isolated by using techniques to identify factors that played a part in the improvement after the coaching training workshop intervention had been conducted. Table 10-4 shows the feasibility of the various techniques that were used to isolate the effects of training and how the each technique applies to National ABC. Participants' estimates were used to isolate the effects of the program on the sales and trend-line analysis was used to isolate the effects of the program on the turnover.

TABLE 10-4. Feasibility of Techniques

Isolation Techniques	Feasible	Not Feasible
Control group		Critical skills are needed immediately on the job for the managers.
Trend-line analysis	Baseline data with which to establish projections is available.	
Forecasting method		Volatile market due to homebuilding industry downturn.
Participant estimate	Obtained easily through pre- and post-survey instruments and through employee satisfaction surveys.	
Employee/supervisor estimate	Obtained easily through post-project survey.	
Senior management estimate	Although subjective in nature, senior management may feel it is necessary to make adjustments in the actual data.	
Customer input	Customer input can be obtained through JD Power surveys.	
Expert estimate		Approach must be utilized with research and explanations to check credibility of data collection and analysis.
Other influencing factors	Ability to calculate influences that improved additional professional development through industry sources and estimations.	

Trend-Line Analysis

A trend-line analysis was used to approximate the impact of training. The effects of the implementation of the Coaching Training Workshop (CTW) was isolated by using techniques to identify factors that played a part in the improvement after the coaching training workshop and core competency model interventions had been conducted. Once the training was implemented, actual performance was weighed against the projected rate, and the trend line was produced, as shown in Figure 10-1.

FIGURE 10-1. Trend-Line Analysis for Turnover Reduction

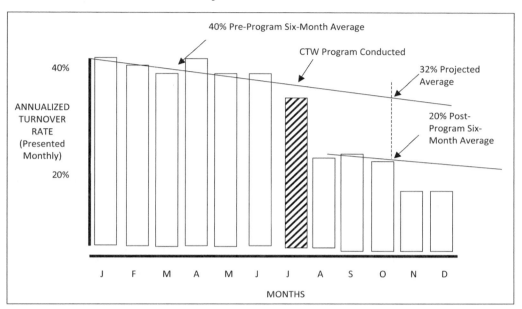

Note: The pre-program six-month turnover averaged 40 percent and the projected program improvement in turnover was 32 percent. Based on the post program six-month turnover average of 20 percent, the benefit resulted in a 12 percent decrease in turnover (32%–20%). The 12% decrease in turnover represents about 6 sales consultant departures that were avoided because of the program. Table 10-5 shows the estimate of turnover costs for the six turnovers avoided, $141,470.

TABLE 10-5. Turnover Cost Estimation

Cost Category	Cost (USD)
Separation Costs	
Cost of Exit Interviewer	$1,800
Admin. Cost Related to Termination	$1,440
Separation Pay (salary and benefits)	$81,490
Increase in Unemployment Tax (marginal rate increase + add tax)	$16,230
Total Separation Costs	**$100,960**
Replacement Costs	
Pre-employment Administrative Costs	$36
Cost of Attracting Applicants	$250
Cost of Interview Process	$9,600
Assessment Cost	$26,400
Background Check Costs	$840
Staff Costs to Meet & Confer	$45
Post-employment Administrative Costs	$3,339
Total Replacement Costs	**$40,510**
Total Turnover Costs	**$141,470**

ROI and Its Meaning

The senior management team suggested that the CTW would produce gains if turnover was reduced and if employee satisfaction and sales were improved. Before the ROI could be determined, the fully loaded costs and benefits derived from the program had to be determined.

Benefits

Phillips suggests "it is helpful to position the ROI calculation in the context of all of the data" (2003, p. 203). As it relates to ROI however, "specific objectives are often set, creating the expectations of an acceptable ROI calculation" (p. 203). Senior management must then be postured to realize the calculation has the ability to show the chain effect of "reaction leading to learning, which leads to learning, which leads to application, which leads to business impact and to ROI" (p. 203). Overall, the expectation of senior management for ROI was 25 percent, based on the approach utilized for all financial standards for the organizations projects.

Tables 10-3 and 10-5 outline the benefits derived from the program. Due to the increase in profits from sales totaling $365,560, as shown in Table 10-3, plus a $141,470 cost avoidance from the 12 percent decrease in turnover as shown in Table 10-5, a total benefit amount for ROI calculation was $507,030.

Costs

In order to keep track of how the program costs were accounted for and to which function expenses were classified under, a cost classification matrix was used. The cost estimation worksheet illustrated in Table 10-6 was reviewed with National ABC's senior management to ensure that the analysis was credible each step of the way. Using this approach to calculate ROI as it relates to the six types of data collected throughout the evaluation process shows the full range of success, including the actual ROI that will provide senior management with credible analysis. A comprehensive analysis includes "business impact, ROI, and intangibles that add to the rich database" (Phillips, 2003, p. 213) from which senior management will make critical decisions for the organization.

Costs were identified using a complete analysis for the coaching training workshop intervention as shown in Table 10-6. Included in the analysis are the program development, program materials, travel expenses for facilitators, facilities and expenses, salaries of participant's involvement in program, training and development overhead, and ROI evaluation cost.

TABLE 10-6. Total Program Costs

Cost Category	Cost (USD)
Analysis/Design/Development Costs Salaries and benefits for HRD staff (no. of people x average salary x employee benefits factor x no. of hours on the project)	45,506
Total Analysis/Design/Development Costs	**45,506**
Delivery Costs Participant cost, salaries and benefits: no. of participants x average salary x employee benefits factor x hours or days of training time (class sessions) Meals, travel, and accommodations (no. of participants x average daily expenses x days of training) Program materials and supplies Facilitator costs (salaries, benefits, meals, travel, outside services) Facility costs (rental and expense allocation) Equipment Expense	46,846 10,200 3,560 80,000 20,500 4,250
Total Delivery Costs	**165,356**
Evaluation Costs Salaries & Employee Benefits--HRD Staff (no. of people x avg. salary x employee benefits factor x no. of hours on project)	9,493
Total Evaluation Costs	**9,493**
Total Program Costs	**220,355**

ROI Calculation

With benefits and costs calculated, the ROI was determined to be 130 percent, far exceeding the 25 percent objective.

$$ROI = \frac{\$507,030^* - \$220,355}{\$220,355} \times 100 = 130\%$$

*Turnover cost avoidance plus sales increase: $141,470 + $365,560 = $507,030

Intangibles

Intangible measures were collected in conjunction with increased confidence of sales managers in utilizing the interventions and job satisfaction of the sales consultants. Any data have the possibility of being converted to monetary values; however, the overriding factor rests on credibility. Employee retention and effective employee development through coaching were the focuses within the CTW training intervention; as a result soft data were needed in the evaluation process (Phillips, 2003). According to Phillips (2003), measures such as employee turnover appear as soft data items more so due to the notion that it is difficult to accurately convert soft data to monetary values. Phillips suggests that "job satisfaction deteriorates to the point where employees withdraw from work or the organization" (2003, p. 147).

Intangible measures consisted of the following:

- Customer satisfaction (JD Power Surveys) was presented as critical measures to "survey data showing the degree to which customers are pleased with the products and services" (Phillips, 2003, p.249) that were sold by National ABC's sales consultants.
- Employee satisfaction (Mercer Consulting Surveys) was noted as one of the most significant intangible measures "most organizations do not, or cannot, place credible values on employee satisfaction data" (Phillips, 2003, p.245) and is generally recorded as an intangible benefit. As shown in Table 10-7, employee satisfaction increased in one year after the program was conducted.

TABLE 10.7 Employee Satisfaction Data

National ABC Employee Satisfaction Survey Previous	Nat. ABC % Fav.	Norm % Diff.
Performance Management	48%	n/a
My performance goals and objectives are clearly defined.	76%	+11%
My last performance review was helpful in identifying actions I could take to improve my performance.	49%	-10%
From what I observe, poor performers in my division are appropriately managed.	29%	-4%
Promotions at Nat. ABC are generally given to the most qualified individuals.	38%	+9%
National ABC Employee Satisfaction Survey— 1 Year after Program	**Nat. ABC % Fav.**	**Norm % Diff.**
Performance Management	56%	n/a
My performance goals and objectives are clearly defined.	84%	+15%
My last performance review was helpful in identifying actions I could take to improve my performance.	59%	+3%
From what I observe, poor performers in my division are appropriately managed.	36%	-2%
Promotions at Nat. ABC are generally given to the most qualified individuals.	46%	+12%

COMMUNICATION OF RESULTS

The actions and timeframes were developed around the identified issues of the action plan. Phillips postulates that "managers will not support activities or processes that they do not fully understand" (2003, p.347). Gaining influence of senior management to solidify support and commitment of stakeholders for the project is imperative. The implementation team had access to the data collection instrument previously developed during the planning phase of the project. The National Training and Development Manager remained focused as it related to understanding the benefits of the cost for the Coaching Training Workshop (CTW) program, which is critical to realizing the impact and communicating the results to the organization. The post-program action plan was presented to the targeted audience that summarized the results from the ROI analysis and feedback on how to effectively coach and develop employees. In addition, expanded ROI analysis and support from all levels of the organization participated in instituting upcoming meeting times based in effective communication of the CTW program.

LESSONS LEARNED

National ABC's commitment to increasing employee learning and development is an ongoing initiative that embraces blended learning solutions. The Coaching Training Workshop (CTW) program increased awareness to the management and supervisory teams the significance of coaching and developing each individual within the organization.

The lessons learned were as follows:

- Building the confidence of senior management must start at the onset of the project.
- The organizational analysis and the needs assessment indicated that performance management training was an appropriate solution and a support of a sponsor/champion was imperative to the success of the program.
- Gaining the buy-in and total commitment of the senior management team to embrace the CTW concept was garnered as the project gained momentum and was successfully implemented.
- Conducting the various surveys and focus groups was challenging at times due to the inconsistency of utilizing web-based pre- and post-training assessments, email, and paper-based documents. Therefore, archiving historical information and templates will serve future ROI Impact studies.

National ABC's participation in a full-blown ROI impact study had never been attempted, and training the team members about the ROI evaluation process was an enlightening experience for all participants.

QUESTIONS FOR DISCUSSION

1. Are the data and results credible? Explain.
2. How can coaching have such a direct impact on sales?
3. What methods other than the trend analysis and participants' estimates could have been used to determine the improvements attributed to the program?
4. Should the profit margin be used in the monetary benefits for sales improvements? Explain.
5. Are the turnover costs accurate? Explain.

REFERENCES

Hustedde, R., and M. Score. (1995). *Force Field Analysis: Incorporating Critical Thinking in Goal Setting.* Milwaukee, WI: Community Development Society. (ERIC Document Reproduction Service No. ED384712). Available online: http://www2.ca.uky.edu/ CEDIK-files/Hustedde_and_Score-_Force_Field_Analysis.pdf.

Management-Issues. (2007). Coaching Hits the Corporate Mainstream. Retrieved on July 10, 2007 from http://www.management-issues.com/contact.asp.

Phillips, J.J. (2003). *Return on Investment in Training and Performance Improvement Programs* (2nd ed.). Woburn, MA: Butterworth-Heinemann.

World at Work. (2007). The Top Five Drivers of Attraction and Retention. Retrieved on July 10, 2007 from http://www.worldatwork.org/.

ABOUT THE AUTHOR

Gwendolyn Brown, PhD, completed her doctorate in education with a specialization in training and performance improvement from Capella University. She has more than 20 years of experience in the human resource development field. Gwen earned her undergraduate degree at Marquette University, completed an MBA with specialized courses in organizational behavior from Case Western Reserve University, earned a master's degree in education with a specialization in instructional design and technology from American Intercontinental University, and completed her doctorate in education with a specialization in training and performance improvement.

Accredited as a senior professional in human resources (SPHR) and as a project management professional (PMP), Gwen has been a training and development manager, instructional designer, adjunct instructor, and consultant in the human resources management, sales management, manufacturing, construction, and information technology service management fields. She specializes in working with organizations that require help in the human performance technology and training and performance improvement areas when leaders want to align appropriate interventions with the goals of the organization, streamline the transfer of critical knowledge and skills, and bridge the gap between theory and practice. Gwen can be reached at P.O. Box 957851, Hoffman Estates, IL 60195; phone: 847-468-8856; email: gxb1024@yahoo.com, or at G-WEN Consulting.com.

11

Selling Skills for Postal Stores Staff
Canada Post

David Soltis and Nancy Donovan

T his case was prepared to serve as a basis for discussion rather than an illustration of either effective or ineffective administrative and management practices. Names, dates, places, and data may have been disguised at the request of the author or organization.

Abstract

The Selling Skills Program consists of a half-day workshop that aims to develop the selling skills of staff at Canada Post. To determine the impact of the program on key performance indicators the Phillips ROI Methodology was applied. The evaluation approach isolated the effects of the solution using a combination of surveys and a control group analysis. Through this evaluation, it was determined that the program exceeded all Level 1 (reaction) targets and achieved its overall learning objectives. A checklist completed five to six months after program delivery validated that learners were applying their skills while on the job. The financial benefits of the program were isolated through a comparative analysis of a trained group versus a control group and yielded a benefit-cost ratio of 1.02 and a ROI of 2.19 percent.

PROGRAM BACKGROUND

Corporate Background

Canada Post Corporation is the Canadian crown corporation that functions as the country's primary postal operator. The corporation has over 70,000 staff and provides service to 14.8 million addresses via traditional "to the door" delivery, supplemented by a 7,000-vehicle fleet in rural and suburban areas. There are 6,500 post offices across the country, a combination of corporate offices and dealerships that are operated by private retailers in conjunction with a host retail business, such as a drugstore.

Program Background

The Selling Skills Program consists of a half-day instructor-led workshop aimed at developing the customer interaction and selling skills of staff at Canada Post. The training program focuses on the application of an interactive selling model during customer engagement. A return on investment (ROI) analysis was completed on this program to satisfy a senior-level stakeholder request for evidence on the program's impact on key performance indicators as well as overall effectiveness of delivery. Program evaluators and senior stakeholders also felt that the results from the study could be used to:

- enhance course marketing materials and highlight the benefits of the program to sites as the training was not considered mandatory
- showcase learning and development's evaluation services and expertise in calculating ROI.

The primary learning objectives of the Selling Skills Program are to:

- identify customer needs and present the benefits of the service being offered
- use effective listening techniques
- apply the Selling Skills model to offer the best solutions for customer needs
- offer each customer complementary products and services more easily
- understand the importance of offering new products and knowing their features and benefits
- use the model to more effectively manage queues.

Evaluation Study Objectives

In order to assess the impact of the Selling Skills Program a full spectrum evaluation study (Levels 1 to 5) was completed. The objectives of the study are listed below:

- **Level 1: learner reaction and planned action:** Collect survey data on learner reaction to the program and establish a course satisfaction rating. Aim to achieve a score of 80 percent or higher on key reaction survey questions including effectiveness of trainer, clarity of learning objectives, applicability of training to role, and so on.
- **Level 2: learning and confidence:** As part of the program learners are required to demonstrate their skills during a scenario-based skill demonstration. The learner's performance is evaluated using a checklist that validates whether he or she is able to demonstrate key selling and customer engagement behaviors. The objective of this level of evaluation was for learners to score 80 percent or higher on the skill demonstration.

- **Level 3: application and implementation:** Learners were observed in their work environment five to six weeks after program completion to determine if they had transferred their knowledge and behaviors to the job. To measure the extent to which skills were being applied, a Level 3 observation was conducted by a third party auditor and results were reported at both the aggregate and site level. The objective of this level of evaluation was for learners to score 70 percent or higher on the observation checklist.
- **Level 4: business impact:** The Selling Skills Program is linked to two key performance indicators: weekly sales and revenue per transaction. The Level 4 objective of the evaluation was to validate if the program led to an increase to weekly sales of 15 percent and an increase to revenue per transaction of 5 percent.
- **Level 5: return on investment (ROI) calculation:** The level 5 objective was to determine if the program benefits exceeded the costs and generated a positive benefit-cost ratio (BCR) of 1.15 and a return on investment (ROI) of 15 percent.

EVALUATION METHODOLOGY

The ROI Methodology was leveraged as the formal evaluation framework to assess the impact of the Selling Skills Training Program. The following guiding principles were applied to the evaluation study:

- Guiding Principle 1: When conducting a higher level of evaluation, collect data at lower levels.
- Guiding Principle 3: When collecting and analyzing data, use only the most credible sources.
- Guiding Principle 4: When analyzing data, select the most conservative alternative for calculations.
- Guiding Principle 5: Use at least one method to isolate the effects of a training solution.
- Guiding Principle 8: Extreme data items and unsupported claims should not be used in ROI calculations.
- Guiding Principle 10: Costs of a solution, project, or program should be fully loaded for ROI analysis.
- Guiding Principle 12: The results from the ROI Methodology must be communicated to all key stakeholders.

The evaluation methodology consisted of five key phases: evaluation planning; developing instruments and collecting baseline data; collecting data during training; collecting, analyzing, and sharing data after training; and calculating return on investment and preparing the final report.

Phase 1: Evaluation Planning

During this phase the objectives for the study were determined in collaboration with the stakeholders of the Selling Skills Training Program. Planning documentation identified the specific measures, data collection methods, and roles and responsibilities for the evaluation study. The ROI study timeline is shown in Figure 11-1. Finally the data isolation method was determined by the project team. The objectives of the study are summarized in Table 11-1.

Phase 2: Develop Instruments and Collect Baseline Data

Following the completion of the planning phase a team developed data collection instruments such as the data collection plan shown in Figure 11-2, and the ROI analysis plan shown in Figure 11-3, to gather data at Levels 1 through 3. A survey to collect data on the learner's reaction to the program and a checklist to be used by instructors when evaluating the skill demonstration component were also developed. Finally, an observation checklist was designed to capture the application of key behaviors while on the job.

TABLE 11-1. Objectives at All 5 Levels

Level of Evaluation	Focus	Measure	Objective
1	Learner Reaction	Score on Evaluation Survey (%)	80%
2	Learning and Confidence	Skills learners are able to demonstrate during the skill demonstration component of program (%)	80%
3	Application and Implementation	Knowledge/skill transferred to the job (%)	70% of skills demonstrated
4	Business Impact	Increase on weekly sales and average revenue per transaction (%)	15% increase in weekly sales
5	Return on Investment (ROI)	Benefit-cost ratio (BCR)	1.15 BCR
		Return on investment (ROI)	15% ROI

Figure 11-1. ROI Study Timeline

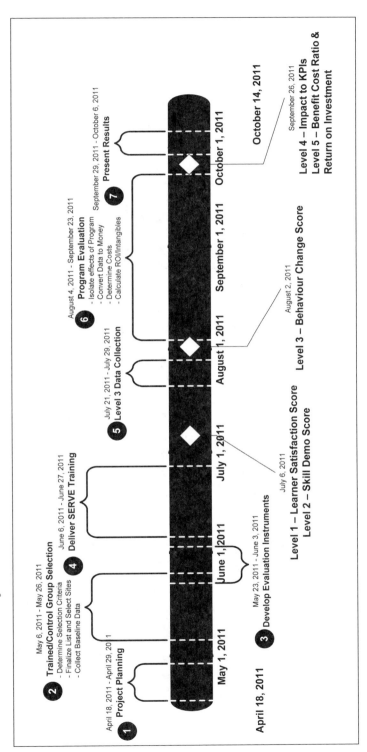

FIGURE 11-2. Data Collection Plan

Program: Selling Skills Program		Responsibility: Donovan/D. Soltis		Date: Thursday, April 7, 2011		
Level	Broad Program Objective(s)	Measures	Data Collection Method/ Instruments	Data Sources	Timing	Responsibilities
1	REACTION and PLANNED ACTIONS • Positive learner reaction	• Learner Satisfaction: 80% of learners indicate that they "Strongly Agree" and "Agree" that the objectives of the course were clear. • Relevance of Material: 80% of Learners indicate that they "Strongly Agree" and "Agree" that the training helped them understand what they need to know to do their job. • Exercises/Skill Demo: 80% of Learners indicate that they "Strongly Agree" and "Agree" that the training prepared them for the work that they will be doing.	• Questionnaire (Online and Paper-Based)	• Participants	• End of program	• Trainer
2	LEARNING AND CONFIDENCE • Learn to use the Selling Skills Model • Demonstrate Selling Skills behaviours	• Observation: Learners complete skill demonstration and score 80%.	• Observation Checklist	• Participants	• End of program	• Trainer

3	**APPLICATION/ IMPLEMENTATION** • 70% of participants use Selling Skills model with customers	• 100% of items checked on checklist • 70% of participants utilize skills from programs	• Observation • Questionnaire/ Audit	• Participant	• 5-6 weeks after program end	• Third Party Auditor
4	**BUSINESS IMPACT** • Increase in revenue per transaction • Increase in weekly sales	• 5% increase in weekly average revenue per transaction per outlet • 15% increase in weekly sales	• Key Performance Indicator Database, Business Reports	• Sales Data	• 3 months after program	• Evaluation Team
5	ROI • 15%	**Baseline Data:**				
		Comments:				

FIGURE 11-3. ROI Analysis Plan

Program: Selling Skills Training Program			Responsibility: N. Donovan / D. Soltis		Date: Thursday, April 7, 2011		
Data Items (Level 4)	Methods for Isolating the Effects of the Program	Methods of Converting Data to Monetary Values	Cost Categories	Intangible Benefits	Communication Targets for Final Report	Other Influences/ Issues During Application	Comments
• 5% increase in weekly average revenue per transaction per outlet • 15% increase in weekly sales	• Two methods will be used to separate the contribution of the program from other factors: Control group Trend analysis	• Select weekly sales and/or revenue per sale • Conversion using profit contribution	**Prorated Costs:** • Analysis • Design • Development • Implementation **General Costs:** • Participant time • Backfill (if higher than participant salaries) • Facilitation Fees (GP trainers) • Materials • Evaluation costs • Travel for trainers • Classroom costs • Administration (contract management)	• Increased customer satisfaction • Reduced turnover	**Senior Level Stakeholders:** • CCO • GM, Retail • GM, L&D • Directors, Retail • Director, L&D **Middle MGMT:** • Customer service • L&D managers • Retail business managers • Retail manager • Franchise/Store • Supervisors • Franchise owners • Participants • National account dealer reps	• Seasonal sales fluctuations • Store size, traffic, sales performance, location • New products & services • Product price increases • Promotions and discounts • Labour disruption • Store age (new vs. mature)	• Engage lines of business resources • Engage labour relations • Confirm franchisees will support evaluation study

Baseline performance data were collected from 142 sites on key variables including weekly sales, average revenue per transaction, and transactions per week. To aid in the selection of sites that would participate in the study, as a trained site or non-trained site (control group), the following data were collected:

- yearly revenue and average revenue per transaction
- square footage of sites
- average number of transactions per week
- site maturity.

After data were collected on all sites in the pool, 12 sites were filtered that were similar in performance. Six sites were selected to be trained, while the other six sites were allocated to the control group.

Phase 3: Collect Data During Training

Once the evaluation instruments were designed, piloted, and approved for use, they were utilized by instructors during the delivery of the training solution. Learners were evaluated during the skill demonstration with the approved checklist. Coaching was also provided to learners to ensure that they grasped product knowledge as well as selling skills behaviors. Finally, learners were able to provide feedback via a paper-based reaction survey.

Phase 4: Collect, Analyze, and Share Data After Training

Once learners completed the program, they applied their knowledge and skills at their respective sites with the intent that these new behaviors would drive increases in revenue. After a period of time, an observation checklist was applied to validate the extent to which the learners were applying their skills while on the job. These observations would take place two to three times per year.

Post-training business performance data were also collected during this period. Once data on the key performance indicators (KPIs) were collected, there was an opportunity to compare the performance of trained stores against non-trained stores in the control group. Through this isolation method, the impact of the program on weekly sales and average revenue per transaction was determined.

Phase 5: Calculate Return on Investment (ROI) and Prepare Final Report

Once the business impact of the solution was determined, the project team calculated the projected costs of the program. Costs were divided into several categories including:

- Participant fees: These fees included the course registration fee, food, as well as backfill costs.
- Instructor fees: This included the trainer's time, food, and incidentals, as well as travel costs.
- Training material costs: Students received printed materials including a workbook, job aids, and fact sheets. These costs were determined on a per student basis.
- Room rental fees: Room and projector fees were factored into the cost sheet.
- Course development costs: The course development costs were also included and amortized over the total number of sites expected to participate in the training program.
- Evaluation study costs: The costs for conducting the program evaluation were included in the final cost calculation.

Once costs for the solution were determined, the financial benefit of the solution was monetized over a period of one year. This process then allowed the evaluation team to calculate the benefit-cost ratio (BCR) and return on investment (ROI). The results were then documented in a detailed report and executive summary. Results were also shared with senior level stakeholders via face-to-face to meetings.

Figure 11-4 provides a high level overview of the evaluation methodology that was applied to the Selling Skills Training Program.

FIGURE 11-4. Evaluation Process Model

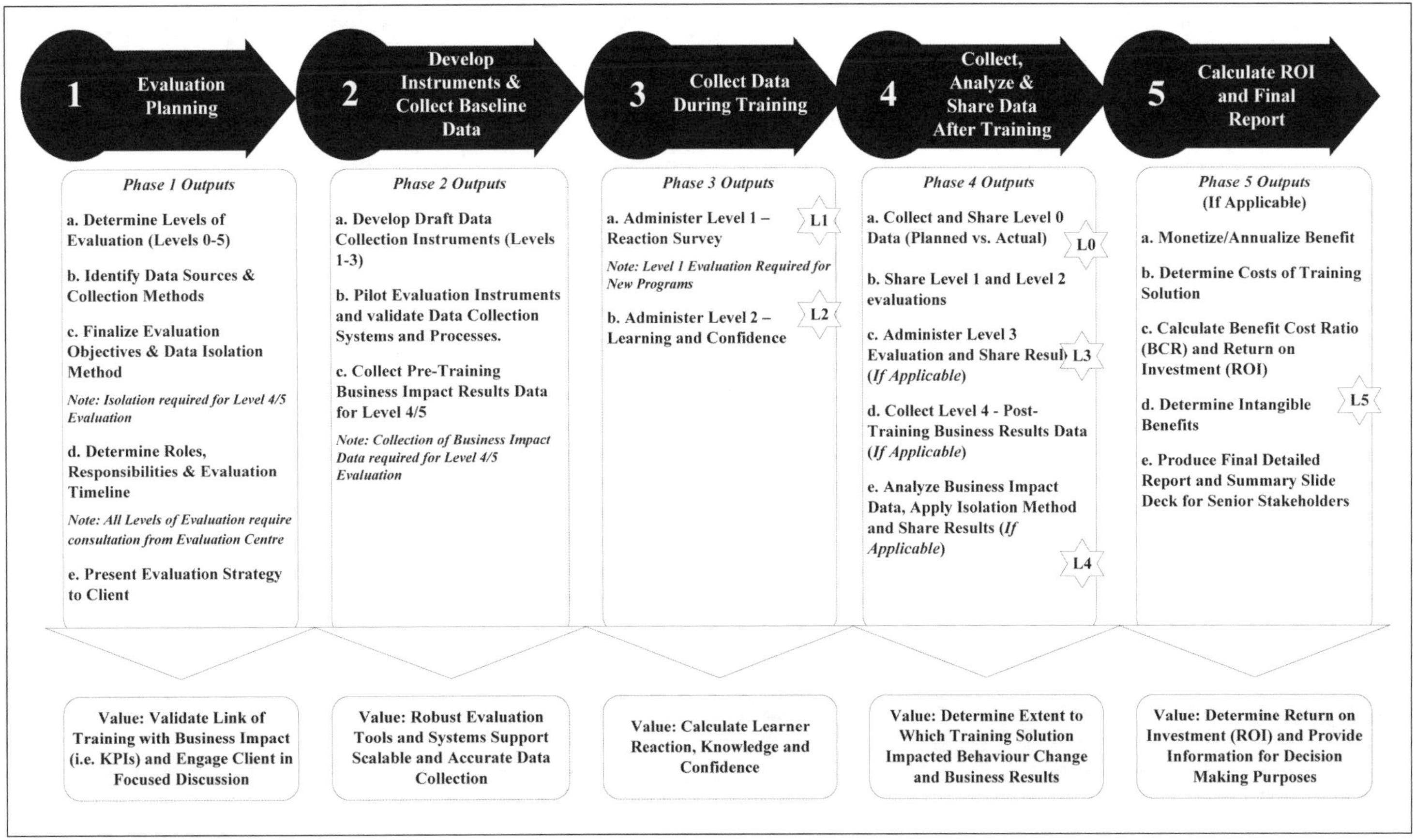

1 Evaluation Planning

Phase 1 Outputs

a. Determine Levels of Evaluation (Levels 0-5)

b. Identify Data Sources & Collection Methods

c. Finalize Evaluation Objectives & Data Isolation Method

Note: Isolation required for Level 4/5 Evaluation

d. Determine Roles, Responsibilities & Evaluation Timeline

Note: All Levels of Evaluation require consultation from Evaluation Centre

e. Present Evaluation Strategy to Client

Value: Validate Link of Training with Business Impact (i.e. KPIs) and Engage Client in Focused Discussion

2 Develop Instruments & Collect Baseline Data

Phase 2 Outputs

a. Develop Draft Data Collection Instruments (Levels 1-3)

b. Pilot Evaluation Instruments and validate Data Collection Systems and Processes.

c. Collect Pre-Training Business Impact Results Data for Level 4/5

Note: Collection of Business Impact Data required for Level 4/5 Evaluation

Value: Robust Evaluation Tools and Systems Support Scalable and Accurate Data Collection

3 Collect Data During Training

Phase 3 Outputs

a. Administer Level 1 – Reaction Survey   L1

Note: Level 1 Evaluation Required for New Programs

b. Administer Level 2 – Learning and Confidence   L2

Value: Calculate Learner Reaction, Knowledge and Confidence

4 Collect, Analyze & Share Data After Training

Phase 4 Outputs

a. Collect and Share Level 0 Data (Planned vs. Actual)   L0

b. Share Level 1 and Level 2 evaluations

c. Administer Level 3 Evaluation and Share Result *(If Applicable)*   L3

d. Collect Level 4 - Post-Training Business Results Data *(If Applicable)*

e. Analyze Business Impact Data, Apply Isolation Method and Share Results *(If Applicable)*   L4

Value: Determine Extent to Which Training Solution Impacted Behaviour Change and Business Results

5 Calculate ROI and Final Report

Phase 5 Outputs (If Applicable)

a. Monetize/Annualize Benefit

b. Determine Costs of Training Solution

c. Calculate Benefit Cost Ratio (BCR) and Return on Investment (ROI)

d. Determine Intangible Benefits   L5

e. Produce Final Detailed Report and Summary Slide Deck for Senior Stakeholders

Value: Determine Return on Investment (ROI) and Provide Information for Decision Making Purposes

EVALUATION RESULTS

Level 1 Evaluation Results

To obtain data on learner satisfaction and planned action, a paper-based survey was designed in collaboration with the training supplier. The survey contained both closed and open-ended questions aimed at gathering data on the training experience. A total of 48 surveys were received from learners. The results from the survey are shown in Table 11-2.

TABLE 11-2. Level 1 Evaluation Results

Survey Question	Level of Agreement*	Target
The objectives of the course were clear to me.	100%	80%
The course materials helped me understand what I need to know to do my job.	100%	80%
The content was presented in a way that made sense to me.	100%	80%
The on-the-job training part of the course helped me to learn.	95.8%	80%
The course seemed to be the right length.	97.9%	80%
The trainer's level of knowledge was appropriate for the course.	100%	80%
The trainer encouraged participation by prompting the class to ask questions.	100%	80%
The trainer was effective when answering questions.	100%	80%
The trainer made the course "real" by creating links between the content and actual job I will be doing.	100%	80%
This training course has adequately prepared me for the work that I will be doing.	100%	80%

*Statistics are based on a 5-point Likert scale. The "actual" statistic represents the percentage of respondents who indicated "Strongly Agree" and "Agree" for each statement.

Overall, participants thoroughly enjoyed their training experience with scores for individual evaluative questions well over the target of 80 percent.

Level 2 Evaluation Results

As part of the training experience, learners were required to perform a skill demonstration in which they assume the role of a selling agent and engage a mock customer in number of interactive scenarios using a simulated workstation, props, and so on. During this interaction the instructor observes the learner's performance and level of application of the Selling Skills model.

Following the completion of the skill demonstration, there was a group discussion on the learner's performance which is combined with coaching from an experienced instructor.

Data are not formally collected on this component of training. However, instructors ensure that learners grasp the basic concepts and are able to demonstrate the appropriate behaviors. Coaching ensures that learners understand their individual areas of improvement.

Level 3 Evaluation Results

To validate that the learning has been applied while on the job, participants are observed in their work environment approximately six to eight weeks after program completion. The observation involves completion of a rigorous checklist that validates the extent to which the learner is applying his or her selling skills during customer engagements.

The learners are graded on five key behaviors that are linked to the program. Scores are assigned at the site level and provide a strong indication regarding the learner's ability to implement and sustain their selling skills on a daily basis.

Sites that participated in the training were successful on the Level 3 observation and achieved an average score of 73.7 percent, exceeding the target score of 70 percent.

Level 4 Evaluation Results

To assess the impact of the training program on key business outcomes, data were obtained from a total of 142 sites. Key indicators included the following:
- total number of transactions per week
- total sales per week
- average revenue per transaction per week.

Additional site-level data was pulled on square footage and as well as maturity. Data were then analyzed to identify the interrelationships between variables which can be summarized as follows:
- **Yearly sales and average revenue per transaction:** As total yearly sales increases the average revenue per transaction increases.
- **L3 observation score and yearly sales:** Sites with a higher Level 3 observation score experience a very slight increase in yearly sales. However, the relationship between these two variables is not strong.
- **L3 observation score and average revenue per transaction:** As the Level 3 observation score increases, there is a slight increase in the average revenue per transaction. However, the relationship between these two variables is not strong.
- **Square footage and yearly sales:** As a site increases in size there is an increase in overall revenue.

- **Square footage and average revenue per transaction:** As square footage increases there is no impact on the average revenue per transaction.
- **Number of transactions and average revenue per transaction:** As the number of transactions increases, the average revenue per transaction decreases.
- **Number of transactions and yearly sales:** As the number of transactions increases, overall yearly sales also increase.

Site Selection Process for Control Group Analysis

Once the interrelationship between key variables was understood it provided the ability to select stores to participate in the ROI study. The following filtering methodology was applied to select sites for the study:

- **Filter 1:** Sites isolated with similar results in yearly sales and average revenue per transaction.
- **Filter 2:** Sites selected with transactions between 40,000 and 50,000 per year.
- **Filter 3:** Stores selected with similar historical Level 3 observation scores.
- **Filter 4:** Stores that were between 426- to 527-square feet were selected for the study.
- **Filter 5:** Stores that have been in operation for at least five years.

This filtering method isolated 12 sites with similar characteristics and levels of performance to be included in the study. From these 12 sites, six were selected to be trained and the remaining six would make up the control group (untrained).

Control Group Comparative Assessment Methodology

The methodology for the control group analysis and comparative assessment can be summarized below:

- Step 1: For each key performance indicator (weekly sales and revenue per transaction) site data were compiled in excel spreadsheets over a period of 26 weeks.
- Step 2: The trained group was then analyzed by creating a scatter plot for weeks one to nine. A trend line was then added and extended to show the pre-business results trajectory. This process is then repeated to establish post training results by creating a scatter plot for weeks 10 to 26. Once again a trend line was added and extended to show post business results trajectory.
- Step 3: Periodic measurements were also taken of the trained group. Results were isolated three weeks prior to training (weeks six to eight) and 11 weeks after training (weeks 19 to 21). Averages of trained sites were used for each key performance indicator over the designated period.
- Step 4: Once pre- and post-business results were established for the trained group, the difference in output was then calculated. This difference

(post-business results—pre-business results) represented the gains made by the trained group.

- Step 5: To cross-compare results of the trained group with the control group, steps 1 to 4 are then completed for the control group sites (untrained).
- Step 6: Once the difference between pre- and post-business results has been determined for the control group, they are compared to the trained group. To account for the seasonal sales peak and gains made by both trained and untrained offices over the period, the results of the control group are subtracted from the trained group. This conservative approach then produces an overall gain/loss for the trained stores when compared against the control group.

Impact to Business Results: Average Weekly Sales

Figure 11-5 shows the average weekly sales results for the trained group (Note: The black vertical line indicates the week that sites attended the Selling Skills Training Program).

FIGURE 11-5. Weekly Sales Pre- and Post-Training Results

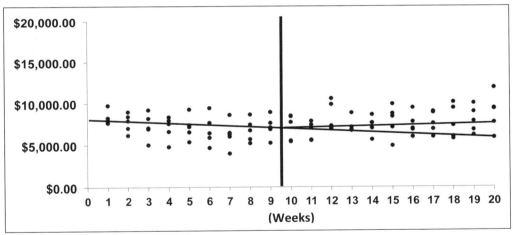

As shown in Figure 11-5, there is a slight increase in the average weekly sales performance of the trained sites. Table 11-3 further validates the improvement made by the trained sites following completion of the training program.

TABLE 11-3. Improvements in Trained Sites

Result Area	Result Description	Weeks Isolated	Average Weekly Sales
Pre-training	3 weeks prior to training	Weeks 6–8	$6,753.94
Post-training	11 weeks after training	Weeks 19–21	$8,489.49
Pre/Post differential	Post-results – Pre-results	N/A	+ $1,735.55

Using a periodic measurement three weeks prior to training and 11 weeks after training, it was determined that the increase to average weekly sales was $1,735.55 (calculation = post-training results – pre-training results).

Figure 11-6 shows the average weekly sales results for the control group.

FIGURE 11-6. Control Group (Untrained) Results

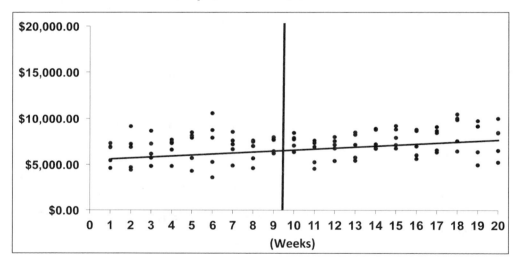

As shown in the Figure 11-6, there is a slight increase in the average weekly sales performance of the control group over the same period of analysis as the trained group.

Table 11-4 further demonstrates the improvement made by the control group.

TABLE 11-4. Control Group Results

Result Area	Result Description	Weeks Isolated	Average Weekly Sales
Pre-training	3 weeks prior to training	Weeks 6–8	$6,785.70
Post-training	11 weeks after training	Weeks 19–21	$8,280.18
Pre/Post differential	Post-results – Pre-results	N/A	+ $1,494.48

Using a periodic measurement three weeks prior to training and 11 weeks after training, it was determined that the increase to average weekly sales was $1,494.48 (calculation = post-training results – pre-training results).

Summary of Findings From Control Group Analysis: Average Weekly Sales

Based on the results from the data analysis, the trained sites and control group saw an increase in their average weekly sales over the same period. However, the increase to average weekly sales made by the trained group exceeded that of the control group. The following formula and calculation summarizes the impact of the program on average weekly sales:

$$\text{Business Impact} = \text{Gains Made by Trained Group} - \text{Gains Made by Control Group}$$
$$= \$1,735.55 - \$1,494.48$$
$$= \$241.07$$

The Selling Skills program saw an increase to average weekly sales of $241.07 per week, which resulted in a gain of 9.24 percent. This exceeded the Level 4 objectives of 5 percent.

Impact to Business Results: Average Revenue per Transaction

Figure 11-7 shows the average revenue per transaction results for the trained group (Note: The black vertical line indicates the week that sites had attended the Selling Skills Training Program).

FIGURE 11-7. Revenue per Transaction: Trained Group

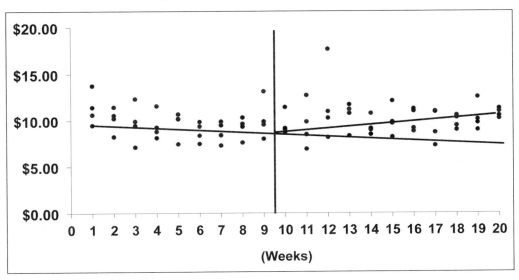

As shown in Figure 11-7, there is an increase in the average revenue per transaction performance of the trained sites.

Table 11-5 further demonstrates the improvement made by the trained sites following completion of the training program.

TABLE 11-5. Improvement by Trained Sites

Result Area	Result Description	Weeks Isolated	Revenue Per Transaction
Pre-training	3 weeks prior to training	Weeks 6–8	$9.31
Post-training	11 weeks after training	Weeks 19–21	$10.76
Pre/Post differential	Post-results – Pre-results	N/A	+ $1.45

Using a periodic measurement three weeks prior to training and 11 weeks after training, it was determined that the increase to average revenue per transaction was $1.45 (calculation = post-training results – pre-training results).

Figure 11-8 shows the average revenue per transaction results for the control group.

FIGURE 11-8. Revenue per Transaction: Control Group

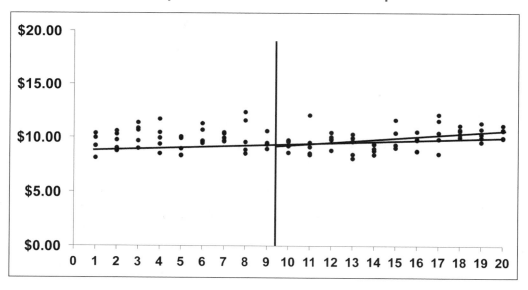

As shown above, there is a very slight increase in the average revenue per transaction results of the control group over the same period of analysis as the trained group.

Table 11-6 further demonstrates the improvement made by the control group.

TABLE 11-6. Control Group Results

Result Area	Result Description	Weeks Isolated	Revenue Per Transaction
Pre-training	3 weeks prior to training	Weeks 6–8	$10.08
Post-training	11 weeks after training	Weeks 19–21	$10.67
Pre/Post differential	Post-results – Pre-results	N/A	+ $0.59

Using a periodic measurement three weeks prior to training and 11 weeks after training, it was determined that the increase to average weekly sales was $0.59 (calculation = post-training results – pre-training results).

Summary of Findings From Control Group Analysis: Average Revenue per Transaction

Based on the results from the data analysis, both the trained sites and control group saw an increase in their average revenue per transaction over the same period. However, similar to the average weekly sales results, the increase to revenue per transaction made by the trained group exceeded that of the control group. The following formula and calculation below summarizes the impact of the program on the average revenue per transaction:

Business Impact = Gains Made by Trained Group – Gains Made by Control Group

= $1.45 - $0.59

= $0.86

The Selling Skills program saw an increase to average revenue per transaction of $0.86 which resulted in a gain of 16.1 percent. This exceeded the Level 4 objectives of 15 percent.

Converting the Data to Monetary Value

This section provides an overview of two options that were explored to convert data to monetary values. The following ROI principles were applied when selecting an option and monetizing the benefit:

- Guiding Principle 4: When analyzing data, choose the most conservative alternative for calculations.
- Guiding Principle 9: Only the first year of benefits (annual) should be used in the ROI analysis.

Option 1 (using average revenue per transaction): To monetize the output using the increase to the average revenue per transaction the gain of $0.86 was applied to the remaining transactions for the year. Table 11-7 shows how the revenue per transaction converted to an overall yearly benefit.

TABLE 11-7. Total Site Benefits

Sites	Average Transactions Per Week	# of Weeks	Total Transactions	Increase to Avg. Rev. Transaction ($0.86) x 40%	Profit Contribution (12% of Sales)
Site 1	1,096	48	52,592.64	$18,091.87	$1,809.19
Site 2	1,008	48	48,374.40	$16,640.79	$1,664.08
Site 3	1,026	48	49,238.40	$16,938.01	$1,693.80
Site 4	1,105	48	53,022.72	$18,239.82	$1,823.98
Site 5	927	48	44,519.04	$15,314.55	$1,531.45
Site 6	869	48	41,708.16	$14,347.61	$1,434.76
Total Annual Benefit for Site					$9,957.26

The overall annual benefit for a site using the average revenue per transaction is $9.957.26. A site profit contribution of 10 percent was applied which was based on a gross margin of 20 percent on products minus all fees and expenses. In addition, an applicability factor of 40 percent was applied to indicate that the average gain of $0.85 would be made on 40 percent of all transactions. This approach ensured that the most conservative benefit would be calculated for the ROI study.

Option 2 (using average weekly sales): The second option considered was to convert the increase to average weekly sales to monetary values.

Average Weekly Sales Gain/Loss per Office for Trained Group: $1,735.56

Average Weekly Sales Gain/Loss per Office for Untrained Group: $1,494.48

Net Increase per Site (Trained – Untrained): $241.08

Site Profit Contribution: (10 percent) of Sales: $24.11

Total Weekly Improvement (six sites): $144.65

Number of Weeks: 48

Total Annual Benefit for Site = $144.65 x 48 = $6,943.10

The overall annual benefit for a site using the average weekly sales is $6,943.10. Similarly to the calculation for option 1, a site profit contribution of 10 percent was applied.

Selected option: Due to the guiding principles of ROI, which stress that a conservative approach be taken to formulate monetary gains of a program, the annualized benefit using weekly sales from the control group analysis was selected for the ROI analysis calculation (i.e., total annual benefit for dealer = $6,943.10).

Calculating the Costs of the Selling Skills Program

Program costs were divided into two main categories, 1) costs paid by site and 2) costs paid by Canada Post. Table 11-8 provides breakdown of the course costs.

TABLE 11-8. Calculating Costs

Cost Item	Unit Costs	Unit Description	# of Units	Total Costs	Cost Applicability Factor	Total Costs
1. Student Fees:						
a. Student course costs	$70.00	Per session	50	$3,500.00	100%	$3,500.00
b. Student back fill costs	$15.00	Per hour	144	$2,160.00	100%	$2,160.00
c. Student food costs	$5.00	Per student	50	$250.00	100%	$250.00
2. Trainer Costs:						
a. Trainer food and incidentals	$81.00	Per day	6	$486.00	60%	$291.60
b. Trainer travel costs	NA	N/A	N/A	$1,000.00	100%	$1,000.00
3. Training Material Costs	$5.37	Per package	50	$268.50	100%	$268.50
4. Room Rental Costs	$180.00	Per room	6	$1,080.00	30%	$324.00
5. Course Development Costs	NA	N/A	N/A	$17,500.00	5%	$875.00
6. ROI Costs	NA	N/A	N/A	$1,210.00	100%	$1,210.00
Total Costs:	$9,879.10					
Site Costs:	$6,794.10					
Canada Post Costs:	$3,085.00					

The costs were calculated with the following assumptions:
- Guiding Principle 10 was applied, which states, "Costs of the solution should be fully loaded for ROI analysis."
- A total of 50 students attended the program for six site locations,
- Total trainer travel costs were allocated at $1000.00.
- Rooms/projectors were payable for 50 percent of the classes.
- Course development costs were allocated at 5 percent based on the fact that six sites out of 142 were targeted for the training program (calculation = 6/142 = 4.23%).
- Only site costs are factored into the ROI calculation.

Level 5 Evaluation Results

The ROI is calculated using the program benefits and costs. The benefit-cost ratio (BCR) is the program benefits divided by cost. In formula form it is:

$$BCR = \frac{\$6{,}943.09}{\$6{,}794.10}$$

$$BCR = 1.02$$

$$\text{Return on Investment (ROI)} = \frac{\text{Net Program Benefits}}{\text{Program Costs}} \times 100$$

$$ROI = \frac{\$6{,}943.09 - \$6{,}794.10}{\$6{,}794.10} \times 100$$

$$ROI = 2.1\%$$

For every dollar spent on training by a site, there is a dollar returned and an additional $0.02 returned. Despite this positive gain the Selling Skills Program is not achieving the BCR target of 1.15 and the ROI target of 15 percent.

COMMUNICATION STRATEGY

Prior to completion of the ROI study, there was an organizational restructure that resulted in a change to the original sponsor of the evaluation study. This resulted in a few unknowns: Would the successor have an interest in knowing the effects of this particular program? Would the overall training strategy change? As the evaluation was in the final stages, the director of sales training recommended that the study continue.

When the final results were calculated, a briefing was provided to the director of sales training to determine the next steps. The informative nature of the results convinced the director that the information was worth presenting to the new executive member, as well as to continue with the intent of the study, namely, influencing stores to take the Selling Skills Program to drive revenue and increase customer service levels. In addition to the director of training, individuals from the client group who provided ongoing revenue and sales data and assisted with the analysis of data (termed, the "data mining team"), played a key role in influencing the executive member to continue with the study.

In a one-on-one meeting, the director of sales training briefed the new executive on the original need and intent of the study and he agreed to view the results.

The ROI consultants presented an executive summary to the senior sponsor and sales strategy team, ensuring that members of the data mining team were also included in this briefing. The presentation provided an overview of the reasons for initiating the study and the criteria used to ensure similarity between the control and test groups. As well, the process for collecting data and the steps taken to assess costs and benefits were explained at a high level, with special mention given to the executive's team who had provided the data for analysis. Finally, the positive result was presented, along with recommendations for next steps, which included an investment in the modification of the course content to make it more accessible (i.e., online) and robust for future learners.

The presentation yielded very positive feedback and a commitment by the new executive to review a proposal by the director of sales training to modify the content of the Selling Skills course.

LESSONS LEARNED

The ROI consultants learned several important lessons while implementing and evaluating the study. The most important lesson was the positive benefit of having developed a supportive stakeholder network within the client and training groups; this network provided continued 'political' support of the initiative during a period of time when there was a change to the original executive level sponsor for the study. The loss of the original sponsor could have caused the study to be stopped. However, the broad support for the evaluation by others in the organization who understood its purpose and value maintained project momentum.

A second lesson learned was the importance of establishing a data mining team. This was a formal role for some experienced and respected members of the client group. Originally, the study sought to measure the impact of the training only on the revenue per transaction of the training program participants; however, upon the recommendation of the client's data team members, weekly sales data were included in the analysis as they felt that it provided even more credibility to the results.

A third lesson learned was the importance of taking time to ensure that the effects of the program could be isolated. The selection of the control and test groups used data points (site locations, yearly sales, number of transactions, square footage) to ensure similar characteristics were shared across all groups. To further reinforce the accuracy of the results from the control group analysis, both a trend-line analysis and periodic measurement technique were applied. This provided stakeholders with a graphical illustration of the program's impact as well as charts detailing the periodic measurements taken prior to and after training.

Finally, the fourth lesson learned was to use the most conservative results from the analysis. When questioned about the positive result of the study, the perception of accuracy was enhanced by the stakeholders when it was revealed that more than one method was used in the isolation of effects of the program, and that only the lowest result was reported in the final study.

RESOURCES

Phillips, J.J., and P.P. Phillips. (2007). *Show Me the Money: How to Determine ROI in People, Projects, and Programs*. San Francisco: Berrett-Koehler.

Phillips, J.J., and P.P. Phillips. (2010). *Proving the Value of HR: ROI Case Studies*. Birmingham, AL: ROI Institute.

Phillips, J.J., and P.P. Phillips. (2007). *The Value of Learning: How Organizations Capture Value and ROI*. San Francisco: John Wiley & Sons.

QUESTIONS FOR DISCUSSION

1. Given the departure of the original sponsor, were the appropriate measures taken to ensure continuation of the study? What would you have done differently?
2. What other methods could have been used to isolate the effects of this program? Would other methods have made the results more or less credible?
3. What other criteria could have been used to ensure similarities between the control and test groups?
4. Discuss the importance of engaging a knowledgeable data mining team. What influence should they have in contributing to the data collection plan?
5. Why is it important to use the most conservative results of a study? What problems do you anticipate if you were to present the "best" results?

ABOUT THE AUTHORS

David Soltis is a results-oriented manager with visible achievements in the healthcare and education sectors. He has served as a Vice Principal for Heritage Academy of Learning Excellence and as the Manager of Training and e-Learning Services Team at the Ontario Telemedicine Network. David is currently the Manager of Learning Analytics, Processes, and Reporting at Canada Post and is a key resource supporting program evaluations and adoption of the corporate learning management system.

David is a Certified Training and Development Professional (CTDP), Project Management Professional (PMP), ROI Professional (CRP) and member of the Ontario College of Teachers. He completed his bachelor of education at the Ontario Institute for

Studies in Education (OISE) and executive MBA at the University of Ottawa, Telfer School of Management.

Nancy Donovan is the Director of Learning and Development at Canada Post Corporation, a Crown corporation that serves as Canada's primary postal operator. In this role she has access to both HR and operations strategies, and she specializes in ensuring alignment between the two by providing measurement of learning programs. By combining her skills and knowledge of business analysis and process management with her ROI accreditation, she drives training process improvement and standardization within a company of more than 65,000 employees.

She holds a bachelor of science degree from Dalhousie University in Halifax, Nova Scotia, and has more than 20 years' experience as a senior-level learning consultant in the private and public sector. In addition to program measurement, her project work has ranged from performance coaching and facilitation to project management and learning solution architecture design.

12

Selling Skills for Retail Sales Assistants

McArthur Sp. z.o.o.

Małgorzata Mitoraj-Jaroszek

T his case was prepared to serve as a basis for discussion rather than an illustration of either effective or ineffective administrative and management practices. Names, dates, places, and data may have been disguised at the request of the author or organization.

Abstract

This case study is a description of an ROI project based on sales training targeted at retail sales assistants in a chain of shoe stores in Poland. A trend analysis was used as a method of isolating the effects of training. The sales training brought overall positive results.

BACKGROUND INFORMATION

McArthur Sp. z.o.o. is a medium-sized trading company, with a network of several shoe shops in large shopping centers in Poland. The senior management felt that the current level of sales was unsatisfactory. In addition to implementing a sales training program, the company conducted a series of mystery shopper surveys to assess the level of customer service and found the results to be very negative.

THE SOLUTION

It was acknowledged that there was an obvious sales training need for store managers, assistant store managers, and sales assistants. The sales training was conducted in nine stores and included the following topic areas: customer service standards, making contact with prospective customers, diagnosing customer needs, offering a solution (i.e., making a shoe presentation), presenting benefits, handling objectives, and closing the sale. In addition, to support and encourage the development of selling skills, managers and assistant store managers took part in tailor-made coaching training. In all, there were 45 participants in the training. Fortnightly, managers were asked to complete a competency assessment sheet for each of their staff members, and send it to the head office for verification by the sales and marketing director. After completing the observation sheet, the managers were asked to conduct coaching meetings with each of their staff members. The whole coaching process took three months.

THE MEASUREMENT CHALLENGE

The guidelines from the senior management were very clear, the aim was to raise the level of sales. To measure the effectiveness of the challenge, the ROI Methodology from the ROI Institute was applied. The process consisted of six areas of measurement: reaction and planned action, learning, application and implementation, business impact, ROI, and intangible measures.

The process includes a comprehensive plan for data collection and analysis, as shown in Figure 12-1. It contains steps leading up to the calculation of ROI, starting from evaluation planning and including types of information needed at each level of evaluation. To complete the process at Level 4, an analysis of intangible benefits is also carried out.

Planning for ROI

One of the important elements of the ROI evaluation is evaluation planning. Two key documents were used: the data collection plan and the ROI analysis plan.

Data Collection Plan

Figure 12-2 shows a completed data collection plan for this project, including all stages of the planning process and data collection. The objectives at Level 1 were identified as: participants indicate a positive response to the training program and complete an action plan at the end of training. The satisfaction level for this objective was a rating between 4.0 and 5.0 on a 5-point scale.

The objectives at Level 2 aimed to check the level of sales skills acquired during the training. At the end of the training, the trainer assessed all participants by a means of a pass or fail aptitude test focusing on the skills practiced. Over 80 percent of the participants passed the test.

At Level 3, two means of evaluation were implemented. The sales assistants were evaluated every two weeks by their managers or by the assistant store managers with a yes-or-no observation checklist for a period of three months. The satisfaction level was set at the implementation level of 80 percent of learned skills in the sales assistants' daily work. In addition, information regarding the implementation of skills was also verified by a mystery shopper survey.

The business impact expected was sales growth, monitored throughout a period of three months after the training was completed. The results of the ROI calculation were expected to be 50 percent.

The data collection plan was a crucial part of the evaluation strategy. It allowed for a very clear outline in terms of the types of information needed, how the data should be collected, and when and by whom it should be collected.

ROI Analysis Plan

The ROI analysis plan was also important to the evaluation. As shown in Figure 12-3, the ROI analysis plan shows how to analyze data at Level 4 (business impact) and convert it to money so a credible ROI calculation can be achieved.

FIGURE **12-1.** The ROI Methodology

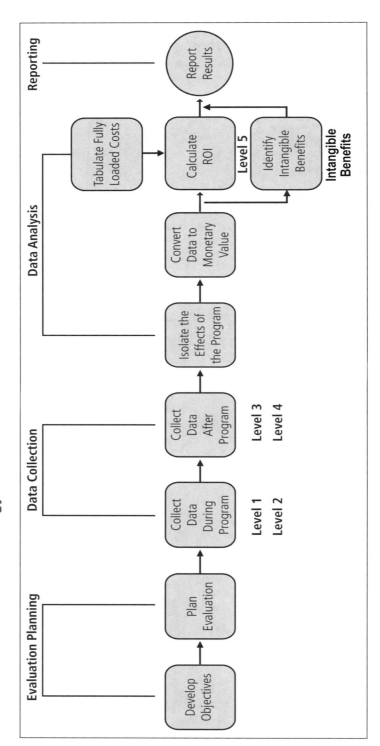

FIGURE 12-2. Data Collection Plan

Program: Increase Sales Results   Purpose: Increase Sales Results   Responsibility: Małgorzata Mitoraj-Jaroszek   Date: 15.04.2011

Level	Program Objectives	Measures	Data Collection Method/Instruments	Data Sources	Timing	Responsibility
1	SATISFACTION/PLANNED ACTION • Positive reaction – four or five • Action plan for store managers	• Rating on a composite of five measures	• Questionnaire	• Participants	• End of program	• Facilitator
2	LEARNING • Shop Assistants: needs analysis skills, handling customer objectives, closing the sale, applying customer service standards • Store Manager: selling, coaching	• Pass or fail on skills practiced	• Test	• Participants	• End of program	• Facilitator
3	APPLICATION/IMPLEMENTATION • Use customer service standards on the job • 80% of shop assistants apply sales techniques • Shop managers apply and use coaching	• Yes-or-no scale • Checklist for observation	• Mystery shopper • Observation	• Manager • Mystery shopper	• Every 2 weeks after the training for a period of 3 months • 3 months after the training	• Małgorzata
4	BUSINESS IMPACT • Increase in sales • Intangible measures: customer satisfaction	• Weekly average sales per store	• Business performance monitoring	• Company System	• 3 months after program	• Head of sales
5	ROI • 50%	Comments:				

235

FIGURE 12-3. ROI Analysis Plan

Data Items (Usually Level 4)	Methods For Isolating the Effects of the Program/Process	Methods of Converting Data to Monetary Values	Cost Categories	Intangible Benefits	Communication Targets for Final Report	Other Influences/Issues During Application
Program: Selling Skills		Purpose: Increase Sales Results		Responsibility: Malgorzata Mitoraj-Jaroszek		Date: 15.04.2011
• Increase in Sales	• Trend Analysis	• Standard value/ profit margin	• Facilitators fees • Program materials • Meals and refreshments • Participant salaries and benefits • Cost coordination and evaluation • Mystery shopper	• Customer Satisfaction	• Program participants • Sales managers • Store managers • Training staff	• N/A

RESULTS

Reaction and Learning

All of the participants (100 percent) who took part in the training completed the evaluation questionnaire. The results are shown in Table 12-1. During the training, participants were evaluated by the trainer using a yes/no test. Eighty percent of the participants received a positive evaluation.

TABLE 12-1. Reaction Questionnaire Results

Participants' Reactions	
This program met the objectives.	4,8
The program was relevant to my work.	4,7
The program was important to my job success.	4,6
The program provided me with new information.	4,4
I will recommend the program to others.	5,0
The program was good investment in me.	4,9
The program met my needs.	4,8
The program was a good use of my time.	4,8
I intend to use the material.	4,7
Overall result	4,7

Note: Participants rated the following on a scale of 1-5.

Application and Implementation

Every two weeks from the end of the training, participants were assessed by their superiors. The process took three months. Managers evaluated the use of sales standards in the sales assistants' daily work. As a result, the study found that 70 percent of the participants used all of the acquired sales standards. Thirty percent did not use one of the acquired standards, closing the sale. Also, 80 percent of store managers effectively conducted on-the-job coaching.

An additional source of information was a mystery client survey. The results after this period were satisfactory. In six of the stores, there was visible improvement, and in three of the stores no changes were observed. (Note: During the evaluation process, staff changes occurred in three of the stores—store managers and sales assistants were dismissed, or resigned on their own.)

Barriers to Success

After completing the sales training program, a focus group was conducted concentrating on the barriers linked to the implementation and application of sales standards. The results of the focus group brought out that the greatest barriers were:

- lack of time to practice some of the skills when there is an increased number of customers in the store (especially true during the weekend rush hours)
- lack of support from immediate superiors, irregular and insufficient amount of constructive feedback.

Store management pointed out that this type of training should be organized more frequently, at the same time stressing that a crucial element of further trainings was to allow the participants to practice in non-standard situations in which they apply the acquired skills. Another crucial observation that was made was that the participants still faced problems with closing the sale. This was the first sales training carried out for McArthur sales assistants, therefore the level of motivation and commitment in this case was extremely high.

Business Impact

It was decided that the business analysis would only take into consideration the results from six of the shops, due to the fact that in three of the stores there was a high employee rotation during the project (this group was excluded from further analysis). Shoe sales were studied in six of the stores for a period of three months after completing the training.

Isolating the Effects of the Program

A key element of the ROI Methodology is isolating the effects of the program on the data. It was decided that in order to do this effectively, a sales trend analysis for a period of three months after the training would be used to compare the results with the same period from the previous year. Actual average unit sales taken starting the week the trainings commenced, during the three-month period was 4 928 pairs of shoes sold. Forecasted average unit sales taken starting the week the trainings commenced, during the three-month period was 3 610,25 pairs of shoes sold, as shown in Figure 12-4.

$$\text{Average ``real''} - \text{average ``forecast''} = 1\ 317,75$$

A group of experts most familiar with the situation indicated that no additional new influences entered during the post-evaluation period. They also indicated that the pre-program influences are still present in the post period.

In all of the stores surveyed, a positive difference was observed between the actual results and the forecasted results. Conducting the same analysis in all of the stores at the same time strengthened the credibility for the increased results.

FIGURE 12-4. Trend Analysis

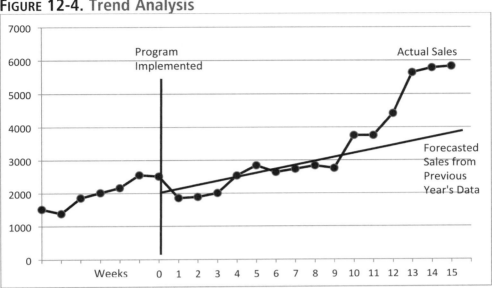

Converting Data to a Monetary Value

To calculate the monetary value of the benefits, the following steps were taken, as shown in Table 12-2. The average price of shoes is 79 PLN, of which 40,29 PLN is the net profit (data supplied by the Sales and Marketing Director). The increase in sales within the three months of the evaluated period was 1 318 units, giving an increase of 439 units per month. Annually, this gives an increase of 5 268 units x the net sales profit of 40,29 PLN. Which gives an overall sum of 212 247,72 PLN.

TABLE 12-2. Steps for Converting Data to Monetary Value

Step 1: Sale value of 1 pair of shoes
Step 2: V = Average price of 79 PLN for 1 pair = net profit 40,29 PLN
Step 3: ΔP = 1 318 units / 3 = 439 units
Step 4: Annual ΔP x12 = 439 x 12 = 5 268 units
Step 5: AΔP x V = 5 268 x 40,29 PLN = 212 247, 72 PLN

Program Costs

Table 12-3 outlines all program costs. The costs take into account the cost of training for nine stores, although the benefits are calculated only on the results of six of the stores.

TABLE 12-3. Project Costs

Item	Total
Facilitators fees	20 000 PLN
Program materials	300 PLN
Meals and refreshments	11 000 PLN
Participant salaries and benefits	18 700 PLN
Cost coordination and evaluation	5 000 PLN
Mystery shopper	5 000 PLN
Total costs	60 000 PLN

ROI Calculation

The ROI and benefit-cost ratio (BCR) were calculated for the project as follows:

$$BCR = \frac{212\ 247,72}{60\ 000} = 3,5 \text{ or } 3,5{:}1$$

The benefit-cost ratio was very satisfying for the customer. ROI was calculated as follows:

$$ROI\% = \frac{212\ 247,72 - 60\ 000}{60\ 000} \times 100 = 253,7\%$$

The ROI interpretation is as follows: each zloty invested returned 2,5 zloty (PLN) in benefits. The training proved to be a good investment and worthy of continuing in the future in order to develop staff sales competence.

The whole process was consistent with the 12 Guiding Principles of the ROI Methodology:

1. When a higher level evaluation is conducted, data must be collected at lower levels.
2. When an evaluation is planned for a higher level, the previous level of evaluation does not have to be comprehensive.
3. When collecting and analyzing data, use only the most credible sources.
4. When analyzing data, select the most conservative alternative for calculations.

5. At least one method must be used to isolate the effects of the solution/project.

6. If no improvement data are available for a population or from a specific source, it is assumed that little or no improvement has occurred.

7. Estimates of improvements should be adjusted for the potential error of the estimate.

8. Extreme data items and unsupported claims should not be used in ROI calculations.

9. Only the first year of benefits (annual) should be used in the ROI analysis of short term solutions.

10. Costs of a solution, project, or program should be fully loaded for ROI analysis.

11. Intangible measures are defined as measures that are purposefully not converted to monetary value.

12. The results from the ROI Methodology must be communicated to all key stakeholders.

Intangibles

An intangible benefit that emerged during the training was an increase in customer satisfaction in six of the shops. A customer satisfaction survey was conducted and mystery shoppers evaluated salespeople for the same criteria. Table 12-4 shows the criteria being examined within the sales staff.

In addition, during the store management training sum up, it was discovered that one of the additional advantages of this training was a much higher level of commitment on the part of the sales assistants. The training also helped to improve communication between the head office and individual stores.

TABLE 12-4. Mystery Shopper Salesperson Evaluation

1.	The sales assistant greeted me with a smile.
2.	The sales assistant made eye contact with me.
3.	The sales assistant offered help too soon (he was pushy).
4.	The sales assistant said good morning.
5.	The sales assistant offered to help me find the right shoes.
6.	The sales assistant presented the benefits of the product.
7.	The sales assistant handled the objections from my side concerning the product, offers, prices, etc.
8.	The sales assistant comprehensively offered and presented alternative products.
9.	The sales assistant suggested I purchase additional products.
10.	The sales assistant informed me of the current promotion.
11.	The sales assistant attempted to close the sale.
12.	The sales assistant informed me about the possibility of refunds / exchanges.
13.	The sales assistant encouraged me to re-visit the shop.
14.	The sales assistant presented the companys loyalty program and encouraged me to take part in it.
15.	The sales assistant was dressed neatly and aesthetically.

COMMUNICATION OF RESULTS

The project results were presented at a meeting with the sales and marketing director and the chairman of the board. The six steps of assessment, the data collection plan, the method of isolating the effects of training, and proposals for the future were presented during the meeting. The overall results of the project were also presented to the participants of the project.

LESSONS LEARNED

Conclusions which emerged during the discussion:

- The training time should be longer (one day is not enough to effectively practice sales competencies).
- The process of coaching should be continuous, not limited to specific projects.
- Before a decision is made about whether to implement training, the motivation level and commitment of participants should be examined (one needs to avoid situations in which the company invests in training employees who may be dismissed in the nearest future or may resign on their own).
- This first ROI project made me realize that this is an extremely practical methodology, which should be applied in companies on regular basis and

function as part of their overall organizational process. The first step that is worth recommending, is choosing individual training programs in order to evaluate them at various levels. My goals are to propose the ROI Methodology to companies in Poland, conduct open training sessions on the ROI Methodology, and to consult and conduct research on the application of the ROI Methodology.

QUESTIONS FOR DISCUSSION

1. How credible is this case study? Explain.
2. What other methods could be used to isolate the effects of the program on the data?

ABOUT THE AUTHOR

Małgorzata Mitoraj-Jaroszek PhD, CRP, has more than 15 years' experience in the training industry. She is the author of various training programs on topics such as training for managers, social skills training, and sales training. Over the years she has worked on multiple consulting projects including the implementation of a formal job evaluation, establishment and implementation of company standards, sales and customer service standards, implementation of the open door policy, setting recruitment processes, and preparing specialists and managers for the role of company trainers. She is also the author of several articles printed in national journals such as "Management and Staff." Her PhD thesis is devoted to management development in organizations, and was presented to the Management Institute at the Jagiellonian University.

About the ROI Institute

The ROI Institute, Inc. is the leading resource on research, training, and networking for practitioners of the Phillips ROI Methodology.

With a combined 50 years of experience in measuring and evaluating training, human resources, technology, and quality programs and initiatives, founders and owners Jack J. Phillips, PhD, and Patti P. Phillips, PhD, are the leading experts in return on investment (ROI).

The ROI Institute, founded in 1992, is a service-driven organization that strives to assist professionals in improving their programs and processes through the use of the ROI Methodology. Developed by Jack Phillips, this methodology is a critical tool for measuring and evaluating programs in 18 different applications in more than 60 countries.

The ROI Institute offers a variety of consulting services, learning opportunities, and publications. In addition, it conducts internal research activities for the organization, other enterprises, public sector entities, industries, and interest groups. Together with their team, Jack and Patti Phillips serve private and public sector organizations globally.

BUILD CAPABILITY IN THE ROI METHODOLOGY

The ROI Institute offers a variety of workshops to help you build capability in the ROI Methodology. Among the many workshops offered through the ROI Institute are:

- One-day *Bottomline on ROI* Workshop—Provides the perfect introduction to all levels of measurement, including the most sophisticated level, ROI. Learn the key principles of the Phillips ROI Methodology and determine whether your organization is ready to implement the process.
- Two-day *ROI Competency Building* Workshop—The standard ROI Workshop on measurement and evaluation, this two-day program involves discussion of the ROI Methodology process, including data collection, isolation methods, data conversion, and more.

ROI CERTIFICATION™

The ROI Institute is the only organization offering certification in the ROI Methodology. Through the ROI Certification process, you can build expertise in implementing ROI evaluation and sustaining the measurement and evaluation process in your organization. Receive personalized coaching while conducting an impact study. When competencies in the ROI Methodology have been demonstrated, certification is awarded. There is not another process that provides access to the same level of expertise as our ROI Certification. To date, more than 7,000 individuals have participated in this process.

For more information on these and other workshops, learning opportunities, consulting, and research, please visit us on the Web at **www.roiinstitute.net,** or call us at **205.678.8101**.

Index

About the Authors

Patricia Pulliam Phillips, PhD, is an internationally recognized author, consultant, and president and CEO of the ROI Institute, Inc. Phillips provides consulting services to organizations worldwide. She helps organizations build capacity in the ROI Methodology by facilitating the ROI certification process and teaching the ROI Methodology through workshops and graduate-level courses. Phillips has a PhD in international development and a master's degree in public and private management. She is certified in ROI evaluation and has been awarded the designations of Certified Professional in Learning and Performance and Certified Performance Technologist.

Jack J. Phillips, PhD, is chairman of the ROI Institute and a world-renowned expert on measurement and evaluation. Phillips provides consulting services for Fortune 500 companies and workshops for major conference providers worldwide. Phillips is also the author or editor of more than 75 books and more than 100 articles. His work has been featured in the Wall Street Journal, Bloomberg Businessweek, Fortune, and on CNN.

Rachel Robinson is senior editor for the ROI Institute. Robinson has served as editor for 10 books with the ROI Institute thus far. She holds an undergraduate degree in English from the University of Alabama at Birmingham. Although much of her career experience lies in the fields of technical and business writing, she has been published in additional disciplines and concentrations.

HOW TO PURCHASE ASTD PRESS PRODUCTS

All ASTD Press titles may be purchased through ASTD's online store at **www.store.astd.org**.

ASTD Press products are available worldwide through various outlets and booksellers. In the United States and Canada, individuals may also purchase titles (print or eBook) from:

Amazon– www.amazon.com (USA); www.amazon.com (CA)
Google Play– play.google.com/store
EBSCO– www.ebscohost.com/ebooks/home

Outside the United States, English-language ASTD Press titles may be purchased through distributors (divided geographically).

United Kingdom, Continental Europe, the Middle East, North Africa, Central Asia, and Latin America:
Eurospan Group
Phone: 44.1767.604.972
Fax: 44.1767.601.640
Email: eurospan@turpin-distribution.com
Web: www.eurospanbookstore.com
For a complete list of countries serviced via Eurospan please visit www.store.astd.org or email publications@astd.org.

South Africa:
Knowledge Resources
Phone: +27(11)880-8540
Fax: +27(11)880-8700/9829
Email: mail@knowres.co.za
Web: http://www.kr.co.za
For a complete list of countries serviced via Knowledge Resources please visit www.store.astd.org or email publications@astd.org.

Nigeria:
Paradise Bookshops
Phone: 08033075133
Email: paradisebookshops@gmail.com
Website: www.paradisebookshops.com

Asia:
Cengage Learning Asia Pte. Ltd.
Email: asia.info@cengage.com
Web: www.cengageasia.com
For a complete list of countries serviced via Cengage Learning please visit www.store.astd.org or email publications@astd.org.

India:
Cengage India Pvt. Ltd.
Phone: 011 43644 1111
Fax: 011 4364 1100
Email: asia.infoindia@cengage.com

For all other countries, customers may send their publication orders directly to ASTD. Please visit: **www.store.astd.org**.